# Lotus Illustrated DICTIONARY of COMMERCE

Complied and Edited by:
**Eric Fernandis**

Lotus PRESS
4735/22, Prakash Deep Building
Ansari Road, Darya Ganj,
New Delhi-110002

Lotus *Illustrated*

# DICTIONARY *of* COMMERCE



***ISBN 81 89093 23 1***

*Published by:*
**Lotus Press : Publishers & Distributors**
Unit No. 220, 2nd Floor, 4735/22,
Prakash Deep Building, Ansari Road, Darya Ganj,
New Delhi- 110002, Ph.: 32903912, 23280047, 09811838000
• E-mail : lotuspress1984@gmail.com www.lotuspress.co.in

*Printed & Published by* : **Lotus Press Publisher & Distributors,** New Delhi-02

# PREFACE

Commerce is a huge subject, which deals with, encourages, serves and promotes national as well as international trade, economic growth and technological advancement. This book provides a wide variety of terminologies, definitions, and abbreviations in a comprehensive style. Moreover, it has sufficiently highlighted the well-known international trade and commerce organisations, their norms and the binding treaties in this arena. It will provide assistance and information to increase competitiveness in economy; will help to plan and conduct business more smoothly. Students and academicians can also find it beneficial as it contains lots of information. It will support people to develop and improve their understanding of the grants of patents and registered trademarks; develop policies and conducts research. Hope, it will assist to promote domestic economic development and the growth of overall businesses.

This precious creation offers a well-coordinated, economical and accessible service to help small businesses increase their potentiality. The focal point here is the trade policy issues concerning commerce. It brings the small business point of view to international trade policy discussions. Through it one can get analysis of foreign market conditions and opportunities, advocacy assistance, general exporting advice, export financing advice, industry analysis, tariffs, regulations, business and practices, etc. This is an unique collection for any interested person in this field. Whether it is participating in critical trade negotiations, managing a mission to overseas markets or advocating on behalf of bidders for international contracts or trade development this book will be of immense importance. From basic manufacturing to high technology and service exports this will be very useful. It will be helpful to monitor trends and developments impacting specific industries, both domestically and overseas.

The aim is to improve our understanding of trade and commerce. Therefore it is possible to generate practicable solutions to today's pressing business situations, so that a healthy and wealthy economy can be maintained. We hope the purpose will be served in every way.

■ **abandon**

refers to the decision not to exercise an option or, sometimes, a clause.

It may also refer to the intentional or unintentional lack of use, maintenance or affirmation process about assets. These assets may include securities, bank accounts, refunds, trademarks and so on. In such cases the property can go to a jurisdiction such as a state or central government.

■ **abandonment**

1. Controlling party giving up rights to property voluntarily.

2. proceeding where a carrier seeks authorisation to stop service over all or part of its route/line, or to give up ownership/control of cargo or vessel.

Shipper or consignee relinquishes damaged freight carrier or refuses to accept delivery. The act of relinquishing title to damaged or lost property to claim a total loss.

■ **abandonment option**

The option of terminating an investment earlier than originally planned.

■ **ability to pay**

refers to the borrower's ability to make interest and principal payments on debts. In context of municipal bonds, refers to the issuer's present and future ability to create sufficient tax revenue to fulfil its contractual obligations, accounting for municipal income and property values.

In context of taxation, notion that tax rates should be determined according to income or wealth.

■ **abnormal returns**

the component of the return that is not due to systematic influences (market-wide influences). In other words, abnormal returns are above those predicted by the market movement alone. Related: excess returns.

■ **about**

about, approx. and circa are terms which when used in a letter of credit, are construed to allow a difference not to exceed 10% more or 10% less than the monetary amount, or the quantity, or the unit price stipulated in the letter of credit.

■ **absolute advantage**

an advantage of one nation or area over another in the costs of producing an item in terms of used resources.

■ **absolute liability**

condition in which a carrier is responsible for all liability and is not protected by normal exemptions found in a bill of lading or common law liability.

■ **absolute priority**

rule in bankruptcy proceedings requiring senior creditors to be paid in full before junior creditors receive any payment.

■ **absorbed**

used in context of general equities. Securities are absorbed as long as there are corresponding orders to buy and sell. The market has reached the absorption point when further assimilation is impossible without an adjustment in price.

■ **absorption**

1. an economic term for the total expenditures by a nation's residents on goods and services.
2. the assumption by one carrier of the charges of another without any increase in the charges to the shipper.

■ **ACATS**

is the Automated Customer Account Transfer Service.

■ **ACB**

refers to Account Cash Balance.

■ **Accelerated Cost Recovery System (ACRS)**

schedule of depreciation rates allowed for tax purposes.

■ **accelerated depreciation**

1. is an accounting technique which provides larger than straight-line depreciation amounts in the early years and smaller than straight-line depreciation amounts in the later years.
2. any depreciation method that produces larger deductions for depreciation in the early years of an asset's life. Accelerated Cost Recovery System (ACRS), which is a depreciation schedule allowed for tax purposes, is one such example.

■ **accelerated tariff elimination**

the reduction of import duties faster than originally had been agreed upon or projected.

■ **acceleration clause**

a contract stating that the unpaid balance becomes due and payable if specific actions transpire, such as failure to make interests payments on time.

■ **acceptance**

contractual agreement instigated when the drawee of a time draft accepts the draft by writing the word accepted thereon. The drawee assumes responsibility as the acceptor and for payment at maturity.

■ **acceptance letter of credit**

a letter of credit which instead of agreeing to pay the beneficiary immediately upon presentation of documents, requires presentation of a time draft drawn by the beneficiary upon the issuing bank or another bank. However, the beneficiary may, in effect, obtain prompt payment by discounting the draft.

■ **accepted draft**

a draft or a bill of exchange accepted by the drawee (acceptor) by putting his signature and accepted on its face. In doing so, he commits himself to pay the bill upon presentation at maturity.

■ **accepting bank**

a bank which by signing 'accepted' on a time draft accepts responsibility to pay when the draft becomes due.

■ **acceptor**

the party that signs 'accepted' on a draft or obligation, agreeing to pay the stated sum at maturity.

## ■ accession

accession is a process by which a country becomes a member of an international agreement (usually an agreement that has already been accepted by other countries).

## ■ accessorial charges

in transportation, those charges made for additional, supplemental, or special services performed in addition to the basic transportation service.

## ■ accessorial services

in transportation, services performed which are additional, supplemental, or special, in addition to the basic transportation service.

## ■ accommodation

an arrangement or engagement made as a favour to another, not dependent upon a consideration received.

## ■ accord and satisfaction

a means of discharging a claim whereby the parties agree to give and accept something in settlement and perform the agreement, the agreement being the accord and its performance the satisfaction.

## ■ account

in the context of bookkeeping, refers to the ledger pages upon which various assets, liabilities, income and expenses are represented.
In the context of investment banking, refers to the status of securities sold and owned or the relationship between parties to an underwriting syndicate. In the context of securities, the relationship between a client and a broker/dealer firm allowing the firm's employee to be the client's buying and selling agent.

## ■ account balance

credits minus debits at the end of a reporting period.

## ■ account executive

the brokerage firm employee who handles stock orders for clients.

## ■ account number

an identification number assigned in its records for purposes of faster and more accurate accounting and record keeping, by banks, institutions and businesses of all kind to their depositors, users, members, subscribers, customers, vendors, or other entities.

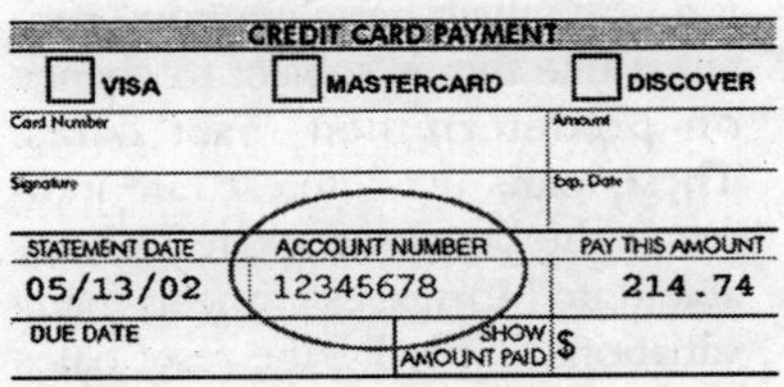


## ■ adequacy of coverage

a test that measures the extent to which the value of an asset is protected from potential loss either through insurance or hedging.

## ■ adhesion contract

a contract with standard, often printed, terms for sale of goods and services, offered to consumers who usually cannot negotiate any changes in the terms and cannot acquire the product unless they agree to them.

## adjustable rate

applies mainly to convertible securities. Refers to interest rate or dividend that is adjusted periodically, usually according to a standard market rate outside the control of the bank or savings institution, such as that prevailing on Treasury bonds or notes. Typically, such issues have a set floor or ceiling, called caps and collars that limits the adjustment.

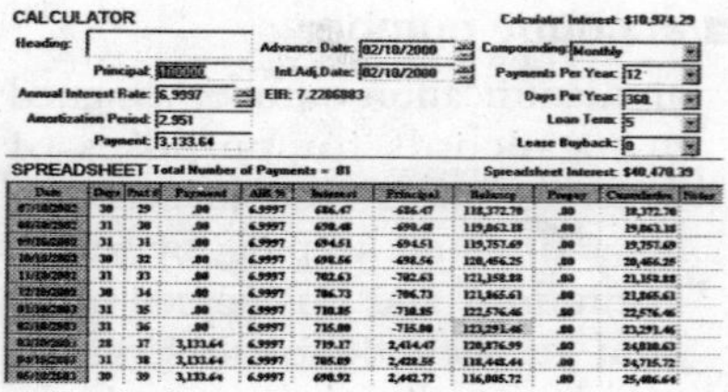


## adjustable rate mortgages

is a loan which has a coupon or interest rate that is subject to change on predetermined reset dates. These loans use interest rate indices as the benchmark rate. Adjustable Rate Mortgages come in many variations. Typically, the reset dates recur every 1, 3, or 5 years; but there are other periods used as well. These loans may have cap and floor features which constrain each reset change in interest rates. There may also be lifetime cap and floor features. Adjustable Rate Mortgages may be strictly amortising though some have negative amortisation features.

## adjusted balance method

method of calculating finance charges that uses the account balance remaining after adjusting for all transactions posted during the given billing period as its basis.

## adjusted basis

price from which to calculate and derive capital gains or losses upon sale of an asset. Account actions, such as any stock splits that have occurred since the initial purchase, must be accounted for.

## Adjusted Debit Balance (ADB)

the account balance for a margin account that is calculated by combining the balance owed to a broker with any outstanding balance in the special miscellaneous account and any paper profits on short accounts.

## Adjusted Gross Income (AGI)

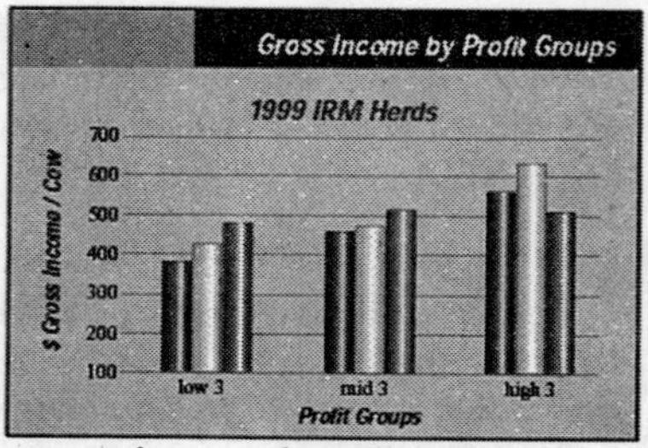


gross income less allowable adjustments, is the income on which an individual is taxed by the central government.

## Adjusted Present Value (APV)

the net present value analysis of an asset if financed solely by equity (present value of unlevered cash flows), plus the present value of any financing decisions (levered cash flows). In other words, the various tax shields provided by the deductibility of interest and the benefits of other investment tax credits are calculated separately. This analysis is often used for highly leveraged transactions such as a leveraged buyout.

Table 5A - Comparing investment locations for 1985 ($w^{us}$ = \$9.54)
Price of Output (p) = \$15
Nominal Interest Rate = 6%

| | US (Invest in 1 unit) | Germany (Invest in 2 units) | Canada (Invest in 2 units) | The U.K. (Invest in 2 units) | Ireland (Invest in 2 units) |
|---|---|---|---|---|---|
| 1) Wage in Country (\$) | 9.54 | 6.57 | 8.29 | 5.33 | 5.21 |
| 2) σ | 1.91 | 1.59 | 0.64 | 1.18 | 0.98 |
| 3) Static PV = (p-w)/r | 91.00 | 140.5 | 111.83 | 161.16 | 163.16 |
| 4) R(Δ) : Value of Excess Capacity | | 57.89 | 27.86 | 72.7 | 73.85 |
| 5) Adjusted Present Value | 124.11 | 198.39 | 139.69 | 233.87 | 237.01 |
| 6) R(Δ) as a % of the Adj. Present Value = (4)/(5) | | 29% | 19.9% | 31% | 31% |

## ■ adjustment

the process of adaptation in an economy that is triggered, for example, by technological developments, changes in demand, or shifting external trade patterns. The changes may involve a reallocation of labour and capital away from uncompetitive products or sectors and into new or other lines of production in which the economy is competitive. In the specific sense used by the International Monetary Fund, adjustment means the adoption of macroeconomic policies, including monetary, fiscal and exchange rate policies, to adjust the level of domestic economic activity to conditions prevailing in the world economy, with the objective of correcting balance-of-payments disequilibria and pursuing domestic objectives such as lower inflation.

## ■ adjustment assistance

financial, training and re-employment technical assistance to workers and technical assistance to firms and industries, to help them cope with adjustment difficulties arising from increased import competition.

## ■ adjustment bond

a bond issued in exchange for outstanding bonds when a corporation facing bankruptcy is recapitalised.

## ■ administrator

the person appointed by the court to manage one's estate when he or she dies without leaving a will. Administrators have the same duties as executors.

## ■ admiralty

any civil or criminal matter having to do with maritime legal issues.

## ■ admiralty court

a court of law that has jurisdiction over maritime legal issues.

## ■ advance

increase in the market price of stocks, bonds, commodities, or other assets.

## ■ advance against collection

a short term loan or credit extended to a seller (usually the exporter) by the seller's bank once a draft has been accepted by the buyer (generally the importer).

## ■ advance arrangements

in transportation, advance arrangements must be made for certain kinds of cargo which require special handling: hazardous cargo, over-weight, over-sized, over-normal quantity, time sensitive, shipped unpacked, live animals, etc. Not every carrier can or will transport every kind of cargo.

■ **advance commitment**

a promise to sell an asset before the seller has lined up purchase of the asset. This seller can offset risk by purchasing a futures contract to fix the sales price approximately.

■ **Advance Computerised Execution System (ACES)**

refers to the Advance Computerised Execution System, run by NASDAQ. ACES automates trades between order entry and market maker firms that have established trading relationships with each other. Securities are designated as specified for automatic execution.

■ **advance funded pension plan**

a pension plan in which funds are set aside in advance of the date of retirement.

■ **advanced charge**

freight or charge on a shipment that is advanced by one transportation company to another, or to the shipper, to be collected from the consignee.

■ **advanced refunding**

is the technique of replacing one bond issue by another. This typically occurs when a municipality can borrow at more favourable terms than the outstanding issue. The new issue's proceeds are used to purchase government obligations which are held in escrow. The income and/or appreciation of these government securities is then used to service the outstanding debt. The escrow may be held until the first call date or maturity of the initial bond issue. If the escrowed funds retire the original issue at the first call date then the issue is pre-refunded. This retirement and replacement process of debt is also known as defeasance.

■ **Advanced Technology Products (ATP)**

products whose technology is from a recognised high technology field, represent leading edge technology in that field and constitute a significant part of all items covered in the selected classification code.

■ **adverse opinion**

an independent auditor's opinion expressing that a firm's financial statements do not reflect the company's position accurately.

■ **adverse selection**

refers to a situation in which sellers have relevant information that buyers lack (or vice versa) about some aspect of product quality.

■ **advice**

1. a report from one party to another informing them of an occurrence with regard to some business transaction: a shipment, a collection, a manufacture etc.
2. a notification by an advising bank on behalf of the issuing bank to a beneficiary informing them of the terms of a letter of credit,

■ **advice of shipment**

notice to local or foreign buyer that shipment has occurred, with packing and routing details. A copy of invoice usually is enclosed and sometimes a copy of the bill of lading.

■ **advised credit**

a letter of credit whose terms and conditions have been notified to the beneficiary by an advising bank on behalf of the issuing bank. The advising bank does not thereby commit itself to pay or guarantee the payment of the letter of credit.

■ **advising bank**

an 'advising bank' is a correspondent of a bank which issues a letter of credit and, on behalf of the issuing bank, the advising bank notifies the beneficiary of the terms of the credit, without engagement on its part to pay or guarantee the credit.

■ **advisory letter**

a newsletter offering financial advice to its readers.

■ **affiliate**

1. a condition of being united, allied, associated, or attached. An affiliate company is one effectively controlled by another.
2. relationship between two companies when one company owns substantial interest, but less than a majority of the voting stock of another company, or when two companies are both subsidiaries of a third company.

■ **affiliated corporation**

a corporation that is an affiliate to the parent company.

■ **affiliated person**

an individual who possesses enough influence and control in a corporation to be able to alter the actions of the corporation.

■ **affirmative covenant**

a bond covenant that specifies certain actions the firm must take.

■ **affordability index**

an index that measures the financial ability of consumers to purchase a home.

■ **affreightment contract**

a contract with a ship owner to hire all or part of a ship for transporting goods. May involve a charter.

■ **afloat**

refers to a shipment of cargo which is currently on board a vessel between ports

■ **aft**

at or towards the stern of the ship or the tail of the aircraft.

■ **after acquired clause**

a contractual clause in a mortgage agreement stating that any additional mortgageable property attained by the borrower after the mortgage is signed will be regarded as additional security for the obligation addressed in the mortgage.

■ **after date**

a notation used on financial instruments (such as drafts or bills of exchange) to fix the maturity date as a fixed number of days past the date of drawing of the draft.

■ **after sight**

a notation on a draft that indicates that payment is due a stated number of days after the draft has been presented to the drawee.

■ **after-hours dealing or trading**

securities trading after regular trading hours on organised exchanges.

■ **after market**

refers to trading in the secondary market following a new securities issuance.

■ **after-tax basis**

the comparison basis used to analyse the net after-tax returns on a corporate taxable bond and a municipal tax-free bond.

■ **after-tax profit margin**

the ratio of net income to net sales.

■ **after-tax real rate of return**

the after-tax rate of return minus the inflation rate.

■ **against actuals**

is a commodity market transaction whereby futures are exchanged or transferred against a cash position.

■ **aged fail**

an account between two broker/dealers that remains intact after 30 days after the settlement date. The receiving firm must adjust its capital as it can no longer treat this account as an assets.

■ **agency**

in context of general equities, buying or selling for the account and risk of a customer. Generally, an agent, or broker, acts as intermediary between buyer and seller, taking no financial risk personally or as a firm and charging a commission for the service. The broker represents a customer buyer/seller to a customer seller/buyer and does not act as principal for the firm's own trading account. Antithesis of principal.

■ **agency basis**

a means of compensating the broker of a programme trade solely on the basis of commission established through bids submitted by various brokerage firms.

■ **agency cost view**

the argument that specifies that the various agency costs create a complex environment in which total agency costs are at a minimum with some, but less than 100%, debt financing.

■ **agency costs**

the incremental costs of having an agent make decisions for a principal.

■ **agency incentive arrangement**

a means of compensating the broker of a programme trade using benchmark prices for issues to be traded in determining commissions or fees.

**agency problem**

conflicts of interest among stockholders, bondholders and managers.

**agency theory**

the analysis of principal-agent relationships, in which one person, an agent, acts on behalf of another person, a principal.

**agent**

is a party who acts on the behalf of another. This occurs when a broker executes a trade for the benefit of the customer. Here, the broker receives a commission.

**aggregate exercise price**

the exercise price multiplied by the number of shares in a put or call contract. The option premium is excluded in the aggregate exercise price. In the case of options traded on debt instruments, the aggregate exercise price is the exercise price of the underlying security multiplied by its face value.

**aggregated shipments**

several shipments intended for one consignee from various shippers that are consolidated and treated as a single consignment.

**aggregation**

process in corporate financial planning whereby the smaller investment proposals of each of the firm's operational units are aggregated and effectively treated as a whole.

**aggressive growth mutual fund**

a mutual fund designed for maximum capital appreciation that places its money in companies with high growth rates.

**aggressively**

used in context of general equities. For a customer it means working to buy or sell one's stock, with an emphasis on execution over price. For a trader it means acting in a way that puts the firm's capital at higher risk through paying a higher price, selling cheaper, or making a larger short sale or purchase than the trader would under normal circumstances.

**AGI**

refers to Adjusted Gross Income.

**aging**

is the concept which assumes that newly issued mortgages tend to prepay slower than mortgages which are older or seasoned. This aging refers to the underlying collateral and not the securities created upon that collateral.

**aging schedule**

a table of accounts receivable broken down into age categories (such as 0-30 days, 30-60 days and 60-90 days), which is used to determine if customer payments are keeping close to schedule.

**agreed valuation**

the value of a shipment that is agreed upon by both the shipper and the carrier to define the freight rate and/or the liability of the carrier.

**agreement among underwriters**

a contract among participating

members of a syndicate that defines the members' proportionate liability, which is usually limited to and based on the participants' level of involvement. The contract outlines the payment schedule on the settlement date.

## Agreement On Trade-Related Aspects Of Intellectual Property Rights (TRIPS)

a WTO agreement that obliges countries to provide minimum standards of intellectual property (IP) protection in national laws and to enforce minimum standards for protecting intellectual property. The TRIPS Agreement covers copyright and related rights (that is, the rights of performers, producers of sound recordings and broadcasting organisations); trademarks including service marks; geographical indications including appellations of origin; industrial designs; patents including the protection of new varieties of plants; the layout-designs of integrated circuits; and undisclosed information, including trade secrets and test data. The agreement sets out the minimum standards of protection to be provided by each member with respect to each of the main areas of intellectual property covered by the agreement. The agreement sets these standards by requiring, first, compliance with the substantive obligations of the main conventions of the World Intellectual Property Organisation, as well as the most recent versions of the Paris Convention for the Protection of Industrial Property and the Bern Convention for the Protection of Literary and Artistic Works, as well as with the Treaty on Intellectual Property in Respect of Integrated Circuits (1989). With the exception of the provisions of the Bern Convention on moral rights, all the main substantive provisions of these conventions are incorporated by reference and thus become obligations under the TRIPS Agreement between member countries. The second main set of provisions deals with domestic procedures and remedies for the enforcement of intellectual property rights, a feature not found in other multilateral IP agreements. In addition, the agreement makes disputes between WTO members concerning TRIPS obligations subject to the WTO's dispute settlement procedures. Finally, the agreement provides for certain basic principles, such as national and most-favoured-nation treatment. Developed country members were required to have implemented all of the obligations under the agreement as of January 1, 1996, while developing country members were permitted a transitional period of an additional four years (until January 1, 2000). Least-developed country members are permitted a transitional period of an additional 10 years (until January 1, 2006) to comply with the obligations of the agreement. In addition, developing countries that, as of 1995, were without patent protection for a given area of technology, especially pharmaceutical or agricultural chemical inventions, have an additional five-year transition (until January 1, 2005) before being required to provide such protection.

■ **Agreement On Trade-Related Investment Measures (TRIMS)**

a WTO agreement that recognises that measures and regulations that governments impose on investments and investors can reduce or distort international trade and may function as disincentives for investors in situations where investment is needed. This agreement clarifies disciplines established in the GATT 1947 provisions that are applicable to certain aspects of investment laws. The objectives of the TRIMS Agreement, as set forth in its preamble, include the expansion and progressive liberalisation of world trade and to facilitate investment across international frontiers so as to increase the economic growth of all trading partners, particularly developing country members, while ensuring free competition. The agreement applies to investment measures related to trade in goods only. Under TRIMS, WTO member countries agreed to eliminate investment measures that limit or force certain types of investments, to offer national treatment to foreign investors and to eliminate quotas and other restraints. The agreement restricts the use of three TRIMS requirements: local content requirements (specifying that some minimum level of local resources be used in operations at foreign-owned plants), trade-balancing requirements (specifying that an investor not import more than a certain proportion of exports, or that a minimum trade surplus be maintained) and foreign exchange balancing requirements (limiting the importation of products used in local production by restricting a firm's access to foreign exchange to an amount related to its exchange inflows).

■ **air cargo**

property of any kind that is transported by aeroplanes (excluding passenger baggage and mail).

■ **air express**

expedited air freight service.

■ **air parcel post**

parcels shipped through the mails to be transported by air.

■ **air pocket stock**

a stock whose price drops precipitously, often on the unexpected news of poor results.

■ **airwaybill**

the shipping document used for the transportation of air freight: includes conditions, limitations of liability, shipping instructions, description of commodity and applicable transportation charges. It is generally similar to a straight non-negotiable bill of lading and is used for similar purposes.

■ **ALCO**

is the acronym for Asset and Liability Committee. Term used frequently in banking industry.

■ **alien corporation**

a company incorporated under the laws of a foreign country regardless of where the company conducts its operations.

■ **alienable**

ability to be transferred or conveyed.

■ **all equity rate**

the discount rate that reflects only the business risks of a project, distinct from the effects of financing.

■ **all in**

refers to an issuer's interest rate after accounting for commissions and various related expenses.

■ **all-cargo aeroplane**

any aeroplane that is used for the sole purpose of transporting cargo or mail.

■ **all-commodity rate**

usually a carload/truckload rate that applies to multiple shipments that move at one time in one vehicle from the consignor to one consignee. An all-commodity rate is established based on actual transportation cost rather than value of service.

■ **alligator spread**

the term used to describe a spread in the options market that generates such a large commission that the client is unlikely to make a profit even if the markets move as the investor anticipated.

■ **all-in cost**

total costs, explicit and implicit.

■ **all-or-none underwriting**

an arrangement whereby a security issue is cancelled if the underwriter is unable to resell the entire issue.

■ **allotment**

the number of securities assigned to each of the participants in an underwriting syndicate.

■ **allowance**

a deduction or discount from the price permitted by a seller.

■ **alongside**

point of delivery beside a vessel, statement designating where the title to goods passes from one party to another.

■ **alpha**

is a measure of the incremental reward (or loss) that an investor gained in relation to the market. Typically, this is measured as performance of a selected portfolio relative to a market benchmark. An enhanced S&P 500 portfolio might have an alpha of .25 which means that the pickup was .25% or a quarter point better than the standard.

■ **alphabet stock**

categories of common stock of a corporation associated with a particular subsidiary resulting from acquisitions and restructuring. The various alphabetical categories have different voting rights and pay dividends tied to the operating performance of the particular divisions.

■ **alternate routing**

routing that is less desirable than the normal, but results in identical terms.

**■ alternative investments**

are usually investments other than mutual funds, certificates of deposit, or direct investments in equities and bonds. Some of these alternatives are: art, collectibles, commodities, commodity funds, commodity pools, derivatives, foreign exchange, hedge funds, oil and gas, precious metals and real estate ventures.

**■ alternative mortgage instruments**

variations of mortgage instruments such as adjustable-rate and variable-rate mortgages, graduated-payment mortgages, reverse-annuity mortgages and several seldom-used variations.

**■ alternative order**

used in context of general equities, order giving a broker a choice between two courses of action, either to buy or sell, never both. Execution of one course automatically eliminates the other. An example is a combination buy limit/buy stop order, where the buy limit is below the current market and the buy stop is above. If the order is for one unit of trading, when one part of the order is executed on the occurrence of one alternative, the order on the other alternative is to be treated as cancelled. If the order is for an amount of more than one unit of trading, the number of units executed determines the amount of the alternative order to be treated as cancelled.

**■ alternative tariff**

in transportation, a tariff with two or more rates for the same goods, to and from the same points, with the opportunity available to the shipper to use the lowest of the charges.

**■ ambac**

is the holding company that provides financial guarantee insurance for both public and private sector clients. This insurance can improve credit ratings.

**■ amendment**

an addition, deletion, or modification of a document.

**■ amortisation**

1. the provision to pay a debt over a period of time.
2. the gradual repayment of borrowings in a series of instalments.
3. a transaction or security where the principal reduces over the life of the agreement.
4. the writing off or reduction in value of an intangible asset over time (c.f.depreciation)
5. allocation of the cost of an asset over its estimated useful life.

**■ amortisation factor**

the pool factor implied by the scheduled amortisation assuming no prepayments.

**■ amortising interest rate swap**

swap in which the principal or notional amount rises (falls) as interest rates rise (decline).

**■ analyst**

employee of a brokerage or fund management house who studies companies and makes buy-and-sell recommendations on stocks of these companies. Most specialise in a specific industry.

■ **and interest**

an indication that the buyer will receive accrued interest in addition to the price quoted for a bond.

■ **angel**

an investment-grade bond. Antithesis to fallen angel. In the context of venture capital, the first investor.

■ **ankle biter**

stock issued with a market capitalisation of less than Rs. 500 million.

■ **announcement date**

date on which particular news concerning a given company is announced to the public. Used in event studies, which researchers use to evaluate the economic impact of events of interest.

■ **annual basis**

the technique in statistics of taking a figure covering a period of less than one year and extrapolating it to cover a full one year period. The process is known as annualising.

■ **annual exclusion**

a tax rule allowing the deduction of certain income from taxation.

■ **annual fund operating expenses**

for investment companies, the management fee and other expenses, including the expenses for maintaining shareholder records, providing shareholders with financial statements and providing custodial and accounting services. For 12b-1 funds, selling and marketing costs are also included.

■ **anticipated holding period**

the period of time an individual expects to hold an asset.

■ **anticipation**

paying what is owed before it is due (usually to save interest charges).

■ **anticipatory hedging**

refers to the placement of a hedge prior to placement of the actual position. Sometimes, this occurs when a firm knows that it will receive investment funds later that day or week and prefers to hedge numerous potential risks at the earlier date. Similarly, a commodity producer may prefer to hedge prior to the harvest of a crop, production of an energy product or processing a raw material into a deliverable lot.

■ **antidilutive effect**

result of a transaction that increases earnings per common share (e.g., by decreasing the number of shares outstanding).

■ **antidumping duties**

additional duties which are assessed on imported goods when those goods are sold to the importing country at a price that is less than fair value, (fair value usually being defined as the price on the exporting country's domestic market or to third countries) and when those imported goods are found to cause or to threaten material injury to industry of the importing country.

■ **antitrust laws**

legislation established by the central government to prevent the formation of monopolies and to regulate trade.

■ **any quantity**

a cargo freight rate that applies to an article without regard to the weight or quantity shipped.

■ **any-interest-date**

a call provision in a municipal bond indenture that establishes the right of redemption for the issuer on any interest payment due date.

■ **any-or-all bid**

often used in risk arbitrage. Takeover bid in which the acquirer offers to pay a set price for all outstanding shares of the target company, or any part thereof; contrasts with two-tier bid.

■ **any-part-of order**

in context of general equities, order to buy or sell a quantity of stock in pieces if necessary. Antithesis of an all-or-none order (AON).

■ **AO or A/O**

refers to As Of. This indicates that while a transaction was processed on one date, it was actually conducted on a different date. Often backlogs or delays in reports or inaccuracies in previous reports trigger this report.

■ **AON**

is a type of order.

■ **applicant**

1. the party at whose request a bank issues a letter of credit.
2. a person who applies for something: a job, a passport, a visa, a license, a ticket etc.

■ **appraisal**

is an expert evaluation of the current, probable market value for a property. It is not necessarily the market value or transaction price.

■ **appraisal rights**

a right of shareholders in a merger to demand the payment of a fair price for their shares, as determined independently.

■ **appreciated property**

property, such as real estate or stock, which has increased in value.

■ **appreciation**

an increase in the value of something, of goods, of currency, of shares of stock, etc.

■ **appropriation request**

formal request for funds for capital investment project.

■ **approved carriers**

refers to armoured car services which are approved by the exchange for the transportation of precious metals.

■ **approved list**

a list of equities and other investments that a financial institution or mutual fund is approved to make.

■ **approx. (approximately)**

same as about and circa; terms which when used in a letter of credit are construed to allow a difference not to exceed 10% more or 10% less than the monetary amount, or the quantity, or the unit price.

## ■ appurtenance

an accessory, adjunct, or appendage connected to a primary property and used in conjunction therewith.

## ■ APR

is the Annual Percentage Rate of Interest.

## ■ apron

1. area of the airport where planes are parked. May be used for loading and unloading of aeroplane.
2. area along the waterside edges of a pier, not under cover, used for loading and unloading of vessels.

## ■ arbitrage

1. is a form of trading which attempts to profit by discrepancies in price due to location, funding, volatility, communications, response to information, or other differences. Typically, the price differences are small and only the quickest, most cost efficient or funding efficient parties participate.
2. a method of taking advantage of the fact that there may be different prices in different markets for identical goods such as gold, foreign exchange or commodities. Simultaneously, one buys in the lower price market and sells in the higher one.
3. the simultaneous buying and selling of a security at two different prices in two different markets, resulting in profits without risk. Perfectly efficient markets present no arbitrage opportunities. Perfectly efficient markets seldom exist, but arbitrage opportunities are often precluded because of transactions costs.

## ■ arbitrage bonds

municipality issued bonds issued intended to gain an interest rate advantage by refunding a higher-rate bond ahead of their call date. Lower-rate refunding issue proceeds are invested in Treasuries until the first call date of the higher-rate issue.

## ■ Arbitrage Pricing Theory (APT)

an alternative model to the capital asset pricing model developed by Stephen Ross and based purely on arbitrage arguments. The APT implies that there are multiple risk factors that need to be taken into account when calculating risk-adjusted performance or alpha.

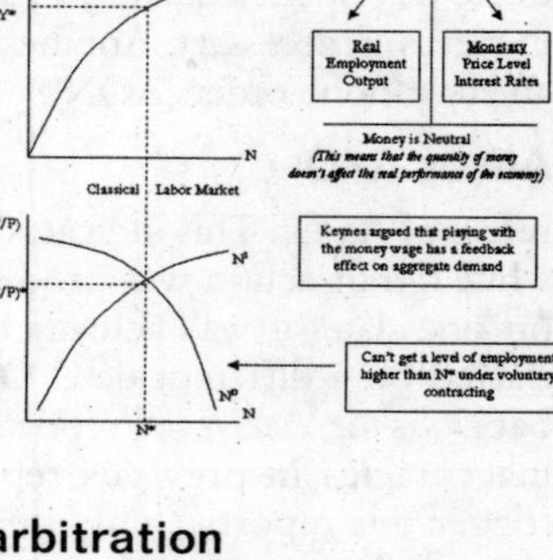


## ■ arbitration

1. a method of settling disputes by reference to an independent

and impartial third party. Arbitration is essentially an adjudication of the arguments of the parties and as such differs from independent expert determination.
2. an arrangement through which two parties to a dispute agree to the appointment of an impartial chairperson or a group of competent persons to decide the disputed issue and agree in advance to abide by the decision rendered.

## ■ Arbitration Panel

is the group of arbitrators selected to resolve a dispute.

## ■ arbitrator

is a person who is selected to resolve a dispute in the financial industry. Usually there are three arbitrators on a panel. The composition of the arbitrators is from a pool of candidates viewed either as Public or Industry.

## ■ as is

indicates goods for sale do not include a warranty , implied or expressed. The buyer takes the entire risk as to the quality or condition of the goods involved and must trust to his own inspection. In sum, the sale is without recourse.

## ■ ascending tops

a chart pattern that depicts that each peak in a security's price over a period of time is higher than the preceding peak. Antithesis of descending tops.

## ■ ASCNI

is Available Separate Consolidated Net Income.

## ■ asian

is an option which uses the averaged prices of the underlying security, index or commodity during its life as the determinant of the pay-off amount.

## ■ Asian Economic Crisis

a series of economic events that resulted in the severe devaluation of a number of Asian currencies and destabilisation of a number of Asian economies, most notably Thailand, Indonesia, South Korea, the Philippines and Malaysia. The Asian economic crisis caused shock waves throughout the global economy. Many economists consider that one factor in the region's difficulties was its economic success during the preceding decade, which featured robust economic growth, increasing capital inflows and macroeconomic management. The substantial capital inflows into the region from the mid-1980s to the mid-1990s led to rapid economic expansion that, in turn, resulted in increased investment and increased local lending based on unrealistically optimistic expectations and economic projections. Structural and policy distortions created fundamental imbalances in these economies that led to the market corrections experienced during the crisis. Some also believe that the macroeconomic difficulties facing the region were not as severe as many regional and international investors feared and that the crisis was exacerbated by the overreaction of market participants, who withdrew investment monies from the region. By 1999, capital inflows into the region had begun to increase again and there were other signs that economies most directly affected by the crisis were beginning to recover.

■ **asian option**

option based on the average price of the underlying assets during the life of the option.

■ **ask**

1. is the price requested, at the minimum, for an order to be acceptable and executed for the seller.
2. this is the quoted ask, or the lowest price an investor will accept to sell a stock. Practically speaking, this is the quoted offer at which an investor can buy shares of stock; also called the offer price.

■ **asked price**

in context of general equities, price at which a security or commodity is offered for sale on an exchange or in the OTC Market.

■ **asked to bid/offer**

used in context of general equities. Usually a seller (buyer) looking to aggressively sell (buy) stock, asks for a capital commitment from an investment bank.

■ **assay**

metal purity test to confirm that the metal meets the standards for trading on a commodities exchange (commodities exchange centre).

■ **assembly service**

a service under which a carrier or a forwarder or a warehouse combines multiple shipments from multiple shippers into one shipment for one receiver.

■ **assessed valuation**

the value assigned to property by a municipality for the purpose of tax assessment. Such an assessed valuation is important to investors in municipal bonds that are backed by property taxes.

■ **assessed value**

is the taxable basis of a property. It is imposed by the municipality. Often it is at a fraction of the market value. Equally important is the rate of taxation on that assessed value. Assessed values may differ substantially from market values and appraised values.

■ **assessment**

1. the valuation or determination as to value of property.
2. the act of apportioning amounts to be paid.
3. an amount assessed or charged, for example: taxes or dues.

■ **asset**

any item of economic value owned by you or your corporation, especially that which could be converted to cash.

■ **asset activity ratios**

ratios that measure how effectively the firm is managing its assets.

■ **asset allocation decision**

the decision regarding how an institution's funds should be distributed among the major classes of assets in which it may invest.

**■ asset allocation mutual fund**

a mutual fund that rotates among stocks, bonds and money market securities to maximise return on investment and minimise risk.

**■ asset backed securities**

is a security backed by notes or receivables against assets other than real estate. Some examples are autos, credit cards and royalties.

**■ asset classes**

categories of assets, such as stocks, bonds, real estate and foreign securities.

**■ asset for asset swap**

creditors exchange the debt of one defaulting borrower for the debt of another defaulting borrower.

**■ asset management account**

account at a brokerage house, bank, or savings institution that integrates banking services and brokerage features.

**■ asset play**

a company with assets that are not believed to be accurately reflected in its stock price, making it an attractive buy or play.

**■ asset pricing model**

a model for determining the required or expected rate of return on an asset.

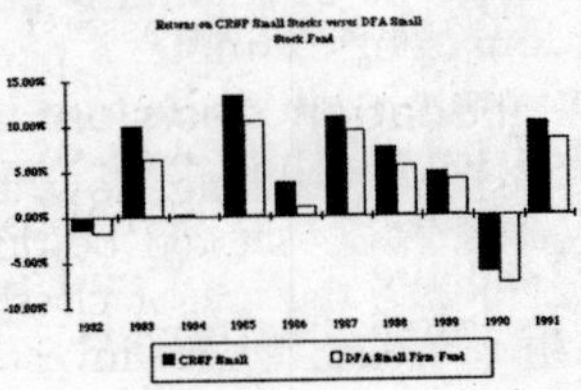


**■ asset substitution**

occurs when a firm invests in assets that are riskier than those that the debt holders expected.

**■ asset substitution problem**

arises when the stockholders substitute riskier assets for the firm's existing assets and expropriate value from the debt holders.

**■ asset swap**

an interest rate swap used to alter the cash flow characteristics of an institution's assets in order to provide a better match with its liabilities.

**■ asset turnover**

the ratio of net sales to total assets.

**■ asset value**

the net market value of a corporation's assets on a per-share basis, not the market value of the shares. A company is undervalued in the market when asset value exceeds market value.

**■ asset/equity ratio**

the ratio of total assets to stockholder equity.

**■ asset/liability management**

the task of managing the funds of a financial institution to accomplish the two goals of a financial institution:

1. to earn an adequate return on funds invested.
2. to maintain a comfortable surplus of assets beyond liabilities. Also called surplus management.

**■ asset-backed security**

a security that is collateralised by loans, leases, receivables, or installment contracts on personal property, not real estate.

**■ asset-based financing**

methods of financing in which lenders and equity investors look principally to the cash flow from a particular asset or set of assets for a return on and the return of, their financing.

**■ asset-coverage test**

a bond indenture restriction that permits additional borrowing if the ratio of assets to debt does not fall below a specified minimum.

**■ assets**

refer to properties owned or due to a person or organisation. Assets are typically viewed in three categories. These three classifications are: Current, Fixed or Long-term and Intangible.

**■ assets**

a firm's productive resources.

**■ assets requirements**

a common element of a financial plan that describes projected capital spending and the proposed uses of net working capital.

**■ assignee**

a party to whom a lease has been assigned.

**■ assignment**

1. is the action for the seller of the option of acquiring the opposite position when an option is exercised. When a put is exercised, the writer receives a long position in securities or a long futures contract. When a call is exercised, the writer receives a short position in the securities or a short futures contract.

2. the transfer of a lease from one party to the other. Once a lease has been assigned, the assignee becomes responsible to the landlord for paying the rent and fulfilling the other obligations of the lease; however, in the event of default, the landlord can require the assignor to pay the rent under the doctrine of privity of contract, where the latter still applies.

3. the receipt of an exercise notice by an options writer that requires the writer to sell (in the case of a call) or purchase (in the case of a put) the underlying security at the specified strike price.

**■ asymmetry**

a lack of equivalence between two things, such as the unequal tax treatment of interest expense and dividend payments.

**■ at par**

a price equal to nominal or face value of a security.

**■ at risk**

the exposure to the danger of economic loss. Frequently used in the context of claiming tax deductions. For example, a person can claim a tax deduction in a limited partnership if the taxpayer can show it is at risk of never realising a profit and of losing its initial investment.

## at sight

a notation on a draft which indicates that payment is due upon its presentation.

## at the bell

in context of general equities, at the opening or close of the market.

## at the close order

in the context of securities, an all or none market order that is to be executed at the closing price of the security on the exchange. If the execution cannot be made under this condition, the order is to be treated as cancelled. In the context of futures and options, refers to a contract that is to be executed on some exchanges during the closing period, a period in which there is a range of prices.

## at the figure

in context of general equities, at the whole integer price (excluding the fraction) closest to the side of the market (bid/ask) being discussed. At the full.

## at the opening order

in context of general equities, market order or limited price order that is to be executed at the opening (and corresponding price) of the stock or not at all and any such order or portion thereof not so executed is to be treated as cancelled.

## authority bond

a bond issued by a government agency or a corporation created to manage a revenue-producing public enterprise. The difference between an authority bond and a municipal bond is that margin protections may be incorporated in the authority bond contract as well as in the legislation that enables the authority.

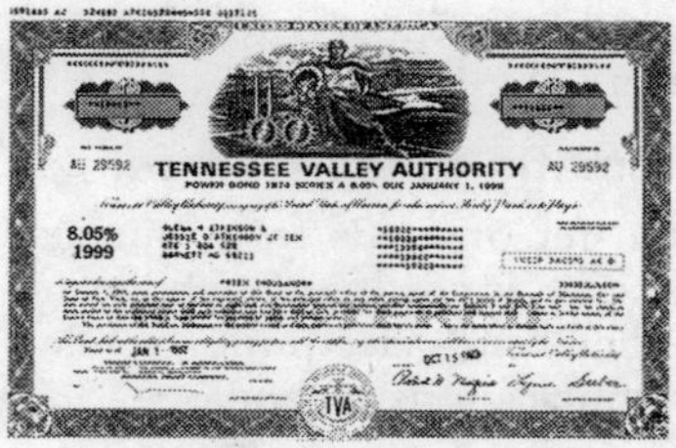


## authorised shares

1. are the number of shares that a corporation may issue. They represent the maximum shares that can be outstanding.
2. number of shares authorised for issuance by a firm's corporate charter.

## auto-correlation

the correlation of a variable with itself over successive time intervals. Sometimes called serial correlation.

## automatic exercise

occurs after an option expires. Each exchange and its clearing house has rules which govern this exercise. There are minimum in-the-money requirements. A holder of an option must inform the clearing house not to automatically exercise an option. These instructions not to exercise may be due to relatively high transaction costs, increases in position limits, or unacceptable alterations in position profiles. Also, after-hours trading indications may suggest dramatically different prices than those used to determine the automatic exercise in-the-money amounts.

■ **automatic extension**

an automatic extension of time granted to a taxpayer to file a tax return.

■ **automatic funds transfer**

a transfer of funds from one account or investment vehicle to another using electronic or telecommunications technology.

■ **automatic investment programme**

a programme in which an investor can invest or withdraw funds automatically. A mutual fund, for example, automatically withdraw a pre-determined, specified amount from the investor's bank account on a regular basis.

■ **automatic withdrawal**

a mutual fund that gives shareholders the right to receive a fixed payment from dividends on a quarterly or monthly basis.

■ **autoregressive**

using past data or variable of interest to predict future values of the same variable.

■ **availability float**

cheque deposited by a company that have not yet been cleared.

■ **available on the way in**

in context of general equities, stock is available to new customer as trade initiated by another customer is about to be consummated (on the exchange floor). Usually said to an inquiring salesperson.

■ **average (across-day) measures**

an estimation of price that uses the average or representative price of a large number of trades.

■ **average accounting return**

the average project earnings after taxes and depreciation divided by the average book value of the investment during its life.

■ **average age of accounts receivable**

the weighted-average age of all the firm's outstanding invoices.

■ **average cost**

in the context of investing, refers to the average cost of shares or stock bought at different prices over time.

■ **average cost of capital**

a firm's required payout to bondholders and stockholders expressed as a percentage of capital contributed to the firm. Average cost of capital is computed by dividing the total required cost of capital by the total amount of contributed capital.

■ **average daily balance**

a method for calculating interest in which the balance owed each day by a customer is divided by the number of days.

■ **average down**

a strategy used by investors to reduce the average cost of shares, in which the investor purchases more shares with a fixed amount of capital as the price of the shares decrease. The investor receives more shares per dollar and decreases the average price per share.

■ **average equity**

a customer's average daily balance in a trading account at a brokerage firm.

■ **average life**

also referred to as the Weighted-Average Life (WAL). The average number of years that each rupee of unpaid principal due on the mortgage remains outstanding. Average life is computed as the weighted-average time to the receipt of all future cash flows, using as the weights the rupee amounts of the principal paydowns.

■ **average maturity**

the average time to maturity of securities held by a mutual fund. Changes in interest rates have greater impact on funds with longer average maturity.

■ **Average Rate of Return (ARR)**

the ratio of the average cash inflow to the amount invested.

■ **average tax rate**

taxes as a fraction of income; total taxes divided by total taxable income.

■ **avoidance of contract**

the legal cancellation of a contract because an event occurs that makes performance of the contract terms impossible or inequitable and that releases the parties from their obligations.

■ **await instructions**

is the designation for a special pairing or matching of transactions. It also refers to additional handling instructions for a transaction for a specific account. These instructions supercede the standard or default instructions.

■ **award**

is the decision of an Arbitration Panel.

■ **away from us**

used in context of general equities, to characterise role of a competing broker/dealer. Trading away from us signifies that stock is bought and/or sold with institutions using other trading firms.

■ **axe to grind**

used in context of general equities. Involvement in a security, whether through a position, order, or inquiry.

■ **back haul**

1. Return transportation movement, usually at less revenue than the original move.
2. Movement in the direction of lighter traffic flow when traffic generally is heavier in the opposite direction.
3. To move a shipment back over part of a route already travelled.
4. The return of a carrier to the original point or area from which its journey began. If a carrier can obtain cargo to carry on the back haul route, that cargo may often obtain a favourable freight rate be-

cause otherwise the carrier would have to return empty.

■ **back office**

is the area or function which relates to the processing, record keeping and other operational aspects of transactions for financial firms.

■ **back order**

that portion of an order that cannot be delivered at the scheduled time, but will be delivered at a later date when available.

■ **back-end load**

refers to charges which are imposed upon the redemption or liquidation of an investment position. Often these charges are on a sliding scale. Sometimes, these charges are viewed as early withdrawal penalties. They are called back-end because they occur at the end of the investment process.

■ **backing away**

occurs when a market maker does not honour its requirement to buy or sell the minimum amount of a security. Sometimes, this action can be suspected by the wilful failure to answer telephones or to update computers.

■ **backwardation**

is the market condition whereby the deferred or more forward delivery months are at a progressive discount to the spot or nearby month. This is also known as an inverted market. This is opposite to a contango or carrying charge market.

■ **bad faith**

the intent to mislead or deceive. It does not include misleading by an honest, inadvertent or uncalled-for misstatement.

■ **bagged cargo**

goods shipped in sacks.

■ **bailment**

a delivery of goods or personal property by one person (the bailor) to another (the bailee) on an express or implied contract for a particular purpose related to the goods while in possession of the bailee, who has a duty to redeliver them to the bailor.

■ **bailout**

is an action taken by others to help a company, organisation or country with its finances. It is an analogy to bailing out a sinking boat. There is considerable debate as to whether the process is a handout, subsidy or a helping hand.

■ **balance of payments**

1. a statement summarising all the economic and financial transactions between companies, banks, private households and public authorities of one nation with those of the other nations of the world over a specific time period. It includes merchandise trade payments, payments and receipts on account of shipping services, tourist services, financial services, government expenditures, short and long term capital movements, interest and dividends, gold movements, etc.

2. a tabulation of a country's credit and debit transactions with other countries and international institutions. These transactions are di-

vided into two broad groups: current account and capital account. The main items included are exports and imports of goods and services (the balance of trade), foreign direct investments, intergovernmental loans, transfer payments, capital inflows and outflows and changes in official gold holdings and foreign exchange reserves.

## ■ balance of trade

the difference in value between a country's total imports and exports over a specific time period.

## ■ balanced economy

a condition of national finances in which imports and exports are equal.

## ■ balanced funds

are mutual funds that invest in both stocks and bonds. The stocks can be both common and preferred. A primary objective is to balance income and growth.

**Balanced Fund Composite**

| *Year* | *APCM Composite Total Return (percent)* | *Benchmark: 50% S+P 500 50% Lehman Govt/Credit* | *Number of Portfolios* | *Total Assets at Year End As of December 31 ($US Millions)* |
|---|---|---|---|---|
| *2000* | *.95* | *1.18* | *4* | *$65.7* |
| *1999* | *9.25* | *9.06* | *3* | *$60.1* |
| *1998* | *21.70* | *19.45* | *2* | *$52.9* |
| *1997* | *22.77* | *21.27* | *2* | *$121.9* |
| *1996* | *11.90* | *12.64* | *2* | *$110.9* |
| *1 Year* | *.95* | *1.18* | | |
| *3 Years* | *10.31* | *9.64* | | |
| *5 Years* | *13.02* | *12.48* | | |

## ■ bale

a large bundle or package of compressed and bound goods, usually with an outer covering, often of burlap.

## ■ bale cargo

cargo shipped in bales.

## ■ ballast

heavy material or water placed in the lower holds of a ship or in strategically placed tanks along the sides to improve its stability.

## ■ BAN (Bond Anticipation Note)

is a short term security issued by a municipality. The security will be paid or redeemed by funds from a new issue. It is a cash management tool.

## ■ bank delivery order to an airline

a letter addressed to an air carrier from a bank who is shown as consignee on an airway bill instructing the carrier to release a shipment. Often airlines will accept as a delivery order a bank's endorsement on the airwaybill, although an airway bill is a non-negotiable document.

## ■ bank draft

a form of check drawn by a bank against its account in another bank.

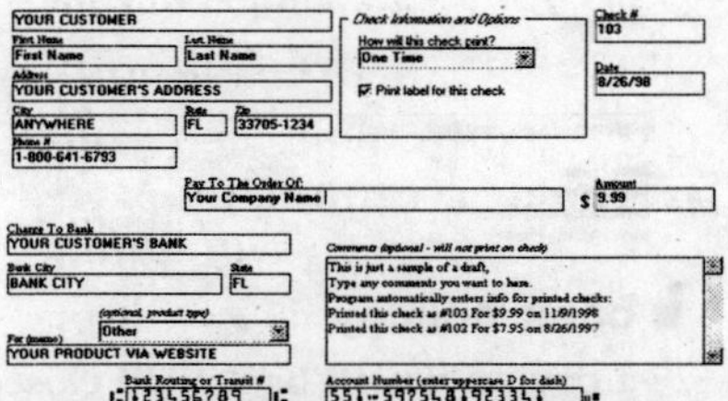


## ■ bank guarantee

an indemnity letter in which the bank commits itself to pay a certain sum if a third party fails to perform or if any other form of default occurs. One use is when a bank wants a carrier to release a shipment which it has financed but the original bills of lading are not yet available for surrender to the carrier.

### ■ bank guarantee letter

is a document by which an approved bank certifies that a put option writer or grantor has sufficient funds at the bank to cover the write. The funds are equal to the exercised value of the put. This value is equal to the strike price multiplied by the number of shares. It effectively reflects an outright purchase of the underlying security at the strike level.

**Sample Bank Letter of Guarantee**

Date:______________

To: United States Amusement Auction
P. O. Box 4819
Louisville, Kentucky 40204
Phone: 502-551-1866

RE: ____________________________
(Name on Company or Personal Check)

Account Number: ____________________________

Dear Sirs,

Please accept this letter as our guarantee of payment of check #(s) __________
drawn on ____________________________
(Name on Company or Personal Check),
Account #____________________________
for amounts to and including $____________________________
(Dollar Amount of Guarantee)

We understand the auction will be held on February 24, 1999 and we will accept checks presented to this bank until ______________, 1999. (At least 10 business days) At which time this guarantee will expire.

Yours Truly,

________________________
(Signature of Authorized Bank Officer)

Bank Name
Bank Address
Bank Telephone Number
Bank Routing Number

### ■ bank holiday

a day on which banks are closed.

### ■ bank market

is the spot and forward markets for currencies. Here, there are known counter parties to the transactions.

### ■ bank note

a promissory note having the appearance of currency, issued by a bank or banker authorised to do so, payable to bearer on demand and intended to circulate as money.

### ■ bank release

a document issued by a bank who is the consignee of a shipment authorising a carrier to deliver a shipment.

### ■ banker's acceptance

a draft calling for payment at a future date on which the drawee is a bank and the bank has agreed to pay by signing accepted on the draft.

### ■ banker's acceptances

are money market instruments which are used to finance import or export transactions. These instruments are essentially checks and represents a bank's promise and ability to pay the face or principal amount on the stipulated maturity date. Maturities are generally less than 3 months. Bankers Acceptances are viewed as money market instruments.

### ■ banker's bank

a bank that is established by mutual consent by independent and unaffiliated banks to provide a clearinghouse for financial transactions.

### ■ banker's draft

a draft payable on demand and drawn by, or on behalf of, a bank upon itself or upon another bank, sometimes a foreign bank, where it maintains an account or a relationship.

**bankruptcy**
the condition of a legal entity that does not have the financial means to pay their incurred debts as they come due.

**bareboat charter**
the charter of a vessel where the charter party has the right to use his own master and crew on the vessel. Pays all operating expenses.

**barge**
a flat bottomed cargo vessel primarily used on rivers and canals. Usually it is towed or pushed but it may be self-propelled.

**bearer**
the person in possession of a negotiable instrument, document of title, or security marked payable to bearer, or the person in possession of one of these documents endorsed in blank.

**bearer bond**
is a security which does not have the owner's name on the certificate. Interest and principal are paid to the person presenting the attached coupons to the agents for payment.

**beggar-thy-neighbour policy**
a course of action through which a country tries to reduce unemployment and increase domestic output by raising tariffs and instituting non-tariff barriers that impede imports and thus improve its own position at the expense of its trading partners.

**belly pits or holds**
compartments beneath the cabin of an aircraft used for the transport of cargo or baggage.

**benchmark**
is the standard to measure, monitor, price or evaluate a security or derivative. The treasury market is the benchmark for the corporate, mortgage backed, international and emerging credit markets. Here, securities are priced in terms of yield pickup relative to a comparable treasury. This comparability is often in terms of maturity though duration or average life become more meaningful for securities which have option characteristics.

**beneficiary**
1. In the case of a letter of credit, the individual or company who is entitled to draw or demand payment under its terms.
2. in the case of insurance, the person entitled to take the proceeds.
3. the person for whose benefit a contract, or trust, or will is executed or enforced.

**benefit**
the amount your insurance company will pay for a service.

**BEO**
is Book-Entry-Only.

**bequest**
to give or leave something by will, typically personal property or assets.

**■ berth**

the place beside a docking area where a ship is secured and cargo can be loaded or unloaded.

**■ bet**

is slang for a market position.

**■ bond equivalent yield**

is the procedure which relates discounted rates such as treasury bills and eurodollars to a bond standard. It is typical for discounted paper to be computed on the basis of a 360-day year whereas bonds are usually based on a 365 day year. If this equivalency is not done then the quoted short-term rates for discounted instruments may be understated.

**■ bond funds**

are mutual funds that invest in credit instruments. There can be distinctions, such as, treasury, international, sovereign, mortgage backed, investment grade corporate and high yield or junk bonds.

**■ bond of indemnity**

a bond to indemnify and save harmless the party to whom the bond is issued against some anticipated loss.

**■ book**

is a term which has several meanings. It can refer to a broker's client list; it may refer to the size and variety of a trader's or trading desk's positions; it may also refer to the process of recording a trade or transaction.

**■ book entry**

is the process or the name given to securities whose ownership and transfer occurs on a computer system.

**■ book runner**

refers to the lead or managing underwriter who runs or maintains the books for the transaction. Often, this underwriter is given total credit for the size of the deal in some metrics. Here, the total value of the deal would be credited to that underwriter as if they solely did the deal. Of course, other parties would receive their renumeration.

**■ book transfer**

is the conveyance or change in ownership without a physical delivery.

**■ booking**

the making of arrangements for a shipment with the representatives of a vessel or airline.

**■ books**

refer to the accounting records or the Official Books and Records of an organisation, person, or financial institution.

**■ bootstrapping**

is the technique to initiate a sample or process. It can use a piece of data to generate or infer other data. These other data are not necessarily observations.

**■ borrow**

is the term which indicates a credit relationship. In securities it can refer to borrowing funds or borrowing securities. When borrowing funds it is for margin for financing purposes. When borrowing securities, it is for short selling or hedging purposes.

## ■ bottom freight

heavy freight that must be loaded on the trailer floor and not on top of other merchandise.

## ■ bottom line

is a term that has several meanings which depend on usage and context.
Often, it refers to the net profitability (profits or losses) of a business.
It may refer to an answer, point of a long commentary, or a conclusion.

## ■ bounties

a compensation paid to persons to induce certain actions. In this class are government payments to producers or exporters to strengthen their competitive position.

## ■ box

has two primary meanings. It can refer to an options strategy or an operations term. For the later, it is the safe, cabinet, or other physical depository for securities which is located in the back office.
When box refers to an options strategy it is the placement of both a bull and a bear spread. One spread is comprised of puts and the other is comprised of calls. Both spreads have the same expiration. It is an arbitrage technique which self-liquidates at expiration. Boxes can be executed as either debit or credit strategies.

## ■ box car

a closed railroad freight car.

## ■ boycott

a concerted refusal to deal commercially with a person, firm, or country.

## ■ brand name

prescription drugs with a trademark or trade name that identifies the product or manufacturer.

## ■ break bulk

1. to unload, sort and reload some/all contents of a vehicle in transit.
To reduce a large shipment of a single commodity to many small shipments, which are then dispersed to various buyers.
2. loose, noncontainerised cargo imported in bulk, usually because of size or weight considerations (such as raw materials or oversized machinery). These shipments are often separated into individual lots and routed to different destinations and/or importers.

## ■ break clause

a clause in a lease giving either or both parties the right to terminate a lease in specified circumstances.

## ■ breakage

1. a monetary allowance that a manufacturer allots for compensation to a buyer for breakage to goods (usually fragile) while in shipment.
2. a fractional amount due to either party in a transaction, for example in computing interest.
3. in marine insurance, breakage refers to breakage of fragile goods

such as glass and china.

### ■ break bulk cargo

cargo that is shipped in packing units such as cartons, cases, crates, bales, or drums, but not containerised.

### ■ breakdown time

a type of penalty pay which is incurred when equipment breaks down.

### ■ breakeven point

is the level whereby an investor neither profits or loses. It is often used in options and other derivatives trading. Aside from transaction costs such as commissions, fees or spreads, there is usually a premium involved. For example, the breakeven point for a purchase call would be the strike price plus the premium to establish the effective breakeven strike price or breakeven level. In the case of a purchased put, it would be the strike price of the put adjusted by the paid premium. The market has to move down through the strike price by an amount equal to the premium paid. This effectively means that the breakeven level is lower than the contract's exercise price.

### ■ breakout

is the departure from a trading range. It can be on the upside or the downside.

### ■ bridge bank

is an organisation which is created to serve as a vehicle to transport damaged loans or securities from an ailing financial institution. Often these nonperforming securities are package into securities or portfolios, which may be, acquired by turn-around specialists or vulture funds at significantly discounted prices. This activity can help improve the creditworthiness of the impaired financial institution because loans or securities in default are no longer held by that institution. This frees up regulatory capital for other purposes and removes impediments for complying with various regulatory bodies and banking laws. It should be noted that from a banking, brokerage or insurance perspective, illiquid or defaulted loans and securities have substantially higher regulatory capital haircuts relative to most other liquid securities.

### ■ bridge loan

is a type of temporary financing which is extended until permanent financing is secured. At that time, funds from the new permanent financing are used to pay off the bridge loan. Sometimes, investment banks have arranged, if not granted, bridge loans in order to participate in a syndicate mandated to raise long-term or permanent financing.

### ■ bridging credit

borrowing ahead of receiving payment for a sale, or short-term credit to a customer pending his or her receipt of funds from another source.

### ■ broker

1. An agent who arranges interstate movement of goods by other carriers.

2. An arranger of exempt loads for owner-operators and/or carriers.
3. One who arranges the buying/selling of goods for a commission.
4. A person who leases owned equipment to a carrier.
5. an intermediary between a buyer and a seller in a highly organised market, as in the case of a stockbroker.
6. broker is the party who acts as an agent for his customer. The broker receives a commission as compensation. This person is also known as an AE, AP, IE, RR, or registered customer support person. Brokers are required to be licensed according to product lines and states when required.
7. one that acts as an agent for others, as in negotiating contracts, purchases, or sales in return for a fee or commission.

## ■ buckets

refers to categories for securities or derivatives. Some buckets refer to maturity classifications, such as, 3, 6, 12 month buckets. There are many other designations as well. The term can also refer to duration adjusted groups, option adjusted groups and other predefined categories which represent a dominant, common feature.

## ■ buffer stocks

commodity stockpiles managed in such a way as to moderate price fluctuations. Goods may be sold from a stockpile when prices reach or approach predetermined ceiling prices and they may be purchased for the stockpile when prices reach or approach predetermined floor levels. Rubber and cocoa are among the commodities considered most likely to benefit from buffer stocks and international commodity agreements exist for both of these products.

## ■ building lease

a long-term lease, imposing an obligation on the lessee to erect one or more buildings on the leased land, which will become the property of the landlord after the lease expires.

## ■ bulk cargo

cargo that is made up of an unpacked commodity; examples include grain, oil and ore.

## ■ bulk carrier

1. vessel that carries bulk commodities such as petroleum, grain, or ore, which are not packaged, bundled, bottled, or otherwise packed.
2. a transporter (usually an ocean-going vessel) of large, heavy cargoes. Dry cargoes are usually mineral ores (such as phosphates or manganese), as opposed to liquid hydrocarbons, a phrase that usually refers to petroleum.
3. a vessel designed for the shipment of bulk cargo.

## ■ bulk freight

freight not in packages or containers such as wheat, petroleum, etc.

## ■ bulk sale

the transfer or sale of substantially all of an inventory of an enterprise in a single transaction, not in the usual course of business.

**bulk solids**

dry cargo shipped loose, such as grain, ore, etc.

**bulkhead**

1. an upright wall in a trailer or railcar that separates and stabilises a load.
2. a cargo restraining partition in a vehicle or vessel.

**bull**

is a person such as an investor, speculator, or strategist who thinks that a stock, index, or market will appreciate in value.

**bull spread**

is an option strategy which is structured to profit from price increases in the underlying market. These spreads can be done for credits or debits. They can be built with calls or puts. When these strategies are done one-for-one, then the purchase of the lower strike and the sale of the higher strike establish the bullish characteristic. Here, the common strategies are vertical, diagonal and weighted spreads.

**bullet**

is a type of credit security which repays the entire principal on the maturity date. Prior to the maturity or prepayment of the bond, interest payments are to be made in accordance with the payment schedule.
Treasury and Corporate bonds pay off in lump sum principal amounts whereas many mortgages pay off on an amortisation basis.

**bundles**

1. are variations of strip trades whereby a trader or risk manager can place a series of calendar month contracts in one transaction. Packs can be bought or sold. They are quoted in quarter basis points from the previous settlement price. These transactions expedite credit market positions and swap hedges and adjustments. One can also trade bundles on a forward basis comparable to other money and credit market instruments.
2. refers to copper cathodes which are strapped together.

**bunker adjustment factor**

an adjustment in shipping charges to offset price fluctuations in the cost of bunker fuel.

**bunker fuel**

the fuel used to power a ship.

**bunker(s)**

1. a compartment (hold) of a ship for storage of fuel.
2. the fuel for a vessel

**burnout**

is a phenomenon in the mortgage market. It represents the tendency of pools to become less sensitive to interest rate declines with the passage of time. While there may have been a surge in prepayments due to declining interest rates, the remaining mortgages do not prepay as quickly as the previous ones in the pools. It is implied that these remaining mortgages are less vulnerable to further accelerated prepayment risks.

**butterfly option spread**

is an options strategy which uses

three strike prices for the same instrument and same expiration date. It can consist of the sale of two at-the-money options (puts or calls) and the purchase of one (put or call) at a higher strike price and the purchase of one (put or call) at a lower strike price.

■ **butterfly trade**

is the sale of two units of a futures contract and the purchase of two units of a futures contract. Here, the contracts are positioned across three different delivery months. One pattern would be buy 1 March, Sell 2 April and Buy 1 May. This strategy is also used in the credit markets.

■ **buy on close**

is an order to make a purchase on the close. It can be a market or limit order.

■ **buy on opening**

is an order to make a purchase on the opening. It can be a market or limit order.

■ **buyer's right to route**

when a seller does not pay freight charges, the purchaser has a right to designate the route for shipment. Seller is responsible for following the buyer's instructions. Complete routing is permitted for rail shipments, but only for the first carrier in motor shipments.

■ **buyer's market**

refers to a situation when a purchaser has greater flexibility and influence in receiving concessions. Often the choices are more plentiful and the prices lower than previously transacted.

■ **buy-in**

occurs when a seller or short seller fails to deliver the securities required to satisfy a transaction's terms. The net financial impact of this transaction is charged to the account of the seller.

■ **buying power**

refers to the amount of securities that can be purchased in a margin account.

■ **buy-side or buyside**

refers to financial organisations which tend to be natural buyers of securities, such as mutual funds, insurance companies and money managers.

■ **cab**

driver's compartment of a truck or tractor.

■ **cable seal**

a heavy steel cable used to secure closed trailer doors. It can only be removed with heavy duty cable cutters.

■ **cabotage**

1. water transportation, navigation or trade along the coasts, between the ports of one nation.
2. inland freight movements confined within the national boundaries of a nation are also sometimes called cabotage.

■ **cab-over**

truck or tractor with a substantial part of the driving cab located over the engine.

**■ cage**

is the area of the back office where securities, checks and limited amounts of cash are processed and held.

**■ call**

1. a demand for early repayment of an obligation, or for the performance of a specific act under a contract.
2. a demand for the payment of money.
3. the act of redeeming a bond earlier than the full term.
4. short for Call Option, a contract giving the holder the right to receive from the issuer a specified amount of a security at a specified price on or before a certain date.
5. short for Margin Call: a call by a future or an options exchange, or by a broker to its clients, for additional collateral to that previously posted when the futures, options, or securities were purchased without posting their full value.

**■ call money**

money lent by banks on a short term basis which the bank, as lender, can call (demand payment at any time, usually on 24 hours notice.)

**■ call option**

is a contract whereby the purchaser, owner or holder is given the right but is not obliged to purchase the underlying security or commodity at a fixed strike price within a limited time frame.

**■ cancel**

is the instruction to terminate an order either in its entirety or partly.

**■ CAO**

is the Chief Administrative Officer.

**■ cap**

is the ceiling, upper limit price, or interest rate which would be paid. It is analogous to a long call position.

**■ capacity load**

1. a trailer loaded to the legal weight limit.
2. a trailer loaded so that no additional piece of freight, equal to the size of the largest piece tendered, will fit into the trailer

**■ capacity to contract**

legal competency to make a contract.

**■ capital**

property or wealth that yields income expressed in terms of money. Also, the accumulated stock of tools, machinery, equipment, buildings and other goods employed, in turn, to produce other goods and services.

**■ capital account**

that portion of a country's balance of payments that includes the inward and outward flow of money for investment and international grants and loans (public and private).

**■ capital goods**

1. durable goods which are used to produce other goods for consumption: for example machinery,

equipment, buildings.
2. also, material used or consumed to produce other goods.
3. industrial products or other goods that are used in the creation of additional wealth, such as machine tools. Capital goods are sometimes called intermediate goods because they only indirectly satisfy human wants (as opposed to consumer goods, which satisfy human wants directly) and they are sometimes called producer goods, because they are used to produce other goods.

■ **capital market**

the market for longer-term loanable funds. The capital market in a country is not one institution; rather, it includes securities exchanges, underwriters, investment banks and insurance companies that canalise supply and demand for long-term capital and claims on capital. The marketing of securities is an important element in the efficient working of a capital market.

■ **capital stock**

refers to all the common and preferred shares, if any, for a corporation.

■ **capital surplus**

refers to the accounting difference between the amount received by the initial sale of a corporation's stock less the par value of that stock. Since many new issues are sold at prices in excess of the par value, the proceeds component can be significant. Other related terms are Paid-In Capital or Paid-In Surplus.

■ **capital value**

the value of an asset, freehold or leasehold, as distinct from its annual or periodic (rental) value.

■ **captain's protest**

a written sworn statement of the master of a vessel to the effect that damage suffered by the ship during the voyage was caused by storm or other peril of the sea, without any negligence or misconduct on his own part.

■ **cargo**

merchandise hauled by transportation lines.

■ **cargo agent**

an agent appointed by an airline or shipping line to solicit and process international air and ocean freight shipments.

■ **cargo manifest**

a list of cargo being transported or warehoused.

■ **cargo sharing**

the reservation and division of maritime traffic between designated trading partners who agree that vessels owned or controlled by either will carry a specified percentage of the cargo moving between them.

■ **cargo tonnage**

the weight of a shipment or of ship's total cargo expressed in tons.

■ **carrying charge**

is the amount to carry an inventory or carry a position for a set period such as a month. In the case of securities it is the funding with an allowance for dividends or interest income. For commodities, it includes storage, insurance and cost of funds.

**■ carrying charge market**

is the implied term structure for a commodity market. It lists progressively higher prices for the more distant delivery months. This progression in prices reflects the assumption of cumulatively higher storage and financing costs over time.

**■ carryover or carryout**

is the amount of inventory or supply which exists at the end of a season or crop year and is added to the supply for the new crop year.

**■ cart**

a four wheeled platform used to move several pieces of freight across the dock at one time.

**■ cartel**

a group of independent producers which regulates production, pricing and marketing by members to maximise market power and limit competition.

**■ case mark**

information shown on the outside of a shipping carton, including destination and contents.

**■ cash**

is a term used in several ways. Sometimes refers to immediate funds, the settlement payment on the trade date, instruments which display high degrees of liquidity and act as cash equivalents, or the spot market.

**■ Cash Against Documents (CAD)**

a term used in collections supported by shipping documents which are released to the buyer only against payment.

**■ Cash Before Delivery (CBD)**

seller assumes no risk and extends no credit because payment is received before shipment.

**■ cash cow**

is a security, investment or a project which generates or throws off lots of funds due to contacts or contracts. Sometimes, the basis for this asset is an excellent customer, a monopolistic market position, or special advantage afforded by patents, licenses, or other economic properties. This cash flow can be used for many purposes. Typically, this situation constitutes the fundamental franchise of a business.

**■ cash equivalent security**

is a term which has several meanings. It often refers to high grade instruments which are very liquid and have very little time to maturity. Among these are treasury bills, commercial paper and bankers' acceptances. In a somewhat broader sense it can include money market shares and short-term municipal paper.

**■ Cash On Delivery (COD)**

buyer pays carrier the price of

goods before they are delivered; seller assumes risk of purchaser refusing to accept goods.

**■ cash sale or cash transaction**

is a transaction which calls for cash payment, delivering and settlement on the same day as the trade. This compares to a Regular Way transaction which are traded on one day and settled on a different day in accordance with industry standards or special terms. These trades are sometimes made to receive a dividend, to be entitled to a rights offering, or to be a shareholder on a record date in order to vote. It should be noted that the settlement process has been shrinking in order to reduce the risk associated with an open trade and its still to be made settlement.

**■ cash settlement**

is the practice of making a final cash payment or adjustment for an open position. This process differs from early or traditional futures markets that required either a futures contract offset or the delivery of a physical commodity. The cash settlement process recognises the insurability factor of risk management products. This trend towards cash settlements reduces instability due to squeezes, weather, or other disruptive variables.

**■ casus major**

an extraordinary casualty such as a fire, shipwreck etc.

**■ category groups**

a classification system which groups various products for statistical, export control or quota control purposes.

**■ cathode**

refers to copper which is in flat bar form and is exchange tradeable.

**■ CATS**

are Certificates of Accrual on Treasury Securities. In a generic sense, the sliced off interest payments or coupons are called strips or zeroes. At those times the discounted bond principal is referred to as the Corpus.

**■ caveat emptor**

let the buyer beware, which is to say the purchaser buys at his own risk.

**■ certificate of inspection**

a certificate issued by an independent third party verifying the condition of cargo or of property.

**■ chargeable weight**

the weight or volume of a shipment used in determining freight charges.

**■ charitable gift annuity**

typically an agreement in which you transfer cash or other assets to a charitable organisation in exchange for its promise to pay you an annuity for life or for a term of years.

**■ charitable trust**

a trust having a charitable

organisation as a beneficiary.

■ **charter service**

temporary hiring of an aircraft or vessel for the transportation of cargo or passengers.

■ **chartered ship**

a ship leased for a stated time, voyage, or voyages.

■ **chassis**

1. a special trailer or undercarriage on which containers are moved over the road.
2. the undercarriage of a vehicle.

■ **cheap**

is a term used in relative value analysis. The cash flow characteristics, when analysed against a benchmark or comparison bond, suggest an under-valued security. This implies that the former security has arbitrage potential against the comparative security.

■ **chock**

a wooden, metal, or rubber wedge used to block the wheels of a trailer at the dock. Also used in trailers to keep floor freight from shifting.

■ **churning**

is an excessive amount of trading of customer funds by a broker. The intent is to generate commission or brokerage fees and not client performance.

■ **CIF**

refers to Cost, Insurance and Freight.

■ **city terminal service**

a service provided by some airlines that involves receiving or delivering cargo at terminals in-town instead of at airports.

■ **claim**

1. a demand of payment.
2. in insurance, a demand for payment of money or property as the result of an insured loss.
3. in transportation, a demand for return of overpaid charges. Also, a demand for reimbursement of losses due to loss or casualty to cargo or failure to deliver.
4. a bill submitted to your insurance company for payment.
5. demand on transportation company for payment due to loss/damage of freight during transit.
6. demand on transportation company for refund on overcharge.
7. demand by an individual/company to recover for loss under insurance policy.

■ **class**

is the total of all options of the same type, put or call, which have the same expiration date.

■ **class rate**

the rate charged for commodities grouped according to similar shipping characteristics. Class Rate applies to numbered/lettered groups/classes of articles contained in the territorial rating column in classification schedules.

## ■ clean draft

a draft with no commercial documents attached.

## ■ clearance

1. the completion of governmental requirements so that a carrier may arrive in a port and unload cargo and passengers, or may lade cargo and passengers and depart for a foreign destination.
2. the accomplishment of the customs formalities necessary to allow goods to be imported or to be exported.

## ■ clearing

is the process of financial guarantee between clearing members. This activity intends to eliminate the risk of contractual or transactional default.
For example, two clients execute a trade through two different clearing member firms. The clients are solvent but at the end of the day one of the clearing members is not. This transaction through a clearing-house would preserve the integrity of the trade.

## ■ close out

is the action taken by a brokerage firm when a client fails to pay for previously purchased securities. Here, the brokerage firm will sell the aforementioned securities.

## ■ closed end investment company or fund

is an investment vehicle that issues shares in a fashion similar to other corporations. The number of shares outstanding is relatively fixed unlike open end investment funds which tend to have variable shares outstanding. Closed End shares can trade at a premium or discount to the net asset value.

## ■ closed-end transaction

a credit transaction with a fixed amount of time for repayment.

## ■ closing or to close for real estate

is the meeting which finalises a real estate transaction. The deed is transferred from the seller to the buyer. Financial settlement is made at that time.

## ■ closing transaction

refers to the sale or purchase of an option contract which offsets a previously established open position.

## ■ CMBS

refers to Commercial Mortgage Backed Securities. These securities are very similar to mortgage backed securities in terms of structure, flexibility and variety of branches or tiers. The key difference is that CMBS are collateralised by commercial properties and not residential mortgages.

## ■ Codes of Conduct

in general usage in trade law, any international agreement that prescribes or recommends standards of behavior by nation-states or multinational corporations is deemed desirable by the international community. For example, the United Nations has encouraged the negotiation of several voluntary codes of conduct (meaning that they are not legally binding), including one that seeks to specify the rights and obligations of transnational corporations. More narrowly, 'codes of conduct' refers to the six agreements that were negotiated during the Tokyo Round to liberalise and harmonise domestic measures that might impede or distort trade: the Agreement on Technical Barriers to Trade, or Standards Code; the Agreement on Government Procurement, or Government Procurement Code; the Agreement on Interpretation and Application of Articles VI, XVI and XXIII of the General Agreement on Tariffs and Trade, or Subsidies Code; the Agreement on Implementation of Article VII, or Customs Valuation Code; the Agreement on Import Licensing Procedures, or Import Licensing Code; and the Agreement on Implementation of Article VI, or Anti-Dumping Code.

## ■ coefficient of variation

is a statistic which is used to determine the degree of relative dispersion. It extends standard deviation analyses. By definition, standard deviations are statistical measures of absolute dispersion. Therefore, it is difficult to compare the variability of two different asset classes or assets within those classes. It is computed by dividing the standard deviation of Asset I by the mean of Asset I. Similarly, the standard deviation of Asset II is divided by the mean of Asset II and so forth. These multiple coefficient of variation can then be compared against one another. By using the coefficient of variation, an analyst can compare variation among relatively high and low priced securities. Similarly, the analyst can evaluate the volatility differences between commodities, currencies, stocks and bond markets.

## ■ coinsurance

is a hedging or risk management term. It refers to the amount of loss that the investor is positioned to take. When a firm is 85 percent hedged, then it is said that the firm is coinsuring the remainder or 15 percent. When an individual holds 100 shares of stock priced at Rs. 80/share and is also a long put with a Rs. 75 strike price, the individual is said to be coinsuring for Rs. 500 or the difference between the market price and the exercise price.

## ■ collar

1. is the combination of a long Cap position and a short Floor position. It is sometimes called a range forward or a fence. Generally, it is structured so that the net cost of the collar is zero or close to zero. This means that the debit expense for the long cap premium is offset by the credit received for the short floor premium. This term is also used to define the prepayment speed range for a credit instrument.

2. an agreement that puts upper and lower limits on the interest rate of a financial instrument or on the price of something and through this device limits the possible

amount of loss or gain from the rise or fall of interest or price of the thing collared

■ **collateral**

1. is the underlying security, mortgage, or asset for the purposes of securitisation or borrowing and lending activities. It is pledged or held in trust.
2. asset pledged by a borrower to secure mortgage. The asset is subject to seizure in the event of default.

■ **collateral trust bond**

is a security issued by a corporation and is secured by other securities. This bond compares to Mortgage Backed Securities which are secured by real property or unsecured bonds. Depending on the underlying collateral and the terms of the issue, these bonds can offer somewhat better financing rates to the issuer.

■ **collateralised obligation**

is the generic term for a structure that carves up the initial cash flow from a similar set of assets into a new and often unique arrangement. By dividing and redistributing the cash flows, both principal and interest, the structure alters the disbursement of the underlying collateral cash flows into several securities. Some of these securities may experience greater stability whereas others may absorb more of the risky characteristics of the underlying assets. Under various circumstances, these structures can improve the credit rating of some of the deal's components.

■ **collect charges**

1. transportation practice where the receiver of the goods pays the freight and charges to the carrier.
2. collection practice where the buyer is expected to pay the bank charges for handling the collection.

■ **Collect On Delivery (COD)**

a service where the purchase price of a shipment is collected by the carrier upon delivery of the shipment and subsequently paid to the shipper.

■ **collect shipment**

shipment where collection of freight charges/advances is made by delivering carrier from the consignee/receiver.

■ **collecting bank**

a bank involved in the collection process. In this process if presentation is made to the drawee, it becomes also the presenting bank.

■ **collection**

1. the presentation for payment of an obligation and the payment thereof.
2. a gathering of similar goods.

■ **collection letter**

customer's written instructions to a bank on how to handle a collection. Many banks have an instruction form for use instead of a letter.

■ **collection papers**

drafts, invoices, printed lists, documents which relate to a shipment and other similar instruments presented to the designated buyer/payee to obtain payment or acceptance.

■ **co-load**

two shipments from different terminals combined to ship as one load.

■ **combination**

1. is an option strategy consisting of multiple parts. These parts can be puts and calls which are arranged as a single position.
2. truck or tractor coupled to one or more trailers (including semi-trailers).

■ **combination aircraft**

an aircraft capable of transporting both cargo and passengers on the same flight.

■ **combined bill of lading**

a bill of lading covering a shipment of goods by more than one mode of transportation.

■ **combined transport**

consignment sent by means of various modes of transport.

■ **comity**

1. in international relations it is the recognition that one sovereignty allows within its territory the legislative, executive or judicial acts of another sovereignty, with due regard to the rights of its own citizens.
2. courtesy, respect and good will.

■ **command economy**

an economic system where the decisions about allocation of resources, production, distribution and consumption are made by a central government authority instead of being determined by market forces. An example was the Nazi economy.

■ **commercial**

refers to a firm in the actual business of growing, mining, processing or otherwise bona fide commercial activity for a commodity market.

■ **commercial counterfeiting**

the production or marketing of goods with the intent of defrauding the purchaser by falsely conveying, directly or indirectly, that the goods are produced by a known and reputable manufacturer. Counterfeit goods are usually distinguished from bogus goods in that, in addition to replicating the legitimate good, they bear a forged trademark. The WTO Agreement on Trade-Related Aspects of Intellectual Property Rights includes provisions to discipline counterfeiting.

■ **commercial invoice**

a document which details the transaction between a seller and a buyer. It minimally should give the name and address of the seller and of the buyer, the date of the sale, a description of the goods sold, the quantity, the unit price, the terms of sale and the total money amount due. If it is an invoice between buyer and seller of different countries it should also indicate the kind of currency.

■ **commercial letter of credit**

an instrument by which a bank substitutes its credit for that of a customer to enable him to finance the purchase of goods or to incur other commitments. The bank issues a letter (or document) on behalf of its client to a supplier and agrees to pay them upon presentation of documentary evidence that the supplier has performed in accordance with the terms of the letter of credit.

## ■ commercial officers

embassy and consular officials who assist their country's citizens and businesses in a foreign country through arranging appointments with local business and government officials and providing counsel on local trade regulations, laws and customs.

## ■ commercial paper

1. an unsecured, short-term instrument. It has a maximum maturity of 270 days. It is issued by companies which have high credit ratings. This instrument is a cash management tool to finance short-term financial needs. It should be noted that corporate downgrades or bankruptcies can severely damage the value of these instruments.
2. negotiable instruments used in commerce. Usually they are short term, unsecured, promissory notes issued by highly rated entities and are traded on the money markets.
3. short-term financial instruments that can be bought and sold, particularly promissory notes that call for the payment of specified amounts of money at a given time.

## ■ commercial set

the documents required to evidence the shipment of goods. Usually includes an invoice, packing list and bill of lading; may include certificate of origin, certificate or policy of insurance and other special documents.

## ■ commercial treaty

an agreement between two or more countries that establishes the conditions under which business may be conducted between their citizens.

## ■ commingling

1. the packing or mingling of various goods subject to different rates of duty so that the value and quantity of each class of goods cannot be readily determined.
2. to combine funds or properties into a common mass.

## ■ commission

1. a board or committee officially appointed to perform certain functions or exercise certain jurisdiction of a public nature.
2. the amount paid by a principal to an agent for their role in the completion of a transaction involving the sale of goods or services.
3. the authority under which one acts, transacts business or negotiates for another.

## ■ commodity

broadly defined, any article exchanged in trade but most commonly used to refer to raw materials, including such minerals as tin, copper and manganese and bulk-produced agricultural products such as coffee, tea and rubber.

■ **commodity code**

the system of identifying a commodity by an assigned number.

■ **commodity pools**

are trading vehicles which combine investment funds from several different persons and trade the sum as one account. This entity is focused on futures and options on futures trading.

■ **commodity rate**

1. a special (usually lower) rate for specific types of goods (usually exempt commodities).
2. a rate lower than class rates, established to cover the movement of a specific customer's freight or for a specific group of customers.

■ **commodity, exempt**

one that may be transported in interstate commerce without operating authority or published rates.

■ **common carrier**

any carrier engaged in the interstate transportation of persons/ property on a regular schedule at published rates and whose services are available to the general public on a for-hire basis.

■ **common fund**

an international institution designed as the centrepiece of the UNCTAD Integrated Programme for Commodities. Its first account (sometimes called its first window and financed from mandatory contributions of member governments) provides funds to help finance buffer stocks maintained under international commodity agreements to stabilise commodity prices. Its second account (sometimes called its second window and largely financed by voluntary contributions) supports research and development and export promotion for selected commodities.

■ **common point**

1. a location serviced by two or more transportation lines.
2. a significant point over which aircrafts fly and report to the air controllers.

■ **Commonwealth of Independent States (CIS)**

a political group comprising the following independent nations, formerly a part of the Soviet Union: Armenia, Azerbaijan, Belarus, Georgia, Kazakhstan, Kyrgysstan, Moldova, Russia, Tajikistan, Turkmenistan, Ukraine and Uzbekistan.

■ **community property**

refers to assets or a method of ownership. Generally, it means that each spouse owns a 50 percent interest in an account. Upon the death of one spouse, the survivor claims his or her ownership of one-half of the asset. The other half will pass in accordance to will or to law.

■ **comparables**

in determining the initial rent, or the market rent during the course of a rent review, parties and those acting on their behalf will consider evidence of rents for similar properties. Comparables may also be used to analyse properties' sale values.

## comparative advantage

a central concept in international trade theory that holds that a country or a region should specialise in the production and export of those goods and services that it can produce relatively more efficiently than other goods and services and that it should import those goods and services in which it has a comparative disadvantage. This theory was first propounded by David Ricardo in 1817 as a basis for increasing the economic welfare of a population through international trade. The comparative advantage theory normally favours specialised production in a country based on intensive utilisation of those factors of production in which the country is relatively well endowed (such as raw materials, fertile land, or skilled labour) and perhaps also the accumulation of physical capital and the pace of research.

## compensation

the principle, central to GATT and the WTO, that any country that raises a tariff above its bound rate, withdraws a binding on a tariff, or otherwise impairs a trade concession must lower other tariffs or make other trade concessions to compensate for the disadvantage suffered by countries whose exports are affected.

## compensatory finance

a loan or transfer of financial resources on concessional terms to a country when its export receipts either total receipts from merchandise exports or receipts from a component of total exports, such as an individual commodity or a stated group of commodities, fall below a predetermined level. The loan, to be repaid according to a previously agreed formula, is intended to stabilise the country's export receipts over an indicated period. Compensatory arrangements exist under the International Monetary Fund and the Lomé Convention.

## competition policy

a framework of rules and regulations designed to foster the efficient allocation of resources as a means of promoting certain objectives, such as economic vitality, consumer welfare and/or other desirable public policy goals. Generally, antitrust laws and other competition laws and policies focus on efficient resource allocation at the national level. The extent to which restraints on competition, public or private, impair cross-border competition is being examined in a variety of international trade and economic forums such as the WTO.

## competitive

refers to a product that can be sold in an appropriate quantity within a specific market because buyers consider its price and quality acceptable, taking account of support services, credit, delivery terms, guaranteed repairs, promotion, or a combination of such factors, in comparison with other available goods.

## competitive rate

rate determined by one transportation line to compete with the rate of another transportation line.

## complex order

is an order which has multiple requirements. It can contain contingencies, stops, stop limits, time instructions and other elements.

## compliance

is the area or the process which has responsibility for firm and employee adherence to the rules and regulations which govern the broker/dealer business. This includes but is not limited to The Powers and Authorities for the firm's position taking and trading limits, guidelines indicated in the employee compliance handbook, registrations, continuing education, sales literature and employee trading activities. Generally, compliance functions are partitioned between registrations and other rules and guidelines. Non-selling employees are usually in compliance to avoid conflicts-of-interest. However, there are exemptions for very small organisations.

## compound option

is an option which is related to another option. A sequence of options such as a call on a subsequent call.

## compradore

an agent in a foreign country employed by a domestic businessman to facilitate transactions with local businesses within the foreign country.

## comps or comparables

refer to pricing or evaluation benchmarking efforts. In real estate the term is used to determine comparable properties for evaluation or assessment purposes. In the securities markets, the term has similar implications for pricing bonds, stocks and derivatives. For credit instruments, it refers to isolating the key pricing characteristics. Among these are issuer, type of collateral or issue, maturity, maturity to first option date, average life, duration, option adjusted duration and so forth. In the case of a simple corporate bond, it would benchmark to a comparable life treasury and adjust for credit rating and other pertinent risk factors by a spread. This spread would be added to the prevailing treasury and indicate what a fair yield would be for the corporate. For equity type securities, the process would involve finding similar companies in the same industry with similar economic profiles and outlooks. Among the considerations would be utility stock or internet stock, growth prospects, cashflow, EPS, value per hit and other determinative factors. Effectively, the process is pricing, marking-to-market, or evaluating by analogy.

## concealed damage

1. damage to the contents of a package which is not evident from

the appearance of the exterior of the package.
2. when goods in an apparently undamaged container are damaged.

## concealed loss

1. loss from a package bearing concealed damage.
2. damage, loss, or shortage of goods within a package which is not apparent from its exterior condition.

## concession

a grant of a position, privilege, or right by a party to a negotiation to induce the other party to yield an equivalent position, privilege, or right. In GATT trade negotiations, a country normally made concessions in the form of reductions in its tariff and nontariff import barriers, in exchange for reductions in the barriers of other countries to its exports. A country's schedule of concessions, accepted as part of its obligations to other contracting parties, would become an integral part of GATT under Article II of the General Agreement on Tariffs and Trade. GATT Article II continues to govern the obligations of country members under the WTO, where it is incorporated by reference into GATT 1994.

## conditional analysis

is the expectational methodology which is probability-based, event-driven and operates within a market environment which has dominant and secondary aspects.

## conditional most-favoured-nation treatment

the extension of concessions by an importing country to other countries that provide equivalent benefits for its exports.

## conditionality

the set of conditions attached to the use of its resources by the International Monetary Fund, involving undertakings and adjustment policies that will restore a sustainable balance-of-payments position within one- to three-year period.

## condominium

refers to a form of real estate ownership. Here, the owner holds title to a specific unit or dwelling while also holding an interest in the property's common areas.

## condor

is an option spread strategy which is akin to a butterfly. Here, there are four different strike prices for the same instrument and for the same date. Condors can be constructed with either calls or puts. They can be either long or short. A long condor entails the purchase of a low strike call, the sale of two different intermediate strike calls and the purchase of a relatively higher strike call.

## confirmation

is a ratification of an order. Usually it is in written form. Verbal confirms must be subsequently validated by a written record of the transaction.

## confirming bank

a bank which engages to honour a

letter of credit issued by another, or engages that such letter of credit will be honoured by the issuer or by a third bank.

**■ congestion**

refers to trading activity which occurs between two visible boundaries. Often this area is tight or relatively narrow in terms of amplitude.

**■ connecting carrier**

a carrier which has direct physical connection with another carrier or forms a connecting link between two or more carriers.

**■ consign**

send goods to a purchaser or an agent to sell.

**■ consignee**

1. the person or firm named in a freight contract to whom goods have been shipped or turned over for care.
2. any person who receives goods shipped from an owner.

**■ consignment**

1. goods or property sent by the aid of a carrier from one person (the consignor) to another (the consignee).
2. entrusting of goods to another to sell as agent for the sender.

**■ consignor**

any person or company that ships articles to customers.

**■ consolidated container**

a shipping container that contains cargo from various shippers for delivery to various consignees.

**■ consolidation**

1. in transportation, the combining of smaller shipments into a single shipment that is sent to a destination point.
2. the reorganisation of corporations to combine two or more into a successor corporation.
3. combining less-than-carload or less-than-truckload shipments to make carload/truckload movements.

**■ consolidator**

a company that provides freight consolidation services.

**■ constant maturity**

is a device which fixes maturities or time to expiration for bonds or derivatives. This fixation of time period enables one to compare and analyse assets or instruments in terms of all other things variable except for time.

**■ consulate**

an office of a country within another country (often there are several, located in the larger commercial centres). These offices represent the commercial interests of the citizens of their country.

**■ consultations**

formal discussions between two or more parties to an agreement with respect to their rights under the agreement. Typically, consultations are requested by a party that believes that its rights under an agreement have been nullified or impaired and are the first and often mandatory step in dispute settlement. If consultations are unsuccessful in resolving the dispute within a specified time, the dispute normally is submitted to a panel for a ruling. The most important multilateral agreements providing for consultations are the WTO's Understanding on Rules and Procedures Governing the Settlement of Disputes and GATT Articles XXII and XXIII.

## ■ consumer goods

1. any goods produced for the express use of individuals rather than the production or manufacturing of other goods.
2. goods that directly satisfy human desires (as opposed to capital goods). An automobile used for pleasure is considered a consumer good. An automobile used by a business person to deliver wares is considered a capital good.

## ■ consumers

individuals or groups that use economic goods and services, thus deriving utility from them.

## ■ consumption

the purchase and utilisation of goods or services for the gratification of human desires or in the production of other goods or services. The consumer may be an individual, a business firm, a public body, or other entity.

## ■ container

a reusable, rigid box in which merchandise is shipped by air, vessel, truck, or rail.

## ■ container freight charge

charge made for the packing or unpacking of cargo from ocean freight containers.

## ■ container load

a shipment of cargo that, according to weight or volume, will fit a standard container.

## ■ container on flatcar

a container without wheels put on railcars for transport inland,

## ■ container part load

a shipment of cargo that according to weight or volume will not fill a standard container on its own but is expected to be shipped in a container, if necessary with other shipments which are also too small to take up a full container themselves.

## ■ container vessel

an ocean going vessel designed specifically to handle the loading, carriage and removal of standard freight containers.

■ **containerisation**

1. using box-like device to store, protect and handle a number of packages as a unit of transit.
2. shipping system based on large cargo-carrying containers that can be interchanged between trucks, trains and ships without re-handling contents.

■ **contango**

is the normal or carrying charge structure for a commodity market. It lists progressively higher prices for the more distant delivery months. This progression in prices reflects implicitly cumulatively higher storage and financing costs.

■ **contingent order**

is an order with at least one contingency attached. Contingencies can be specific times or events.

■ **contraband**

any product that a nation has made unlawful to possess, produce, transport, import, or export.

■ **contract carrier**

1. excluding common carriers, any person who under contract will transport passengers or goods for agreed upon compensation.
2. any carrier engaged in interstate transportation of persons/ property by motor vehicle on a for-hire basis, but under continuing contract with one or a limited number of customers to meet specific needs of each customer.

■ **contract rates**

rates which are part of a total contract negotiated between shipper and a carrier.

■ **convenience yield**

is the assumed or expected benefit of holding a long position in a physical commodity. This holding is to satisfy existing near-term delivery commitments or to maintain uninterrupted manufacturing processes. It highlights the marginal value of an inventory relative to the anticipated usage. High convenience yields tend to occur in inverted or backward markets. In these situations, the costs of being without the physical commodity are greater than the premium paid to hold the commodity. A positive convenience yield is greater than the sum of the financing plus other storage carrying costs.

■ **conventional**

tractor with the engine in front of the cab.

■ **conventional tariff**

a tariff established through a convention (or international agreement) resulting from tariff negotiations and, hence, not subject to modifications by national action.

■ **convergence**

is the behaviour of a cash commodity or the underlying security instrument and the derivative moving towards one another.

■ **conversion**

is the action of transforming a security into another security. A convertible bond, when exercised, will convert into the stipulated number of common shares.

■ **convertibility**

the attribute of being exchangeable, such as a currency freely able to be exchanged for another, or as preferred stock or bonds to be exchanged for common stock.

■ **convertible**

is a security which can be exercised into another security. Examples of convertibles are bonds, preferred stocks, warrants and some swap agreements. Convertibles are related to options because they have specified spans for exercise, conversion price levels which approximate strike prices and there are inherent premium structures. These premiums are related to volatility considerations.

■ **convertible bond**

is a credit instrument which is convertible into equity. Usually, this conversion is done at the discretion and exercise of the bond holder and not the corporation. However, there may be forced conversions due to stipulated events such as takeovers or call options in favour of the issuer. Generally, convertible bonds are coupons paying but there are zero coupon convertible bonds as well. These bonds tend to have lower-than-market rates of interest in exchange for a potential equity stake for the bondholder.

■ **convertible preferred**

is a preferred stock which is convertible into common stock.

■ **convertible securities hedge funds**

generally look to purchase the bonds or preferred securities and sell common shares against these long positions. The intent is to hedge interest or dividend paying securities with low or no dividend common shares. In the event of a default the bonds and other securities have priority over the common shares. Also, the bonds or preferred stocks usually generate positive cash flows whereas the short positions are generally not responsible for dividend payments. Therefore the fund should have a positive cash flow and protected by relative seniority position in corporate securities. These funds also use warrants and options as portfolio instruments.

■ **convexity**

is the second derivative of the price/yield curve for a bond.

■ **cooperative or co-op**

refers to a form of real estate ownership. Here, the property is owned by shareholders. Each shareholder owns proprietary rights to a specific unit or dwelling while also owning an interest in the entire property. In many places, loans for such properties are effectively personal loans securitised by the shares of ownership. This is different from the usual real estate mortgage loan which is directly secured by the underlying real property.

The term can also refer to a business arrangement whereby parties of similar interest combine their activities. One example of this would be a farmers' cooperative to market grain or produce; operate and own storage facilities; or operate and own equipment.

■ **copyright**

an exclusive right conferred by a government for a specified period to the creator of literary or artistic works such as books, maps, articles, drawings, charts, photographs, musical compositions, motion pictures, recordings, or computer programs. The WTO Agreement on Trade-Related Aspects of Intellectual Property Rights incorporates all substantive trade-related protection afforded under the Bern Convention for the Protection of Literary and Artistic Works, clarifying that computer programs are protected as literary works and compilations of databases as intellectual creation. Protection extends for the duration of the life of the author plus 70 years and includes rights of translation, reproduction, public performance, broadcasting, adaptation and arrangement and rental.

■ **core inflation**

the basic level of inflation over a period of time as opposed to temporary fluctuations.

■ **core labour standards**

core labour standards are human rights agreed by the International Labour Organisation and other groups to include freedom of association, the right to organise and bargain collectively, a prohibition on forced labour, a prohibition on discrimination in employment and a prohibition on exploitative child labour. Founded in 1919, the ILO is the United Nations' specialised agency established to promote social justice and internationally recognised human and labour rights.

■ **corner**

refers to a market condition whereby an individual or group of individuals have gained control of a commodity or market.

■ **correlation**

is the statistical relationship between two variables. It indicates how they move together and not necessarily casual relationship.

■ **correspondent**

is a financial institution which performs activities or services for another financial institution. Sometimes, this arrangement occurs because of a lack of physical presence in a particular geographic area. Other times it may be due to an outsourcing or need for specialised services such as clearance and physical transfers of securities.

■ **cost basis**

the original value of an asset, such as stock, before its appreciation or depreciation.

■ **cost plus**

a pricing method where the purchaser agrees to pay the production cost of the good plus a fixed percentage to the seller for profit.

## Council of the European Union

usually referred to as the Council of Ministers, one of the official institutions of the European Union. (It should not be confused with the European Council of the European Union.) While the European Commission is charged with proposing legislation, the Council of Ministers has the power to adopt it, although in certain cases only with the approval of the European Parliament. Depending on the matter at issue, the Council of Ministers must take decisions either by qualified majority voting or by unanimity. The Council of Ministers is made up of representatives usually government ministers from all EU member states. As a result, the council is a forum in which EU member states attempt to assert their interests. The Council of Ministers, which is based in Brussels, Belgium, addresses the major areas of EU policy, including agriculture, economy, environment, foreign affairs, finance, industry and transport.

## Counter Trade (CT)

arrangements under which the sale of goods or services from one country to another are linked to sales in the opposite direction. Countertrade arrangements frequently characterise East-West trade. Such transactions include:

1. unterpurchase contracts that stipulate that the vendor must purchase goods from the importer equivalent in value to a specified percentage of the value of the exported goods;
2. verse countertrade contracts that require an importer to export goods equivalent in value to a specified percentage of the value of the imported goods;
3. obligation that can be sold to an exporter in a third country;
4. y-back (or compensation) arrangements through which a company selling equipment, licenses, technology, or a turnkey plant agrees to accept in full or partial payment products manufactured with such equipment, licenses, technology, or plant;
5. earning agreements between two countries that agree to purchase specific amounts of each other's products over a certain period of time, using a designated clearing currency in the transactions;
6. arrangements that permit the sale of unpaid balances in a clearing account to be sold to a third party, usually at a discount, that may be used for producing goods in the country holding the balance;

## country of departure

the country from which a shipment of goods, a carrier, or a passenger has or is scheduled to depart.

## country of destination

the country that is the ultimate destination for a shipment of goods. For a carrier, it is the country in which it intends to complete its current voyage or flight.

## country of dispatch

the country from which a cargo is shipped.

## country of export destination

the country to which goods are going in order to be consumed, further processed, or manufactured, as presumed by the shipper at the time of exportation.

## country of exportation

the country from which goods are shipped with intention to separate them from the mass of goods in that country.

## country of origin

the country in which goods were produced, mined, grown or manufactured.

## country risk

the financial risks of a transaction which relate to the political, economic, or social instability of the country of the debtor and is over and above the credit risk of the borrower.

## coupon

is the contractual rate of interest on a credit instrument.

## courier

1. attendant who accompanies shipments.
2. express company which handles shipments of documents and small packages on an expedited basis and may or may not have the shipments accompanied by attendants,

## covenant

the word is used in two senses. First, in the strict legal sense, it refers to clause in the lease requiring the tenant (or landlord) to do something or to refrain from doing something. Second, it is used in the wider sense to denote the worth of a tenant (or, bearing in mind the doctrine of privity of contract, that of previous assignors) and hence the risk of default, which will have a bearing on the value of the lease.

## coverage

the services and benefit level your insurance company will pay.

## covered warrant

is a derivative contract written against the underlying stock position. However, these warrants are not issued by the corporation of the underlying security but they are offered by investment underwriters. There are also put and call warrants written against indices, baskets and other securities.

## covered write

is the sale of an option against a position in the underlying instrument. Often this is the sale of a call against a long position in the stock. It could also be the sale of a put against a short position in the stock. Here, if the put is exercised, a long stock position is assigned to the seller of the option. Then this newly acquired long position is offset by the previously held short position. The covered write can also apply to warrant and other option positions.

## ■ CPT

an international commercial term (Incoterm), meaning Carriage Paid To, that is used in international sales contracts to signify that a seller must clear for export and pay the freight and all associated costs to transport goods to a destination named by the buyer. While the seller is responsible for the risk of loss or damage that might be incurred in conveying the goods to a carrier, such risk is transferred to the buyer when the goods are delivered to the carrier. The seller is not obligated to contract or to pay for insurance.

## ■ crack spread

is the purchase of crude oil against the sale of the refined products. In futures trading, it is the simultaneous purchase of crude oil futures versus the sale of heating oil and gasoline futures. The spread differentials reflect the potential refining margins or profitability. The spread computes the cost of the raw commodity input, crude oil and its refined products, gasoline and heating oil.

## ■ credit

a promise of future payment, usually with interest, given in exchange for present delivery of money, goods, or services. Interest is set at a rate that varies with the risk involved and with the reputation as a risk that a particular borrower enjoys with an actual or potential lender.

## ■ credit crunch

occurs when credit availability is so restricted that normal economic or financial activity is adversely influenced. It is a more extreme case of credit rationing which has tightened.

## ■ credit rationing

occurs when the terms of a borrowing relationship become more restrictive. For example, higher margin requirements for security transactions indicate tighter credit requirements. Sometimes, credit rationing may occur in some industries and not in others to promote or discourage specific types of activities. Credit rationing can occur when interest rates have been trending either up or down. In the latter, defaults often prompt new and higher margin requirements. Thus, credit availability is more limited and interest rates can move higher in the near-term as cash demands increase.

## ■ credit risk

is the risk related to counterparty failure. It is a key concern for Over-the-Counter transactions. This compares to listed trades passing through a clearinghouse.

## ■ credit spread

is an option position whereby the end result is a credit. For example, the investor who places a vertical bear call spread receives a credit. Similarly, the trader who places a vertical bull put spread receives a premium credit.

**crop**

is the yield or harvest of a planting or other agricultural or animal husbandry activity.

**crop year**

is a time span which does not necessarily correspond to a calendar year. A crop year commences with the beginning of the harvest and continues until the start of the next harvest. Each crop has its own specifications.

**cross dock**

transfer of freight from one trailer to another at a terminal.

**cross hedge**

is the use of a futures or other derivative contract as a risk management tool where the specifications of the underlying and the derivative do not match. However, there should be a reasonable economic rationale for doing this action.

**cross trade**

is a transaction that is not exposed to the public by outcry or usual trading practices. This type of matching trade is permissible provided it is done in accordance with the rules and regulations of the particular exchange and other regulatory organisations. The letter X can indicate this type of transaction on a ticker tape. It may be also used on a ticket or blotter.

**crush spread**

is the purchase of soybeans against the sale of the processed products. In futures trading, it is the simultaneous purchase of soybean futures versus the sale of soybean oil and soybean meal futures. The spread differentials reflect the potential processing margins or profitability. Here, the spread implies that the cost of the raw commodity input, soybeans, is cheap to its processed products.

**cumulative preferred**

is a security which maintains priority in the receipt of dividends relative to common shares. It also maintains the right to collect or recover any dividends that were not paid due to temporary cash shortages.

**currencies and major foreign market hedge funds**

invest in securities and derivatives which go across borders. These funds try to capitalise on interest rate differentials between currencies, varying investment climates for different countries, relative volatilities in equity or credit markets and variations of the other hedge fund themes.

**currency**

the circulating media of exchange in a country. Prior to World War I, currency generally meant coins and paper money. But with the expanding use of credit instruments, it has come to include cheques drawn on bank accounts, postal money orders and prepaid travellers cheques that usually require identification of maker or endorser. Most business transactions are carried out by means of bank cheques.

■ **current account**

that portion of a country's balance of payments that records current (as opposed to capital) transactions, including visible trade (exports and imports), invisible trade (income and expenditures for services), profits earned from foreign operations, interest and transfer payments.

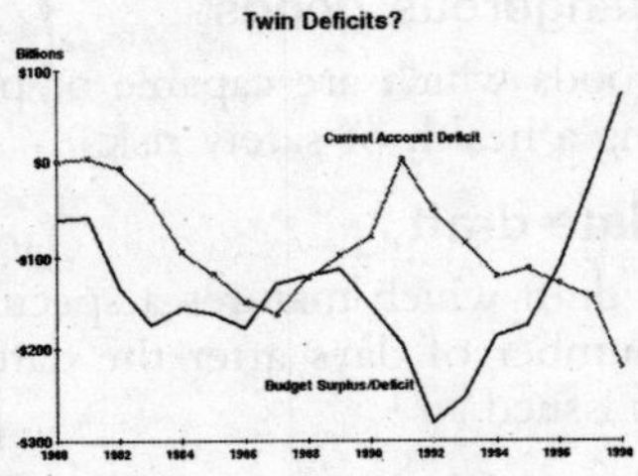


■ **current assets**

refer to properties or items which are expected to be paid or sold within a year. The specific list is broad but can be categorised as cash, cash equivalents, securitised liquid investments, accounts receivable, inventories and securities maturing within a year.

■ **current liabilities**

refers to obligations due and payable within a year.

■ **current principal factor**

is the statistic which is multiplied against the initial principal amount to indicate the current outstanding principal amount.

■ **current principal value**

is the adjusted outstanding amount of mortgage indebtedness. It is computed by multiplying the initial principal amount by the Current Principal Factor. This factor reflects any accretions in part due to negative amortisation, any ordinary principal payments and accelerated principal payments. Greater divergence between the ordinary expectation for principal and current principal amount is a reflection of the prepayment events.

■ **current ratio**

refers to the amount of an entity's current assets divided by the amount of current liabilities.

■ **customs**

the government service which is responsible for the administration of Customs law and the collection of duties and taxes relating thereto and which has responsibility for the application of other laws and regulations relative to the importation, transit and exportation of goods.

■ **customs area**

a geographic area, usually but not

necessarily identical to one or several contiguous national political jurisdictions, applying a particular tariff schedule on goods entering or leaving the area.

■ **customs bond**

a bond that, in certain circumstances, importers must post to effect the entry of imported goods. A customs bond usually must be guaranteed by an approved surety. The bond acts as a security in order to ensure the collection of duties and taxes owed on imports and to facilitate compliance with other importation requirements. Customs bonds fall into three general categories: single entry bonds, continuous bonds and carnets.

■ **customs broker**

a specialist in customs procedures who acts on behalf of importers for a fee.

■ **customs classification**

the particular category in a tariff nomenclature in which a product is classified for tariff purposes. Also, the procedure for determining the appropriate tariff category in a country's nomenclature system used for the classification, coding and description of internationally traded goods. Most major trading nations classify imported goods in conformity with the Harmonised Commodity Description and Coding System, also called the Harmonised System.

■ **cyclic or cyclical analysis**

is the study of recurring, preferably periodic, movements in prices or other time series.

■ **DAF**

an international commercial term, meaning Delivered At Frontier, that is used in international sales contracts to signify that the seller must clear for export, pay for the freight and bear all costs and risks for the carriage of goods to a named destination at a frontier but before the customs border of the adjoining country. A DAF contract is used primarily when conveyance of the goods is by rail or road.

■ **damages**

1. a loss or harm to a person or their property.
2. the pecuniary compensation or indemnity which may be recovered by any person who has suffered loss, detriment or injury to his person, property or rights through the unlawful act, omission, or negligence of another.

■ **dangerous goods**

goods which are capable of posing a health or safety risk.

■ **date draft**

a draft which matures a specified number of days after the date it is issued.

■ **date of issue**

the arbitrary date on a contract or on a financial instrument fixed as the date from which the term runs. (Neither the actual date on the instrument, nor the date the instrument was actually signed, nor the date the instrument was executed, nor the date the instrument was delivered, are considered to be the Date of issue or the issuance date.)

## ■ dated date

is the date from which interest accrues on a newly issued municipal security.

## ■ day order

is an order to trade securities, derivatives or futures which expires at the end of the trading day for which it was entered.

## ■ day trader

is a market participant who has a same-day transaction horizon. Often the positions are held for minutes or hours but they are offset by the end-of-the-market-day.

## ■ day trading

is the investment, speculation or risk management approach which is limited to intraday activity with little or no overnight carrying of positions.

## ■ dealer

is an organisation which transacts trades on the behalf of its proprietary account. This activity is opposed to a broker which transacts trades for the account of its customer. The dealer is usually compensated by the spread.

## ■ debit spread

is an option position whereby the end result is a debit. For example, the investor who places a vertical bull call spread pays a net premium or is debited. Similarly, a risk manager who places a vertical bear put spread is charged a net premium or is debited.

## ■ debt

refers to a relationship which obliges a borrower to pay interest and principal. The terms are often in writing and define the relationship. Indentures and mortgage notes are common types of these written instruments of indebtedness.

## ■ devaluation

refers to the action taken by a country via its central bank or monetary board which reduces the value of its currency vis a vis other currencies. Often, the result is more abrupt than would occur within a floating rate framework.

## ■ devanning

the unloading of cargo from a shipping container.

## ■ developed countries

a term used to distinguish the more industrialised nations including most OECD member countries
from developing or less developed countries. The developed countries are sometimes collectively designated as the Group B countries or the North, because most of them are in the Northern Hemisphere.

**■ developing countries**

a broad range of countries that generally lack a high degree of industrialisation, infrastructure and other capital investment, sophisticated technology, widespread literacy and advanced living standards among their populations as a whole. The developing countries are sometimes collectively designated as the Third World and sometimes as the South, because a large number of them are in the Southern Hemisphere. All of the countries of Africa (except South Africa), Asia (except Hong Kong, Singapore, South Korea and Taiwan) and Oceania (except Australia, Japan and New Zealand), Latin America and the Middle East are generally considered developing countries, as are a few European countries (Cyprus, Malta, Turkey, Poland and Hungary, for example).

**■ diagonal spread**

is the purchase and sale of puts or calls for the same instrument but for different strike prices and different delivery dates. These strategies can be done for debits or credits. Also, they are bullish or bearish depending on the relationship of the purchased to sold strike price. When the lower strike is purchased and the higher strike is sold then the strategy has a bullish configuration. When the lower strike is sold and the higher strike is purchased then the strategy has a bearish configuration.

**■ differential**

an amount added to or deducted from a base shipping freight rate between two given locations to determine a new rate to or from some other point or via another route.

**■ differential export tax**

a multi-tier export tax usually structured so that the tax on exports of a raw material exceeds the tax (if any) on exports of processed goods made from the raw material, thereby creating an incentive to process the raw material domestically.

**■ direct investment**

defined in the International Monetary Fund's 'Balance of Payments Manual' as investment that is made to acquire a lasting interest in an enterprise operating in an economy other than that of the investor, the investor's purpose being to have an effective voice in the management of the enterprise.

**■ Direct Mail Collection (DMC)**

a seller may forward his documents and instructions for collecting payment directly to a collecting bank in a foreign country, without going through the intermediary of the seller's own domestic bank.

**■ direct tax**

a tax that is levied on the wealth or income of individuals. Income, wealth and inheritance taxes and social security charges are examples of direct taxes.

**■ discharge**

1. to release, liberate, annul, unburden, disencounter, dismiss. To ex-

tinguish an obligation, terminate all employment of a person, release, as from prison or military services.
2. the unloading of passengers or cargo from a vessel, vehicle, or aircraft.

## discharging

the unloading of cargo from a carrier, or of the contents from a container.

## discount

is the negative differential against the spot price. It can refer to an interest rate, price difference, amount under par, or other similar relationship.

## discount points

type of fee that you pay to the lender. One point is equal to one percent of the loan amount.

## discount rate

is the interest rate used for adjusting for the time value of money for Net Present Value, Option Pricing or other Market Models.

## discounted bill

an accepted draft against which a loan is made and the interest is deducted immediately.

## discounted cash flow

an investment appraisal technique which takes account of the time value of money by assessing the present value of future income and expenditure. It is often used in valuing an investment or to show the viability of a project.

## discounting

1. the sale at less than original price of a commodity or monetary instrument, often for immediate payment.
2. a loan by a bank with a deduction of the interest in advance.

## distressed securities

refer to issues in bankruptcy or other severely impaired securities which have very low credit ratings.

## distribution

refers to selling often coincident with market tops or consolidations. It also refers to the liquidation, partial or entire, by insiders, control people, or major investors. The term also refers to a disbursement out of a retirement plan or mutual fund.

## distribution service

a transportation service that accepts a shipment from a shipper and at destination separates and sorts the packages and distributes them to many receivers.

## distributions

refers to the various underlying or assumed probabilistic processes. A few distributions are: the Binomial, the Normal and the Uniform.

## distributor

an agent who sells for a supplier at wholesale and usually maintains an inventory of the supplier's products.

## diversion

any change in the routing of a shipment once it has been received by the carrier at point of origin and prior to delivery at destination.

## dolly

a piece of equipment with wheels used to move freight with or without a tractor.

**domestic exports**

exports of goods which were grown, produced, mined, or manufactured in the country from which exported.

**domestic system of production**

the system of economic production that prevailed in Europe in the 16th and 17th centuries, prior to the Industrial Revolution, under which merchants supplied materials and sometimes tools and machines to workers who produced finished goods in their homes and turned them over to the merchants.

**domicile**

that place where a person or organisation has their principal residence with intent to make it their permanent home.

**don't know**

is a term used by brokers, dealers and traders when there are transaction comparisons. When a transaction does not match up on a party's books or records then a DK notice is sent to the other party.

**door-to-door**

shipping service from shipper's door to consignee's door.

**double taxation**

refers to corporate income which is subject to both corporate taxes and individual taxes. Frequently, it is viewed as the case whereby the company's income is taxed and the distribution of that income in the form of a dividend paid to the shareholder is taxed again.

**double-column tariff**

a customs tariff schedule with two columns of rates, one for preferred trading partners and one for imports from others.

**down payment**

part of the purchase price that the buyer pays in cash and does not finance with a mortgage.

**down-and-in**

is an option feature by which a derivative contract becomes active when an indicator, such as price, drops through a trigger point or threshold. Related topics are Down-and-Out, Up-and-In and Up-and-Out.

**down-and-out**

is an option feature by which a derivative contract dies or ceases to exist when an indicator, such as price, drops through a trigger point or threshold. Related topics are Down-and-In, Up-and-In and Up-and-Out.

**downgrade**

is the lowering, reduction, or negative change in an company's or country's credit rating. Often it can refer to one or more issues.

**downstream dumping**

1. the sale of products below cost or below fair value by a producer to another producer in its own domestic market by whom the product is then further processed and exported to another country at a price lower than would otherwise be charged and thus causing injury to that country.
2. also known as input dumping,

the practice of exporting an end-product containing an input that has been purchased at less than normal value.

**■ down-tick**

refers to a trading transaction which is executed at a lower price than the preceding one. It is also known as a Minus-Tick.

**■ dray**

a vehicle used to haul cargo or goods, usually drawn by a horse.

**■ drayage**

the charge made for hauling freight via carts, drays or trucks.

**■ drayage**

transporting freight by truck, primarily in local cartage.

**■ drip or drips**

refer to Dividend Reinvestment Programs whereby an investor acquires additional shares of the corporation by having the dividends automatically reinvested.

**■ drive axle**

the axle(s) which are connected to the engine by a drive shaft and power the vehicle. Also called power axle.

**■ driver collect**

refers to a shipment for which the driver must collect freight charges at the time of delivery.

**■ drop shipment**

at the request of a wholesaler, a shipment of goods from a manufacturer directly to a dealer or consumer, avoiding delivery to the wholesaler.

**■ drop-off**

the delivery of a shipment by a shipper to a carrier for transportation.

**■ dry-bulk container**

a shipping container designed to carry unpackaged free-flowing dry solids such as grain or sand.

**■ dry-cargo container**

any shipping container designed to transport goods other than liquids or gasses.

**■ DSO**

refers to Days Sales Outstanding or Day's Sales Outstanding. It measures the relationship of Accounts Receivables relative to Sales. Different users apply time factors to adjust for quarterly or annual views.

**■ dual exchange rate**

the existence of two exchange rates for a single currency for use in different circumstances as mandated by the government.

**■ dual pricing**

1. the selling of identical products in different markets for different prices.
2. selling identical products for different prices in different markets. Dual pricing often reflects export subsidy and dumping practices.

**■ dual trading**

occurs when a member of an exchange trades for both his own personal account and executes customer orders as well. Sometimes, it is viewed that the potential for a conflict of interest may be present.

■ **dub**

a 28-foot trailer designed to be pulled two or three at a time by one tractor. Also referred to as a pup or doubles.

■ **due on sale**

is a clause which requires the immediate and full payment of the existing mortgage in the event of a transfer of ownership, sale, death, or some refinancings. This clause is usually specific as to what events will trigger the repayment of the mortgage.

■ **dumping**

the sale of goods in a foreign country at less than fair value (a price lower than that at which it is sold within the exporting country or to third countries) and which thereby materially injures, or threatens to materially injure, that industry in the foreign country.

■ **dunnage**

1. materials placed around cargo to prevent shifting or damage while in transit.
2. term used for cardboard, empty pallets, plywood, foam rubber, air bags, or other items used to cushion or protect freight while in transit.

■ **durable goods**

any product which is not consumed through use.

■ **durable power of attorney**

a written legal document that lets an individual designate another person to act on his or her behalf, even in the event the individual becomes disabled or incapacitated.

■ **duty suspension**

a unilateral nonapplication of a customs duty, or its application at a reduced level, usually on a temporary basis.

■ **early exercise**

is the exercise of an option by its owner prior to the expiration date.

■ **earnest money**

is a deposit made towards the purchase of real property. In some locales it is viewed synonymously with the Binder. Other places consider it as an additional deposit towards the purchase. Here, the amount can be quite large. Often it would accompany a signed sales contract prior to the closing or settlement.

■ **easement**

a right to use another person's property.

■ **eastern account**

refers to an undivided underwriting account.

■ **east-west trade**

referred to trade between the former Soviet Union and the socialist countries of Eastern Europe (East) on the one hand and the developed market economy countries of Western Europe, North America and Japan on the other (West).

■ **ebit**

refers to Earnings Before Interest and Taxes.

■ **ebitda**

refers to Earnings Before Interest, Taxes, Depreciation and Amortisation.

■ **ecns**

Electronic Communications Networks. These platforms, islands or mechanisms serve trading, investing and risk management purposes.

■ **economic development**

the process of growth in total and per capita income, especially in developing countries, accompanied by increased infrastructure, more industrial activity, improved agricultural practices, migration of labour from rural to urban industrial areas, rising literacy, broadened employment opportunities and gradually diminishing reliance on official development assistance.

■ **ed**

refers to the eurodollar futures and options on futures contracts.

■ **edge act corporations**

banks that are subsidiaries either to bank holding companies or other banks established to engage in foreign business transactions.

■ **effective date**

is the day that a new issue begins trading in the secondary market. This marks the transition from the initial issuance or Primary Market to the Aftermarket or Secondary Market.

■ **effective duration**

measures the percentage change in price for a 1 percentage point or 100 basis point change in interest rates.

■ **effective strike price**

is the adjusted level of the option contract exercise price. A key adjustment is for time value either paid or received.

■ **effective tariff rate**

the concept that effective protection reflected in a tariff rate is the sum of the protection for the component parts of the final manufactured unit. This concept implies that the nominal tariff rate of the finished good significantly understates the de facto protection for the value added in the production process. Several academic studies in the late 1960s and early 1970s established the theoretical basis for the effective tariff rate concept, but most trade policy experts see little practical utility in the theory, since the many different circumstances affecting the component parts comprising most industrial products make it difficult to establish their actual effective rates.

■ **efficiency**

narrowly, the input-output relationship between the quantity of materials used and the quantity of goods produced. More broadly, economic efficiency implies the best result (taking quality as well as quantity into account) in the production or distribution of goods and services at the least cost. Most economists believe the reduction of barriers to trade contributes to international economic efficiency by encouraging countries to specialise in the production of those goods and services in which they have a comparative advantage, thus making the world's most competitive goods and services available to consumers outside the area that produces them.

## ■ elasticity

refers to the economic concept of the ability or comparative ease to adjust supply or demand within a changing economy.

## ■ electronic commerce

1. a system of integrated communications, data management and security services that allow business applications within different organisations to automatically interchange information.

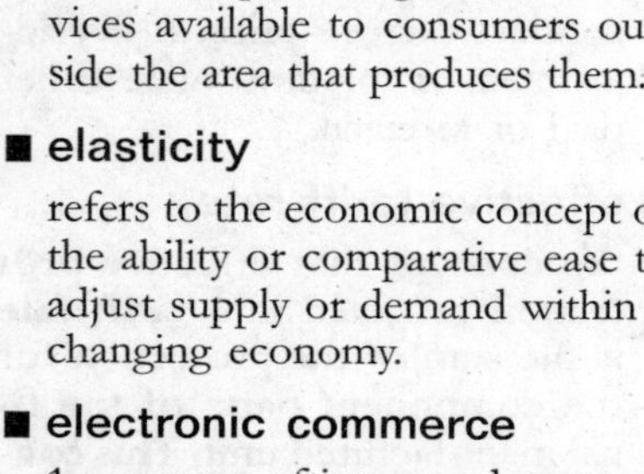


2. any activity that utilises some form of electronic communication in the inventory, exchange, advertisement and distribution of and the payment for goods and services. All forms of commercial transactions are based upon the transmission of digitised data, including text, sound and visual images.

## ■ Electronic Data Interchange (EDI)

electronic transmission of data and information according to particular protocols.

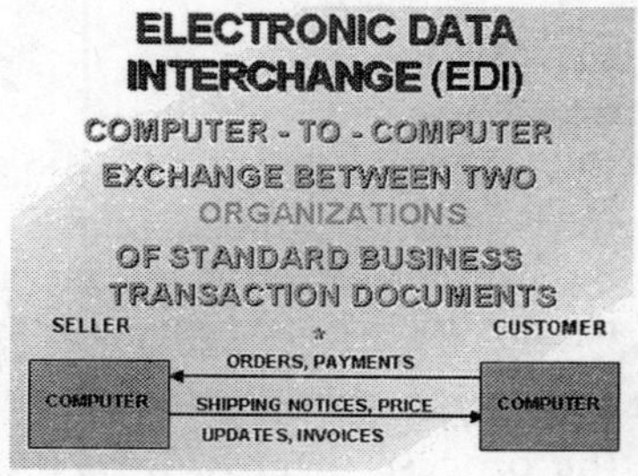


## ■ electronic funds transfer

system of transferring funds from one account to another by electronic means.

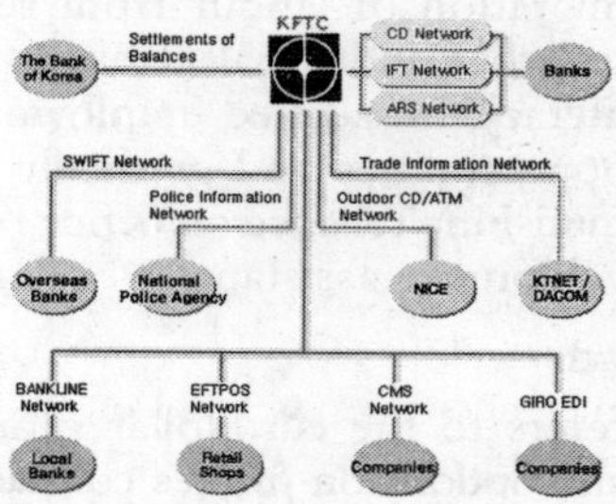


## ■ electronic trading

is the process whereby customers or their representatives can directly enter orders and receive reports and statements via the internet. It can also include trading with terminals over dedicated telephone lines.

## ■ embargo

a government prohibition of exports or imports with respect to specific products or specific foreign countries.

**embedded option**

is an option whose characteristics are implied but not explicitly specified. One notable example is the option granted a mortgagor (home owner) by the lender. The mortgagor has the right to prepay the mortgage at any time but is not required to do so in any specified manner.

**emerging markets**

is a term which broadly categorises countries in the midst of developing their financial markets and economic infrastructures. This development is viewed in terms of freer, more liquid markets, which facilitate trade. Privatisation of former state owned or administered businesses is a key factor in this process.

**emerging markets funds**

are investment vehicles, either open-end or closed-end, which invest in countries whose economies are becoming more capitalistic. Often this emergence is from socialistic, communistic or other tightly controlled economic systems. There are also Hedge Funds which participate in emerging markets.

**emerging markets hedge funds**

narrow their investment horizon to issues in markets which are not as mature or liquid as the previous group. However, these less developed markets are believed to offer greater risk adjusted rates of return. A general perspective is akin to getting in on the ground floor.

**EMU**

is the European Monetary Union.

**en route**

in transit (referring to goods, passengers, or vessels).

**endowment**

a fund owned by an individual that is to be used for a specific purpose.

**entrepot**

an intermediary storage facility (often in an intermediate country) where goods are kept temporarily for distribution.

**entrepot trade**

the import and export of goods which receive no further processing but are distributed from the entrepot facility which is chosen for its location and lack of restrictions on trade,

**entrepreneur**

a person who assumes responsibility for organisation, management and risk in the production of goods and services. In theory, his or her enterprise should make a profit if it is economically efficient and should incur losses if it is not.

**entry**

1. that documentation required to be filed with the appropriate customs officer to secure the release of imported merchandise from customs custody.
2. the act of filing that documentation.

**entry documents**

the documents required to complete

customs entry to secure the release of imported merchandise.

### ■ equalisation

in transportation, a money allowance given the customer if the transport company picks up the goods at origin points or delivers them to destination points other than those named on the bill of lading.

### ■ equilibrium

a state in which economic forces that are likely to cause change in opposing directions are in perfect balance, so that change is unlikely. A market is in equilibrium if the quantity of a product that consumers will buy at the prevailing price exactly matches the amount suppliers will sell at that price.

### ■ equipment trust certificate

is a security which is collateralised by specific equipment, often capital in nature. The title is held in trust until the obligation is satisfied. However, the borrower is permitted to use the item provided there are no defaults precluding usage.

This security operates in a manner similar to a mortgage or hypothecation agreement.

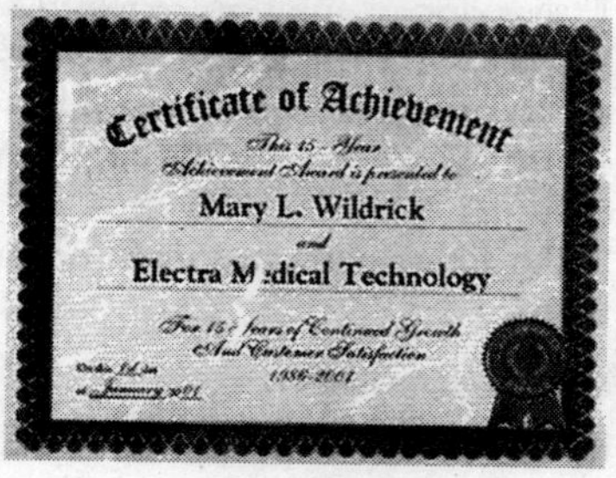


### ■ equitise a margin call

is an event whereby a previously unsatisfied margin call is eliminated by an effective transfer of ownership. In 1998, Long Term Capital Management transfered a portion of ownership to its creditors. In some respects, it was a debt for equity swap. The immediate benefit to the previous creditors is that the regulatory capital requirement is not impaired by a default. It also extends the horizon for position liquidation.

### ■ equity

fairness, justice. Also, the value of property beyond the total amount owed on it.

### ■ equity hedge funds

try to long position themselves in stronger or outperform issues while selling short weaker or poorer prospect securities. Variations of this are: trading large cap issues versus small caps; using derivatives for enhanced returns; specialising in programme trading; or using leverage to magnify returns.

### ■ ERM

refers to Enterprise Risk Management.

### ■ error

is a mistake in terms of quantity, type of order, side of market (purchase or sale), security, or other condition of a trade.

### ■ error account

is the destination for the temporary placement of a trade

which was involved in an error transaction. Firms will either take immediate market action to correct the error, or sometimes will keep the position there as they work it out.

### escape clause

1. a provision in a bilateral or multilateral commercial agreement permitting a signatory nation to change their obligations when imports threaten serious harm to the producers of competitive domestic goods.
2. a provision in a contract or other document permitting parties to avoid liability for nonperformance under certain conditions.

### escrow

is a fund held by a third-party custodian.

### ESOP

is the Employee Stock Ownership Plan. It is similar to a profit sharing plan, but here only the stock of the employer is purchased with the contributions.

### estate tax

a tax imposed at one's death on the transfer of most types of property.

### Estimated Rental Values (ERV)

an estimate of the rental which a property is likely to command in the open market at a given time.

### euro

the common currency of those European Union countries that have elected to participate in the third stage of economic and monetary union. The euro was launched on January 1, 1999, with 11 participating countries (Austria, Belgium, Finland, France, Germany, Ireland, Italy, Luxembourg, Netherlands, Portugal and Spain) converting their previous currencies at an irrevocably fixed conversion rate. The geographic area of the participating countries is popularly referred to as the Euro Zone. The euro replaces the ECU (European currency unit) as the unit of account for the European Union. Existing national notes and coins will continue to circulate until July 1, 2002. Euro notes and coins will begin to circulate on January 1, 2002.

### eurobond

a bond issued in a Euro-currency, usually Euro-dollars

### European Union (EU)

the overarching entity encompassing the modern attempt at European integration. Created by the Treaty on European Union (also known as the Maastricht Treaty), which entered into force on November 1, 1993, the European Union is often described as a building supported by three pillars. Specifically, the pillars include the European Community (essentially the European Communities as they existed in pre-Maastricht Europe), the Common Foreign and Security Policy (establishing common foreign policy positions and developing a common defence policy) and Justice and Home Affairs (principally providing for cooperation between police and other authorities on crime, terrorism and immigration issues). Some confusion exists as to when the terms European Union, European Community and European Economic Community (EEC) may be properly used. The delimitation between these entities is far from clear, but generally, EU, EC and EEC may not be used interchangeably. As noted, the EC continues to constitute part of the EU; however, the EC possesses a legal personality while the EU currently does not. As a result, the term EU should be used when referring to the system as a whole. The term EC is most properly used when referring to the laws and institutions falling within the first pillar of the EU. The term EEC should be used only when referring to the historical entity that preceded the EC.

## ■ ex

is derived from Latin and refers to without or not included.

## ■ ex works

it is a sale term where the title to goods passes to the buyer when they leave the vendor's dock and consequently at that point the liability for loss or damage and the expenses of shipment also pass from vendor to buyer.

## ■ exception

1. a shortage, overage, or damage to a shipment.
2. a notation of such conditions on a freight bill, bill of lading or unloading checksheet.

## ■ exchange controls

the rationing of foreign currencies, bank drafts and other instruments for settling international financial obligations by countries seeking to ameliorate acute balance-of-payments difficulties. When such measures are imposed, importers must apply for prior authorisation from the government to obtain the foreign currency required to bring in designated amounts and types of goods. Since such measures have the effect of restricting imports, they are considered nontariff barriers to trade.

## ■ exchange for physicals

is an ex-pit transaction whereby physical commodities or actual financial instruments are exchanged for futures contracts. This flexible technique is permitted for bona fide hedging transactions. This procedure allows for grades, quantities, locations and delivery dates which are different from those stipulated for good delivery under the standard contract rules.

■ **exchange rate**

1. the price of one currency expressed in terms of another.
2. the price (or rate) at which one currency is exchanged for another currency, for gold, or for Special Drawing Rights.

**How interest rates affect the economy**

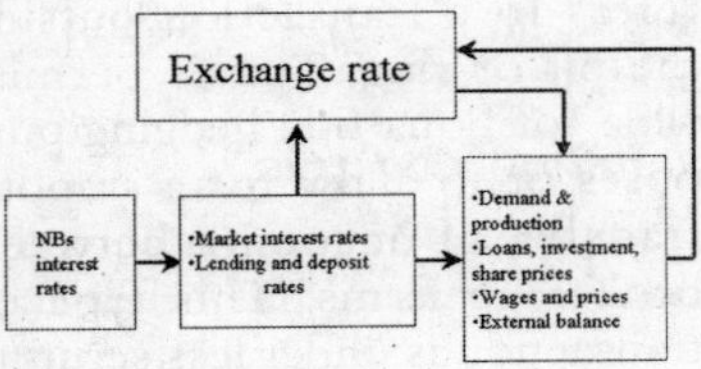


■ **excise tax**

taxes on the manufacture, sale, or consumption of goods, or upon licenses to pursue certain occupations, or upon corporate privileges. In current usage it covers various license fees imposed by government and practically every internal revenue tax from any source except the income tax.

■ **exculpatory clause**

1. a contractual clause that releases one party from liability in case of wrong doing by the other party involved.2. a contractual clause which excuses a trustee from liability where he executes a power in good faith.

■ **ex-dividend**

refers to a transaction in which the new purchaser of a stock is not entitled to the recently declared dividend. This occurs because the new purchaser did not own the security on the record date.

■ **executor (or personal representative)**

the person named in a will to manage the estate. This person will collect the property, pay any debt and distribute your property or assets according to the will.

■ **exempt securities**

are issues which are not bound by the filing provisions of the Securities Act of 1933. Exempt securities include treasury and municipal notes and bonds, bank securities and nonprofit organisation securities.

■ **exercise**

is the action taken by the holder of an option or convertible security to convert his derivative position into the underlying security, commodity or futures. In the case of the option the exercise of a call would give the owner of the call the underlying instrument or cash settlement adjustment. In the case of a convertible bond, the owner of the bond terminates that contractual relationship in exchange for shares in the corporation. The owner of the option is the only one that exercises. However, there are mandatory exercises for expiring options that are in-the-money by more than the stipulated threshold amount. Also, there may be built-in event options that take priority over the owner of the securities right to exercise. Nevertheless, this nesting of options still defers to rules that establish which party holds which options.

**exercise price**

is the predetermined level at which an optional underlying instrument is priced upon its exercise. The exercise price is also called the strike price.

**expected excess return**

is equal to the nonmarket or alpha return plus the beta-adjusted market or systematic return. Since beta relates an asset's return to the market, the alpha distinguishes it from the market. Algebraically, this is presented by the expression for a straight line or excess return equals $\alpha$ (alpha) + $\beta$ (beta)X (market return).

**expected value**

is viewed as an anticipated, theoretical or fair value for an instrument.

**expected volatility**

is the forward looking aspect of volatility or variability.

**expediting**

moving shipments through regular channels at an accelerated rate.

**expiration**

is the date stipulated for the cessation of the life of an option. It is also the formal acknowledgment of the option's termination.

**expiry**

is the expiration date of a derivative.

**expiry date**

the end, specifically: the cessation; termination by lapse of time as the expiration of a lease, insurance policy, or statute. Coming to a close or termination. The expiry date is the date on which these events occur. It is the last date that options or warrants can be executed.

**ex-pit**

refers to a transaction outside the pit or ring. This is permissible for bona fide hedging purposes or to allow for a smooth transfer of accounts between brokerage firms. This type of transaction is under less scrutiny than ordinary transactions because there is no public offering of the positions.

**explicit option**

is an option whose strike and expiration are clearly stated. There is a direct payment for this specific option contract. In the case of an implied option, the price adjustment is reflected in the instrument such as a mortgage.

**export**

to send or transport goods out of a customs territory.

**export broker**

a firm that specialises in bringing foreign buyers and domestic sellers together for a fee but usually does not participate in the actual business transaction.

**export control**

the establishment of procedures for the governmental control of exports for statistical or strategic purposes.

■ **export draft**

a documentary order in the form of a draft drawn on the importing party to pay the seller for the exported goods.

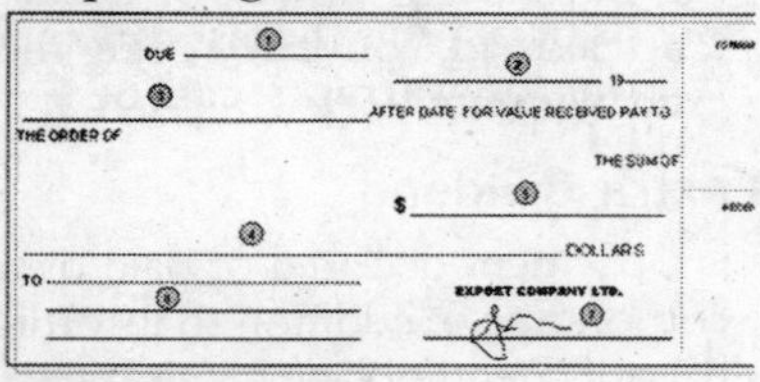


■ **export duty**

a tax imposed by some nations on their exports.

■ **export letter of credit**

when importer has arranged with bank for letter-of-credit financing of purchases, he applies for issuance of individual letters of credit to cover purchase contracts as made.

■ **export license**

a license issued to exporters by governments to permit them to export certain goods to certain countries. Such goods may be of strategic importance, or simply in short supply, or are controlled to comply with foreign agreements.

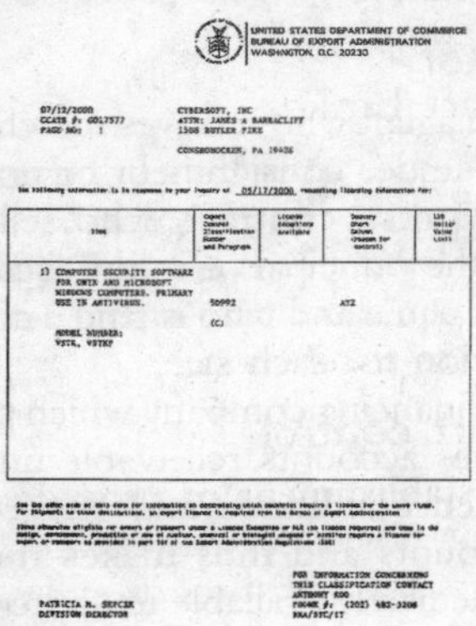


■ **export management company**

a private firm that serves as the export department for several manufacturers and handles the exporting aspect of the business for a commission or fee.

■ **export merchant**

a company that buys domestic and foreign products and sells to foreign purchasers. Usually an export merchant is able to compete because of specialised knowledge of the products in which they deal, detailed knowledge of foreign markets and expertise in international trading techniques.

■ **export processing zone**

industrial parks designated by a government to provide tax and other incentives to export firms.

■ **export promotion**

public or private sector support for foreign sales through such activities as trade missions and trade fairs, based on available market information and analysis.

■ **export quotas**

specific restrictions or ceilings imposed by an exporting country on the value or volume of certain exports to protect domestic producers and consumers from temporary shortages of the goods affected or to bolster their prices in world markets. Some international commodity agreements explicitly indicate when producers should apply such restraints. Export quotas are also often applied in orderly marketing agreements and voluntary restraint agreements and to promote domestic processing of raw materials in countries that produce them.

■ **export restraints**

restrictions which a nation places upon its exports, often to avoid more burdensome restrictions being applied by the importing nations.

■ **export statistics**

the statistics that cover the exports from one country to other countries.

■ **export subsidies**

government payments to induce exportation by domestic producers.

■ **export trading company**

a corporation organised for the principal purpose of exporting goods and services.

■ **exporter**

an individual or company that ships goods from one country to another in the course of trade.

■ **ex-rights**

refers to a transaction which the new purchaser of a stock is not entitled to participate in the recently declared rights offering. The mechanics are similar to ex-dividend conditions. Here, the exclusion point in time is known as the ex-rights date.

■ **extending**

is a term to indicate an increase in the duration of mortgage backed and related securities. Generally, it is a consequence of slower-than-expected prepayments.

■ **external value**

the purchasing power of a currency abroad, converted using the exchange rate.

■ **extra dividend**

is a payment declared or paid by a corporation in addition to its ordinary dividend policy. It can reflect a distribution of profits which are considered extraordinary.

■ **extradition**

the surrender by one state or country to another of an individual accused or convicted of an offence within the jurisdiction of the other.

■ **extrinsic value**

is the time value component of an option premium.

■ **facilitation**

1. programmes designed to expedite the flow of international commerce.
2. the act of freeing more or less completely from obstruction or hindrance.

■ **factor**

1. an agent who receives merchandise under consignment or under a bailment contract, who sells it for the principal or in the factor's own name and who is paid a commission for each sale.
2. a financing company which purchases accounts receivable under agreed conditions and at agreed discounts and thus makes funds immediately available to approved sellers.

## factorage

the commission or other compensation paid to a factor.

## factor's lien

the right of a factor to retain possession of designated assets of the principal until the factor receives full compensation from the principal.

## fair value

is viewed as the indifference point from a modelling perspective as to whether to buy or sell an instrument or market. If the market price were higher than fair value it would suggest selling the security. If the security was trading at less than fair value it would suggest buying it. When coupled with related derivative instruments, the approach becomes an arbitrage one.

## fair value difference

is the disparity between an instruments trading price and its computed value.

## FAS

an international commercial term (Incoterm), meaning Free Alongside Ship, that is used in sales contracts to signify a seller's obligation to pay the costs and assume all risks for transporting goods from his or her place of business to the point of embarkation where a vessel or plane selected by the buyer will accept the goods. In trade statistics, FAS value means that the import or export figures are calculated on this basis, regardless of the nature of individual transactions reflected in the statistics.

## fast market

is a trading condition when prices change quickly and volume is dramatic. At these times, the price reports are behind and a trading range of prices is substituted for price dissemination. Often special rules apply at such times.

## fat tails

describes the appearance of a probability curve which has a higher-than-normally-expected occurrence of observations in the remote areas, or tails, away from the mean.

## feeder

in intermodal moves, a pickup/delivery vehicle or ship.

## feeder vessel

a vessel which is part of a cargo network in which the larger, faster vessels only call at the major ports at both ends of the area being covered and the smaller ports are served by the smaller feeder vessels which transfer the cargo to and from the major port terminals and thus keep the larger vessels filled closer to capacity and spare them the expense and loss of time in loading and unloading in the subsidiary ports.

■ **fill or kill**

is an order that must be immediately executed in its entirety or it is cancelled. There are no partial fills with this type of order.

■ **financial instrument**

a document which has a monetary value or is evidence of a monetary transaction, such as drafts, bills of exchange, cheques and promissory notes.

■ **financial market**

market for the exchange of capital and credit in an economy.

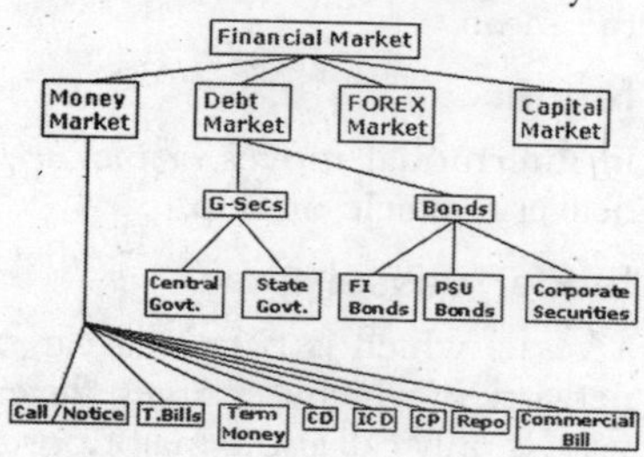


■ **fineness**

is a measure of the purity of a precious metal such as gold. Three 9s or .999 shows the relative purity of gold. Here, there would be an .001 part of impurity for the specimen.

■ **FIR**

is the Futures Initial Requirement. It refers to the amount of the original margin or performance bond.

■ **fire sale**

refers to the rapid disposition of positions. This often occurs at less than fair value versus transactions conducted under more favourable or orderly conditions.

■ **First In, First Out (FIFO)**

warehouse term meaning first items stored are the first used.

■ **first notice day**

is the day when notices or intents to make a delivery are permitted.

■ **first world countries**

western, industrialised, non-communist countries, were the previously accepted criteria, but in view of the emergence of Japan as an economic power and the rising status of Russia and China, industrialised is probably the only remaining valid criterian for a first world country at this time.

■ **fishy back**

transporting motor carrier trailers and containers by ship.

■ **five dragons**

term used to describe the emerging economies of Hong Kong, Singapore, South Korea, Taiwan and Thailand.

■ **fixed assets**

refers to items such as buildings, furniture, memberships and long-term leases. Typically, these properties are not intended for sale or disposal within a year.

■ **fixed charges**

1. charges which do not increase or decrease with a change in volume.

2. expenses that have to be borne whether any business is done or not.

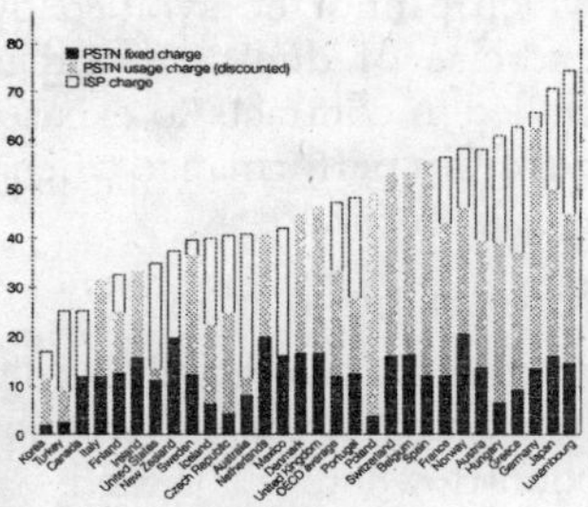


■ **fixed exchange**

1. when Governments or their Central Banks administratively set the exchange rate for their currency.
2. an administratively set exchange rate where no rate fluctuations are permitted.

■ **fixed rate**

the interest rate (i.e., the percentage) applied to the outstanding principal remains constant throughout the life of the loan.

■ **fixing**

the setting of a price by a known method at regular times. For example, the establishment of an official exchange rate, interest rate, or security or commodity price.

■ **flag**

a reference to the country of registry of a vessel.

■ **flag of convenience**

the national flag flown by a ship that is registered in a country other than that of its owners. (Usually arranged in order to save taxes and operating expenses)

■ **flat**

is a condition where a bond is traded without accrued interest.

■ **flat market**

is a term structure whereby the various delivery months are basically trading at the same price level or yield.

■ **flight of capital**

the movement of capital to another country to avoid loss.

■ **'flip flop' arbitration**

a form of arbitration under which the arbitrator bases his award on the submission he considers most reasonable. It is claimed that this encourages parties to be more reasonable in their submissions and reduces polarisation.

■ **floating**

free determination of rates based on supply and demand, for example exchange rates or interest rates.

■ **floating rate**

refers to the condition whereby exchange rates are relatively free to change. It can also refer to an interest rate which changes relatively quickly or frequently.

■ **floor**

is the lower limit price or interest rate.

■ **floor broker**

is a member of an exchange who executes orders for others.

■ **flotation**

is the initial offering of stock to the public.

■ **FOB (Free on Board)**

an international commercial term,

meaning free on board, used in international sales contracts. In an FOB contract, a buyer and a seller agree on a designated FOB point. The seller assumes the cost of having goods packaged and ready for shipment from the FOB point, whether this is his/her own place of business or some intermediate point. The buyer assumes the costs and risks from the FOB point, including inland transportation costs and risks in the exporting country, as well as all subsequent transportation costs, including the costs of loading the merchandise on a vessel. If the contract stipulates FOB vessel, the seller bears all transportation costs to the vessel named by the buyer, as well as the costs of loading the goods on that vessel. The same principle applies to the abbreviations FOR (free on rail) and FOT (free on truck).

### ■ FOB destination

freight costs paid to the destination point, title transfers at destination.

### ■ FOB factory

title to goods and transportation responsibility transfers from seller to factory.

### ■ FOB vessel

title/transportation costs transfer after goods are delivered on vessel. All export taxes/costs involved in overseas shipments are assessed to the buyer.

### ■ force majeure

a condition of superior or irresistible force such as Acts of God, including earthquakes and floods, which cannot be avoided by the exercise of due care and is included in contracts to excuse parties from performance when such events occur.

### ■ foreign bond

an international bond usually denominated in the currency of the country where it is issued.

### ■ foreign commerce

trade between individuals or legal entities in different countries.

### ■ foreign currency

the currency of any foreign country which is authorised by that country as the medium of circulation.

### ■ foreign exchange contract

a contract for the sale or purchase of the currency of one country to be paid for with the currency of another country, specifying an amount, an exchange rate and delivery date.

### ■ foreign exchange earnings

the proceeds from a country's exports of goods, services and capital, normally denominated in convertible currencies.

### ■ foreign exchange rate

the rate or price of the currency of one country in terms of the currency of another.

### ■ foreign flag

the national identification of a carrier registered in a foreign country. A vessel flies the national flag of the country in which it is registered and it may be registered in a country different from that of its owner.

## foreign income

income gained by residents of one country from another country.

## foreign investment

direct and portfolio investment. Foreign direct investment is the ownership or control, directly or indirectly, by one person of 10 percent or more of the voting securities of a foreign incorporated business enterprise or an equivalent interest in a foreign unincorporated business enterprise. Portfolio investment is any international investment which is not direct investment. It would generally represent an interest in a business enterprise that is less than 10 percent of the business enterprise's voting securities or equivalent interest.

## foreign market value

it is the price at which merchandise is sold at wholesale in the principal markets of the country from which it is exported.

## foreign remittances

the transfer of any funds across national boundaries.

## forfeiture

forfeiture of a lease occurs when the landlord exercises his right to regain possession against the wishes of the tenant, where there is a breach in a condition of the lease, or a breach of a covenant.

## forklift

mechanical vehicle used to move freight on the dock. Also known as lift-truck, towmotor, or hi-lo.

## forward

is a market similar to futures in terms of deferred deliveries. However, notable differences include the lack of contract standardisation, the lack of a central clearinghouse, the potential for substantial counterparty risk, but it allows contractual term customisation and deliveries at times, points and grades other than those listed for futures contracts. It is also used to refer to the bank currency market.

## forward foreign exchange

an agreement to purchase or sell an amount of foreign currency at a future date at a predetermined price.

## forward market

a market in which contracts for future deliveries of goods and securities on a specified date are entered into at fixed prices. The contracts themselves are popularly known as futures. Many commodity exchanges, wool, cotton and wheat, for example, have established forward markets that permit interested parties to hedge against changes in the prices of the raw materials they use or deal in.

## forwarding agent

a firm specialising in shipping goods abroad. Payments made for insurance and other expenses are charged to the foreign buyer.

## foul bill of lading

a bill of lading issued with notations on it which limit the carrier's liability; for example, a notation that the goods were received damaged, or short, or improperly packaged.

**■ FRA**

is a Forward Rate Agreement.

**■ fractional currency**

any currency that is smaller than a standard money unit.

**■ FRCMO**

is a Floating Rate Collateralised Mortgage Obligation.

**■ Free Alongside (FAS)**

selling term in international trade. Selling party quotes price including delivery of goods alongside overseas vessel at exporting port.

**■ free in and out**

a pricing term indicating that the vessel operator is responsible for the cost of loading and unloading.

**■ free list**

a schedule of items in a customs tariff that are not subject to the payment of duties.

**■ free market**

a market in which there is unrestricted trading of goods with prices determined by supply and demand. Internationally, there is an unrestricted movement of goods in and out and it is unhampered by the existence of tariffs or other trade barriers.

**■ free port**

an area where imported goods may be brought without payment of duties.

**■ free riding**

has several meanings. It can refer to a customer account which engaged in purchases and sales without paying for the securities. There are several exceptions for some markets which may permit day-trading waivers or no reconciliation until final settlement or reciprocal closeout of position.
It can refer to an underwriter withholding a portion of a hot issue for the benefit of its own account.

**■ free time**

1. the time allowed shippers and receivers to load or unload rail cars before demurrage or detention.
2. the time allowed consignees to take physical delivery of cargo before storage or demurrage is assessed.

**■ free trade**

a theoretical concept that assumes international trade unhampered by government measures such as tariffs or nontariff barriers. The objective of trade liberalisation is to achieve freer trade rather than free trade, it being generally recognised among trade policy officials that some restrictions on trade are likely to remain in effect for the foreseeable future.

**■ free zone**

an area within a country (a seaport, airport, warehouse, or any designated area) regarded as being outside its customs territory. Importers may therefore bring goods of foreign origin into such an area without paying customs duties and taxes, pending their eventual processing, transshipment, or re-exportation. Free zones were numerous and prosperous during an earlier period when tariffs were high. Some still exist in capital cities, transport junctions and major seaports, but their number and prominence have declined as tariffs have fallen in recent years. Free zones may also be known as free ports, free warehouses, free trade zones and foreign trade zones.

## free-astray

1. a shipment or part of a shipment which has been dropped off at a wrong location by a carrier.
2. a shipment that is mis-routed or unloaded at the wrong terminal and is billed and forwarded to the correct terminal free of charge.

## Freedom, Commerce and Navigation Treaty (FCN)

a bilateral establishment treaty defining the legal and commercial rights of the citizens of each country under the laws of the other.

## freeholder

one holding an estate in fee simple, absolute in possession.

## freight

1. all merchandise, goods, products, or commodities shipped by rail, air, road, or water, other than baggage, express mail, or regular mail.
2. the compensation paid for the transport of goods.

## freight charge

the charge assessed for transporting cargo.

## freight claim

1. a demand upon a carrier for the repayment of overcharge.
2. a demand upon a carrier for cargo loss or damage.

## freight forwarder

1. an individual/company that accepts less-than truckload (LTL) shipments and consolidates them into truckload lots on a for-hire basis.
2. an agent who helps expedite shipments by preparing the necessary documents/making other arrangements for moving freight.

## freighter

a ship or aeroplane used primarily to carry cargo.

## FRM

is a Fixed Rate Mortgage.

## FRN

is a Floating Rate Note.

## front office

is the area or function which relates to trading, investing, or sales activities for a financial firm. Orders start here, flow through the middle office, if any and get processed by the back office.

## front-end load

refers to charges which are imposed upon the purchase or acquisition of an investment position. Many times these charges are on a sliding scale. Sometimes, these charges are viewed as impediments to early withdrawals. They are called front-end because they occur at the beginning of the investment process.

## frozen account

occurs when a client fails to pay for securities within the allotted time. Subsequent transactions can only occur if the account has sufficient funds or securities on deposit to complete the transactions. The frozen status or freeze can be removed only after the account complies with existing rules and regulations for an established time frame.

## full repairing and insuring (FRI) lease

an FRI lease requires the tenant to pay all running costs, e.g., maintenance, rates and insurance.

## fundamental analysis

is the research approach which considers economic and monetary factors. For securities, it evaluates the company as well as the industry and economy. For commodities, it looks at supply and demand in terms of actual usage, production and inventories, among other things.

## fungibles

goods that, for commercial purposes, are identical with other goods and interchangeable in all situations.

## futures commission merchant

is a firm which is registered to do customer business in the futures and options-on-futures business. This customer business relates to the taking of orders for contract execution.

## futures contract

a contract for the future delivery of a specified commodity, currency or security on a specific date at a rate determined in the present.

## futures contract equivalency

serves two key purposes. First, it converts the hedgeable positions into standardised units. Secondly, it allows these standardised units to be used as building blocks. When used as building blocks, option characteristics can be more clearly established. For example, an initial equivalency for treasury notes and bonds is the conversion factor. It relates various coupons and maturities into economically deliverable, not necessarily perfectly priced, units.

## futures contracts

are instruments predicated on a cash commodity or currency, a financial instrument, or an index. These are standardised contracts which are traded on organised exchanges. Also, these contracts are subject to industry and exchange regulations and government regulatory bodies and laws. The standardisation is one of the key factors which differentiates these instruments from forward contracts. Other factors are the standardisation of margin or performance bond procedures and the high degree of anonymous offset. Futures contracts can be offset by a trade opposite to the initial transaction and EFP, or a good delivery. Good deliveries can be satisfied by either the delivery of the actual commodity or financial instrument or by a final cash payment for Cash Settlement markets.

### g

is the Commodity Futures Symbol which represents the February Delivery Month.

### G-7

is the Group of Seven Nations. The membership consists of Britain, Canada, France, Germany, Italy, Japan and the United States of America.

### GAAP

is the acronym for Generally Accepted Accounting Principles.

### gamma

is the second derivative of an option. It measures the expected change in the delta given a change in the underlying instrument.

### gang

maritime: A group of longshoremen under a supervisor who are assigned to load or unload a portion of a vessel.

### gangway

1. the opening through which a ship is boarded.
2. a platform connecting quarterdeck and forecastle of a ship.

### gantry crane

a specialised crane which travels on a structure which can span a wide area and raises and lowers cargo. Some of them span the deck of a vessel.

### GAP

is the term used to described differences or imbalances in asset and liability categories or buckets.

### GARCH

is Generalised Autoregressive Conditional Heteroskedasticity (ARCH). It is a time series approach which models volatility as a function of both previous returns and previous volatilities.

■ **GARP**

refers to Generally Accepted Risk Principles.

■ **gateway**

1. a major airport or seaport;
2. the port where customs clearance takes place;
3. a point at which freight moving from one territory to another is interchanged between transportation lines.

■ **GDRS**

a Global Depository Receipts.

■ **gearing**

is a measure of exposure. It relates the number of warrants that can be purchased for the same price of the stock. For example, if the stock is trading at 150 and the warrants are trading at 30, then the gearing is 5.00 or 5-to-1.

■ **geisha bond**

bond issued on the Japanese market in currencies other than yen.

■ **general account**

refers to the assets held by the insurance company to back their obligations for guaranteed or fixed-dollar benefits and contracts. Here, the insurance company is at risk.

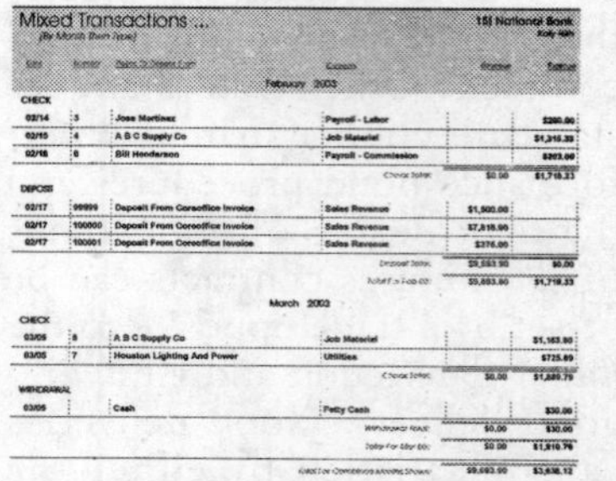


General Agreement on Tariffs And Trade (GATT)

refers both to the de facto international organisation headquartered at Geneva, Switzerland, through which the contracting parties consulted on a day-to-day basis regarding the application of GATT provisions and the 1947 General Agreement on Tariffs and Trade that gave birth to it. Because the U.S. Senate would not ratify the Havana Charter of 1948, which would have created an International Trade Organisation (ITO) as a specialised agency of the United Nations system similar to the International Monetary Fund and the World Bank, the GATT organisation became the key international institution concerned with multinational trade negotiations. The Interim Commission of the ITO (ICITO), which was established to facilitate the creation of the ITO, subsequently became the GATT Secretariat. By 1993, there were 103 GATT contracting parties, accounting for approximately 85 percent of world trade and some 30 additional countries and dependencies applied GATT provisions on a de facto basis. The organisation provided a framework for negotiations called rounds within which contracting parties negotiated to lower tariffs and other barriers to trade and a consultative mechanism that could be invoked by governments seeking to protect their trade interests. Over the years the GATT organisation evolved through several rounds of multilateral negotiations. With the Tokyo and Uruguay Rounds, the focus of trade liberalisation shifted from lowering tariffs to the elimination of nontariff barriers to trade. The Uruguay Round, which was the most recent round, lasted from 1986 to 1994 and led to the creation of the World Trade Organisation, which, on January 1, 1995, replaced the GATT organisation.

## ■ General Agreement On Trade In Services (GATS)

a WTO agreement that is the first multilateral agreement to provide legally enforceable rules covering all international trade and investment in the service sector (except for those services provided in the exercise of governmental authority). GATS is designed to reduce or eliminate governmental measures that prevent services from being freely provided across national borders or that discriminate against locally established service firms with foreign ownership. Thus, GATS expands generally accepted notions of international trade to place trade in services on the same footing as trade in goods. GATS consists of a framework agreement that lays out the general principles and obligations for trade in services (including most-favoured-nation treatment, market access and national treatment) that apply to all WTO members in much the same way as the GATT does for trade in goods. Attached to this framework agreement are annexes dealing with rules for specific service sector (movement of natural persons, air transport, financial services, maritime and telecommunications) national schedules negotiated during the Uruguay Round listing each member's specific undertakings with respect to its service sectors. The agreement also provides for exceptions to the principles of national treatment and most-favoured-nation treatment. First, governments can choose the services in which they make market access and national treatment commitments; second, they can limit the degree of market access and national treatment they provide; third, they can take exceptions even from the MFN obligation, in principle only for 10 years, in order to give more favourable treatment to some countries than to WTO members in general. Finally, GATS provides a forum for further negotiations to open services markets around the world.

## ■ general average

1. loss that affects all cargo interests on board a vessel as well as

the ship herself.

2. an internationally accepted rule of the sea which says when a peril threatens the survival of the ship, there may be sacrificed (thrown overboard) any cargo or supplies or ships' furnishings and any expense incurred necessary to save the ship. If the vessel is saved, all cargo owners, ship owner and owners of the freight revenue share pro rata in the loss.

■ **general cargo rate**

the rate a carrier charges for the transportation of cargo which does not qualify for a lower special class or commodity rate in the carrier's tariff.

■ **general cargo vessels**

a vessel designed to handle breakbulk cargo such as bags, cartons, cases, crates and drums, either individually or in unitised or palletised loads.

■ **general commodity rate**

in a maritime tariff, a freight rate applicable to all commodities except those for which specific rates have been filed.

■ **general imports**

the total physical arrivals of merchandise into one country from foreign countries during a period of time..

■ **general liability**

unlimited responsibility for an obligation, such as payment of debts of a business.

■ **general partnership**

a partnership where all partners have joint ownership. They share the profit, losses and management equally and each has personal liability for all the debts.

■ **general tariff**

a tariff that applies to countries that do not enjoy either preferential or most favoured nation tariff treatment.

■ **Generalised System Of Preferences (GSP)**

a programme providing for free rates of duty for merchandise from beneficiary developing independent countries and territories to encourage their economic growth.

■ **generic**

prescription drugs that do not carry a trademark or trade name.

■ **gift tax**

tax on gifts generally paid by the person making the gift, rather than the recipient.

■ **gold exchange standard**

a monetary system adopted by some countries which did not have enough gold to go onto the gold standard so they deposited their gold with one of the leading gold standard countries and made their currency more or less freely convertible to the currency of that country.

## gold reserves

gold retained by a nation or its central banks contributing to the nation's creditworthiness in the issuance of bonds and currency, although there may be no commitment by it to exchange gold for its currency.

## gold standard

a monetary system whereby every form of currency issued by a country is convertible on demand into its legal equivalent in gold or gold coin

## gold/silver ratio

refers to the monetary conversion rate between one ounce of gold and the appropriate ounces of silver. You divide the one-ounce price of gold by the current silver price, for the same delivery time and determine the number of silver ounces required for this equation. This measurement goes back at least to a bimetallic monetary standard.

## gondola car

an open railway car with sides and ends, used principally for hauling coal, sand, etc.

## goods

merchandise, supplies, raw materials, wares, commodities, products. The meaning may vary in various situations but for purposes of a contract for storage or transportation, or with reference to collateral for security, it means all things treated as movable.

## good-till-cancelled

is an order which remains in effect until it is executed or cancelled. The cancellation can be predetermined such as in two months (giving a specific time) or left open and not specifying any time. However, many brokerage firms and traders may require ratification of all open orders at the end of the month or other time span of their choosing to minimise errors.

## grades

refers to the quality of a potentially deliverable commodity. It can refer to sulfur content for crude, country of origin for coffee or cocoa, or other distinguishing factors which influence the item. Often there is a schedule of premiums and discounts to adjust the invoice or delivery price for grade differences.

## graduated payment mortgage

is a mortgage which frequently has relatively low payments in its early life. These relatively low payments are often insufficient to amortise the principal. Therefore, with the passage of time the payment schedule is stepped-up to paydown the early negative amortisation, service, the interest requirement and paydown the total principal balance.

## graduation

the presumption that individual developing countries are capable of assuming greater responsibilities and obligations in the international community, within the context of the WTO or the World Bank, for example as their economies advance, through industrialisation, export development and rising living standards. In this sense, graduation implies that donor countries may remove the more advanced developing countries from eligibility for all or some products under the Generalised System of Preferences. Within the World Bank, graduation moves a country from dependence on concessional grants to nonconcessional loans from international financial institutions and private banks.

## grains

refers to the commodity futures markets for corn, oats and wheat. A broader definition would include soybeans.

## grandfather clause

a provision in a legal instrument, such as GATT, that allows countries that accede to it to maintain preexisting domestic legislation inconsistent with provisions of that instrument.

## grantee

One to whom a grant is made; a grant being the giving or permitting as a right or privilege, an authority, a power, a license, or a property.

## grantor

the person who transfers assets into a trust for the benefit of another.

## grants

is the process of initially selling or writing an option.

## green

is a mortgage backed securities term which indicates mortgages which are not seasoned yet. Typically, a mortgage that is less than 30 months old is considered green.

## green card

a popular name for an identity card (visa) issued by the U.S. Immigration and Naturalisation Service entitling a foreign national to enter and reside in the United States as a permanent resident.

## green shoe

refers to an underwriting allotment which is in excess of the first stipulated share amount. Depending on demand and/or market stabilising functions, an underwriter can exercise this option for additional shares. Many new deals now have this option included. Usually, the green shoe is limited to an additional 15 percent of new shares. It was named after the company for which it was the focus of the deal.

■ **grid**

fixed margin within which exchange rates are allowed to fluctuate.

■ **gridlock**

is a condition whereby trading activity ceases or becomes extremely constrained. Frequently, the spreads between bids and offers widen dramatically and volume dries up. Therefore, there are very few, if any, trades.

■ **gross**

1. 12 dozen or 144 articles.
2. total (as in Gross Weight.)

■ **gross domestic product**

a measure of the market value of all goods and services produced within the boundaries of a nation. It excludes income from external enterprises or investments.

■ **gross estate**

the total property or assets held by an individual.

■ **gross national product**

a measure of the market value of all goods and services produced within the boundaries of a nation plus receipts from foreign business activities and investments beyond the national boundaries.

■ **gross weight**

the total weight of a package or a shipment, including goods and packaging.

■ **group of 8 (G-8)**

the heads of state or government of the leading industrial democracies who have met annually since 1975 to coordinate economic policies to achieve sustained economic growth with price stability, to foster stability in exchange markets and to promote adjustment in external imbalances. The group also addresses other pressing international economic issues that affect global economic performance. In 1973 and 1974, the finance ministers of the United States, Japan, Germany, France and the United Kingdom met informally in a group referred to as the Group of 5. In 1975, when the group became a group of heads of state, what was then called the Group of 6 comprised the United States, Japan, Germany, France, Italy and the United Kingdom. Canada joined the group in 1976, transforming it into the Group of 7. The group has recently come to be known as the Group of 8 because, since the end of the Cold War in 1992, Russia has been attending these meetings where it has participated at an ever higher level. In recent times, representatives of the European Union have also attended as observers.

■ **growth funds**

are mutual funds that invest in stocks of companies which are expected to outperform most other firms. This outperformance is predicated on faster growth than comparable firms in the same industry. Also, these industries can be those which are expected to experience growth rates in excess of an average.

**Top growth funds this quarter**

| LARGE-CAP GROWTH | % RETURN |
|---|---|
| Rydex Velocity 100 | 78.85% |
| ProFunds UltraOTC | 78.25% |
| Potomac OTC Plus | 46.69% |
| ASAF ProFund Managed OTC | 46.41% |
| Touchstone Aggressive Growth | 41.41% |
| **MID-CAP GROWTH** | |
| Van Wagoner Emerging Growth | 66.10% |
| Van Wagoner Post-Venture | 61.37% |
| Van Wagoner Mid-Cap Growth | 46.74% |
| Dominion Insight Growth | 37.25% |
| TCW Galileo Aggressive Growth Eq | 32.39% |
| **SMALL-CAP GROWTH** | |
| ARK Social Issues Small-cap Eq Inst | 49.21% |
| Van Wagoner Micro-Cap Growth | 37.28% |
| Reserve Small-Cap Growth | 31.56% |
| UM Small-Cap Growth | 30.37% |
| Kopp Emerging Growth | 30.32% |

### ■ guts

is the purchase or the sale of two in-the-money options. For example, a long guts consists of the purchase of a low strike call and the purchase of a high strike put. A short guts position consists of the sale of the high strike put and the sale of the low strike call.

### ■ h

is the Commodity Futures Symbol which represents the March Delivery Month.

### ■ hallmark

1. originally an impression made on gold and silverware introduced in the beginning of the fourteenth century in England to identify the quality of the metal used. Later, a mark to identify the maker and year of production.

2. figuratively, a distinguishing characteristic.

### ■ harbour fees

charges assessed to users for use of a harbour, used generally for maintenance of the harbour.

### ■ harbour master

an officer who is commander of harbour activities and directs the berthing, etc. of ships in a harbour.

### ■ hard loan

a foreign loan that must be paid in hard money.

### ■ hard money

currency of a nation having stability in the country and a reputation abroad for economic strength and as a result it has wide and ready acceptability on world markets.

### ■ harmonisation

the process of making procedures or measures applied by different countries

especially those affecting international trade more compatible, as by effecting simultaneous tariff cuts applied by different countries so as to make their tariff structures more uniform. Most proposals for harmonising tariffs envisage relatively large cuts in high tariffs and smaller cuts in lower tariffs, as contrasted with the linear reduction formula used in the Kennedy Round, which called for identical percentage cuts for all applicable tariffs. Tokyo Round tariff cuts increased tariff harmonisation among the developed countries.

## ■ Harmonised System (HS)

a multipurpose international goods classification system designed to be used by manufacturers, transporters, exporters, importers, customs, statisticians and others in classifying under a single commodity code goods moving in international trade.

## ■ hatch

the opening in the deck of a vessel which gives access to a cargo hold.

## ■ haulage

1. the local transport of goods.
2. also the charge(s) made for hauling freight on carts, drays or trucks.
3. also called cartage or drayage.

## ■ hazardous materials

a substance or material which has been determined to be capable of posing an unreasonable risk to health, safety and property when transported in commerce.

## ■ head lessee

where a sub-tenancy (or series of subtenancies) exists, the highest leaseholder in the chain (who pays head rent to the freeholder).

## ■ headline rent

the rent apparently being paid, which may not take account of concessions such as rent-free periods.

## ■ heavy crude oil

is petroleum with a high specific gravity and a low API gravity. It has a relatively high proportion of heavy hydrocarbon products or fractions.

## ■ heavy lift

any article deemed by rules in a vessel's tariff to be beyond a certain weight. It may be too heavy for the ship's tackle and require special equipment such as a floating crane.

## heavy lift charge

in a maritime tariff, a charge made for lifting heavy articles to load or unload them.

## heavy lift vessel

a vessel with heavy lift cranes and other equipment designed to be self-sustaining in the handling of heavy cargo.

## hedge

1. to reduce one's risk of loss by compensating transactions on the other side. For example, buy goods for future delivery priced in a foreign currency. Hedge by buying the foreign exchange needed at the rate then in effect. Or, another way of hedging is to buy a forward exchange contract. In both cases the buyer will have a known cost in its own currency. This is a hedge against the risk of foreign exchange fluctuation, it is not a hedge against a change in the price of the goods.
2. action taken by a buyer or seller to protect his or her business or assets against a change in prices. A miller, for example, might buy a quantity of wheat to convert into flour at a given point in time and agree at the same time to sell a similar quantity of wheat that he does not own, at the same price, for delivery at a designated future point in time. If the price of wheat falls, he will lose on the flour while making a profit on the wheat he can later buy at the lower price. But if the price of wheat rises, he will make an extra profit on his flour, which he will have to sacrifice by purchasing wheat at the current high price. In either case, his production profits are protected.

## hedge funds

are alternative investment vehicles. Hedge fund trading styles are quite variable from one fund to another. Some are Macro Funds which place positions on movements in broad economic groups such as currencies, credit, equity and derivatives markets. Others are more focused on narrow Specialties, such as Convertible Securities or Mortgage Backed Securities. These funds operate as limited partnerships. There are limitations on the number of partners, minimum financial standards and commitments and liabilities.

## hedge properties

are features considered necessary for a good risk management position. There are four basic properties and they are: Economic Validity, Reasonable Correlative Movements, Convergence and Consistent Basis Behaviour.

## hedge ratio

the amount of future exchange contracts, options, or underlying financial instruments, purchased or sold against a position to accomplish a hedge of the position.

## hedging

is the process of protecting a position. It is the placement of a position to offset an exposed cash or physical market position.

## hedging paradox

is when favourable basis movements do not guarantee a favourable global result for the hedge. Also, it can occur when the basis behaviour is unfavourable yet the hedge is still beneficial.

## heteroskedasticity or heteroscedasticity

is the condition where the residual variance is no constant. This tends to happen in cross-sectional analyses. It also occurs in various consumer, income, risk and size of firm studies.

## high density

high density cargo is cargo whose weight is high compared to its volume. A vessel tariff in which freight is charged according to weight or volume, whichever yields the highest freight charge, will result in high density freight being charged on a weight basis.

## historic volatility

is the statistical measurement of the underlying instrumentís price variability over some defined time frame such as 10, 20 30, or 50 days.

## hitchment

in maritime situations, if the tariff of the steamship company provides for it, portions of a shipment originating in different places may be joined together under one bill of lading from one shipper to one consignee at one destination.

## hold

1. The interior of a vessel below deck where cargo is carried.
2. to delay; to pause (verb); a delay; a pause (noun).
3. A verb with multiple other meanings than those noted above such as: to retain, to contain, to maintain, to bind, to bear, to own.

## hold for pickup

freight to be held at the carrier's destination location for pickup by the recipient.

## hold harmless contract

an agreement by which one party accepts responsibility for all damages and other liability that arise from a transaction, relieving the other party of any such liability.

## Ho-Lee option model

is an Arbitrage Free Model which uses an estimated spot curve to evaluate embedded options in credit or fixed income securities.

## homoskedasticity or homoscedasticity

is the condition of constant residual variance.

## honour

to accept a bill of exchange; or to pay a note, cheque or draft at maturity.

## horizontal export trading company

an export trading company which exports a range of similar or identical products supplied by a number of manufacturers who may be competitors on the domestic market.

■ **horizontal spread**

is a spread which is composed of two puts or two calls on the same underlying instrument. It is called horizontal because both options have the same strike or exercise price but two different expiration dates. Generally, the trade is placed with the nearby option sold and the deferred option purchased. This is an attempt to capitalise on the acceleration in time value decay for the nearby relative to the deferred contract month.

■ **hostile**

often refers to an unsolicitated and unwanted bid by the target company. It rejects this bid and indicates that the company does not want to be acquired by that bidder.

■ **hot issues**

are stocks which trade at an immediate premium relative to their initial offering price on the effective date. There are restrictions and prohibitions regarding trading in these issues. These constraints apply to brokerage firm employees and their immediate families. Other parties may also be subject to such constraints.

■ **house air waybill**

1. a bill of lading issued by a freight forwarder for consolidated air freight shipments.
2. an airway bill issued by an airfreight forwarder by which the forwarder assumes the risk and obligations of being the carrier.

■ **hub and spoke routing**

air cargo routing pattern that feeds traffic from many places to a central airport where it is sorted and rerouted on other aircraft to final destinations.

■ **hull**

the outer shell of a vessel.

■ **hump**

an essential feature of a railcar sorting yard . The hump is that part of the track which is elevated so that when a car is pushed up on it and uncoupled, it runs down the other side by gravity and is switched onto the siding where a train is being made up for the desired destination.

■ **hurricane bonds**

are issued to pass on unacceptably high risks to speculators. In exchange, these speculators may receive potentially greater-than-market rates of return. These bonds have characteristics comparable to those for risky collateralised obligation trances.

**■ hybrid**

is a security which has mixed characteristics. One example is a convertible bond. It can have a coupon and pay interest and therefore partially behave like a credit market instrument. However, its conversion feature also imbues the instrument with equity characteristics.

**■ hybridisation**

is the act or process of creating a new instrument which has two or more credit, equity, currency or commodity characteristics.

**■ hypothetication agreements**

are legal documents which define the pledging of collateral. A mortgage defines the collateral for a real estate loan or Note and a securities hypothecation agreement permits margin accounts and futures accounts by stating what is being pledged to cover positions, debit balances, or even deficit balances. Generally, this document allows the owner to enjoy the usage of the property provided that no default occurs. In the event of a default the property can go to the creditor to satisfy the claim. The residual value, if any, would then go to the owner.

**■ IB**

is an Introducing Broker. Depending on the financials and election, Introducing Brokers can be effectively self-guaranteeing or Guaranteed by the Clearing Firm with which they are affiliated.

**■ implied conditions**

certain implied conditions are not written into marine insurance policies, but they are so basic to the understanding between the underwriter and the assured that the law gives them much the same effect as if written. (In many other types of contracts there also may be implied conditions, for example a seller of goods implies that they are fit for the purpose they purport to serve.)

**■ implied price**

is the price computed by a model which considers a comparable benchmark, volatility and spread adjustment. It is used in the absence of a current market price.

**■ implied repo rate**

is influenced by the cost of funds, tax rates, deductibility of carry charges, yields, the time to expiration and organisational constraints. It indicates the implied rate of return for specified investments. While many quote services list an assumed or benchmark Implied Repo Rate, there are many because each investor has his or her own schedule of financing costs and investment opportunities.

**■ implied volatility**

is the current volatility or the level of volatility required to generate an option premium given a known market price for the underlying, an interest rate, an expiration date and a strike price.

**import**

the act of bringing or causing any goods to be brought into a customs territory.

**import credit**

a commercial letter of credit issued for the purpose of financing the importation of goods.

**import duty**

customs duty which is collected in connection with the importation of goods.

**import license**

an import license (or import permit) is an authorisation by a competent authority for the importation of goods which are subject to restriction.

**import quota**

a protective device establishing limits on the quantity of a particular product that may be imported into a country.

**import quota auctioning**

the process of auctioning the right to import specified quantities of quota-restricted goods.

**import relief**

any of several measures imposed by a government to temporally restrict imports of a product or commodity to protect domestic producers from competition. Or, any of several measures to strengthen domestic producers such as subsidies, educational assistance to workers, training assistance to workers, low interest loans to producers, tax relief to producers etc.

**import restrictions**

any one of a series of tariff and non-tariff barriers imposed by an importing nation to control the volume of goods coming into the country from other countries.

**import sensitive producers**

domestic producers whose economic viability is threatened by competition (quality, price or service) from imported products.

**import substitution**

a national economic strategy to build up a domestic economy by emphasising the replacement of imports by domestically produced goods.

**importer**

the individual, firm or legal entity that brings goods, or causes goods to be brought from a foreign country into a customs territory.

**imports**

the inflow of goods and services into a country's market for consumption. A country enhances its welfare by importing a broader range of higher-quality goods and services at lower cost than it could produce domestically. The expansion of world trade since the end of World War II has therefore been a principal factor underlying a general rise in living standards in most countries.

**imports for consumption**

the total of merchandise that has physically cleared through the customs of a country either entering domestic consumption channels immediately or entering after withdrawal for consumption from bonded warehouses or from foreign trade zones.

## ■ impost

1. A tax, especially an import duty.
2. To classify an impost in order to fix the duty. (rarely used). (Note: an imposter is one who imposts. Another definition of an imposter is a pretender but that is not the meaning intended here.)

## ■ impound

to seize or hold; or to place in custody by order of a court.

## ■ in bond

storage of goods in custody of government/bonded warehouse or carrier from whom goods can be taken only upon payment of taxes/duties to appropriate government agency.

## ■ in bond shipment

an import or export shipment which has not been cleared by Customs and is transported, stored, or handled with security to the government provided by indemnity bonds.

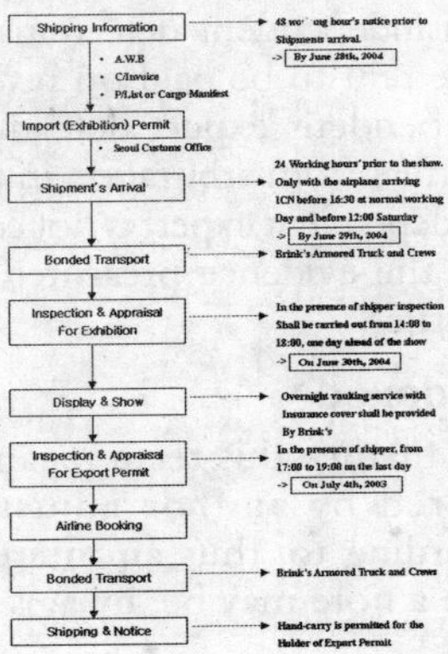


## ■ incentive

a motivational force that stimulates people to greater activity or increased efficiency.

## ■ income

money or its equivalent, earned or accrued, arising from the sale of goods or services.

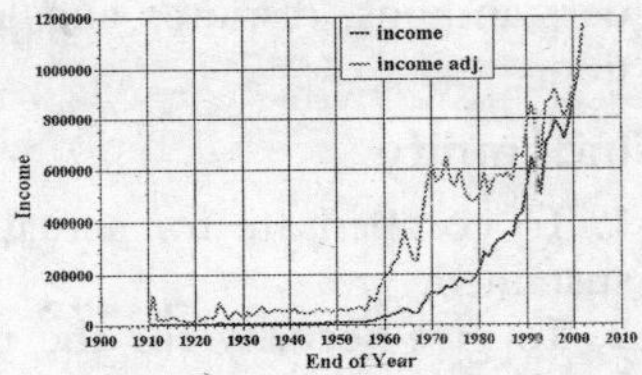


## ■ income bonds

refer to securities which promise to repay the principal when due. However, these bonds differ from other bonds in that they promise to pay interest only when it is earned. This type of bond is very similar to many kinds of preferred stock. However, an advantage can be the tax deductibility of the interest charge when paid versus a preferred dividend payment. These bonds are sometimes known as Adjustment Bonds. The quality of these bonds generally is not as good as investment grade issues because there is an additional contingency on the payment of interest.

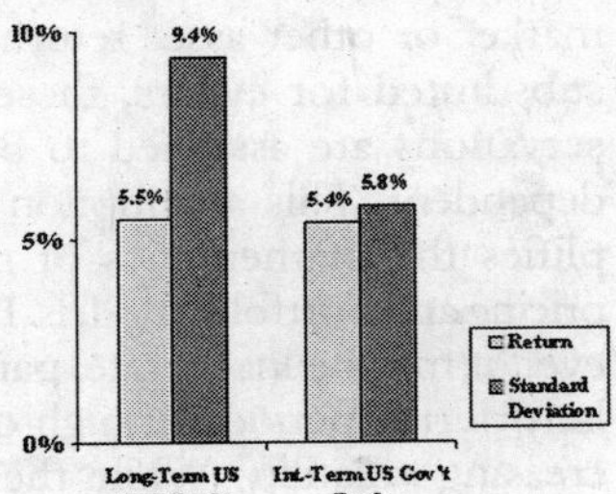

**incoterms**

an abbreviation of International Commercial Terms published by the International Chamber of Commerce. It is a set of rules for the interpretation of the most commonly used trade terms in foreign trade which parties to a contract can agree upon to avoid misunderstandings, disputes and litigation.

**indemnify**

1. To compensate for actual loss sustained.
2. To give security for the reimbursement of a person in case of an anticipated loss falling upon him.

**indemnity**

1. a compensation to make a person whole from a loss already sustained.
2. a contract or assurance by which one engages to secure another against an anticipated loss.

**independence**

is a very important concept in probability and statistics. When the occurrence or nonoccurrence of an event has no impact or statistical influence on another event then the events are said to be independent of one another. When stock market or other asset returns are substituted for events, these observations are assumed to be independent. This assumption simplifies the mathematics of many pricing and portfolio models. However, it may be inaccurate, particularly during periods of high or increasing volatility. While the majority of observations may fall within the defined assumption, the occurrence of big change days has been demonstrated to occur more frequently than normally expected. Moreover, these relatively large price or rate changes tend to cluster within relatively narrow time frames. As a quick illustration, if a three standard deviation event is normally expected to occur once every 40 years or 10,000 trading days then the likelihood of two such events in a short time frame is expected to be 1 in 100,000,000 (10,000 x 10,000). This clearly has not been the case. It is critical to take into account the statistical interdependence for Value at Risk Programmes, hedging and derivative pricing models.

**independent action**

the right of a conference member to depart from the common freight rates, terms or conditions of the conference without the need for prior approval of the conference.

**independent expert determination**

an independent determination of the rent to be paid on review. Independent expert determination differs from arbitration in that the independent expert is not confined to the evidence presented by the parties.

**indexed**

in finance this term means measured by and/or adjusted according to, thus an interest rate on a note may be, by agreement, indexed i.e., adjusted according to the market at time the interest is due. Or a note denominated in a foreign currency may have its exchange rate indexed, adjusted according to the market rate in effect at the time of payment.

### ■ indexed currency borrowings

borrowings in a foreign currency where the rate of interest is linked to an agreed scale and/or the rate of exchange at repayment is linked to an agreed scale.

### ■ indexed currency option note

note denominated and paying interest in one currency but whose redemption value is linked to an exchange rate for another currency.

### ■ indication of interest

occurs when a client states his or her interest in purchasing a new issue before its effective date. This interest is non-binding.

### ■ industrial policy

traditional government policies intended to provide a favourable economic climate for the development of industry in general or specific industrial sectors. Instruments of industrial policy may include tax incentives to promote investments or exports, direct or indirect subsidies, special financing arrangements, protection against foreign competition, worker training programmes, regional development programmes, assistance for research and development and measures to help small business firms. Historically the term industrial policy has been associated with at least some degree of centralised economic planning or indicative planning, but this connotation is not always intended by its contemporary advocates.

### ■ industrial revolution

the emergence of the factory system of production, in which workers were brought together in one plant and supplied with tools, machines and materials with which they worked in return for wages. Narrowly speaking, the Industrial Revolution was spearheaded by the rapid changes in the manufacture of textiles, particularly in England, between about 1770 and 1830. More broadly, the term applies to continuing structural economic change in the world economy. Before the Industrial Revolution, the domestic system of production prevailed in the 16th and 17th centuries.

### ■ integrated tariff

the system used by a shipping conference to charge agreed upon rates for services.

### ■ intellectual property

ownership as evidenced by patents, trademarks and copyrights conferring the right to possess, use, or dispose of products created by human ingenuity.

### ■ interchange agreement

an agreement that specifically lays down the terms of leasing or temporarily borrowing equipment from a carrier. A frequent use of an interchange agreement is between an ocean carrier and a trucking company when the trucking company takes a container from the pier for delivery to the consignee.

**■ interchange point**

a location where one carrier delivers freight to another carrier.

**■ interest**

a sum paid for the use of borrowed capital, usually expressed in terms of a rate or percentage of the capital involved (the interest rate), which is normally higher when the risk (including both the risk of non-payment and the probability of inflation) is greater.

**■ interest only**

is a security whose value is predicated on a discounted interest rate structure. Typically, this is a CMO type derivative product. Prepayment activity is a dominant evaluation factor.

**■ interest rate**

is either the coupon or floating rate attached to a credit instrument or lending operation.

**■ interest rate risk**

is the risk associated with changes in general interest rate levels or yield curves.

**■ interest rate swap**

is the contract whereby one party typically agrees to exchange a floating rate for a fixed coupon rate. There are many variations to this theme. Some of these other swaps can be cross border, fixed-for-fixed, or floating-for-floating. The common denominator to these transactions is the swapping of cashflows and not principal amounts. There are predetermined periodic adjustments in cash flow payments.

**■ interim rent**

a landlord may apply to the court to fix an interim rent when he has given notice of termination of a tenancy or where the tenant has served notice of a request for a new tenancy on the landlord.

**■ interline freight**

freight moving from origin to destination over two or more transportation lines.

**■ interline shipping**

the movement of a single shipment on two or more carriers.

**■ intermarket trading system**

is the network which links the trading floors of several registered exchanges. It encourages competition in issues listed on the American or New York Stock Exchanges with the other participating regional exchanges. The competitive edge occurs if there is a better price out in the network than on a particular exchange. If so, then a broker or market maker can execute at that better price.

■ **intermediate corporate bonds**

are investment grade notes and bonds issued by corporations. The maturities range between 1 to 10 years. These securities encompass banks, other financial institutions and industrial issuers.

■ **intermodal compatibility**

the physical capability of a shipment of goods to be transported from one form of transportation to another.

■ **intermodal transport**

coordinated transport of freight using multiple methods of transportation.

■ **intermodal transportation**

using more than one mode to deliver shipments. For example, rail or ocean vessel carriage of tractor-trailer containers.

■ **International Commodity Agreement (ICA)**

an international understanding, usually reflected in a legal instrument, relating to trade in a particular commodity and based on terms negotiated and accepted by most of the countries that export and import commercially significant quantities of the commodity. Some commodity agreements, such as those for coffee, cocoa, natural rubber and sugar, have centered on economic provisions intended to stabilise the market price within a negotiated price range for the commodity through the use of buffer stocks, export quotas, or both. Of these, only rubber currently has economic provisions as part of the agreement. Other commodity agreements (such as existing agreements for jute and jute products, olive oil and wheat) seek to promote cooperation among producers and consumers through improved consultations, exchange of information, research and development and export promotion.

■ **International Development Association (IDA)**

an affiliate of the World Bank, established in 1960, that extends concessional loans to the least developed countries and other relatively poor countries to finance long-term high-priority development projects. IDA resources are contributed by 33 donor countries. The World Bank would not be able to make loans to many of the poorest countries, including most countries in Africa, without IDA resources.

■ **International Finance Corporation (IFC)**

an affiliate of the World Bank established in 1956 to promote commercial enterprises in developing countries through loans and equity financing comparable to those extended by investment banks. It also facilitates the establishment of partnerships between private investors, wherever they may be located and capital markets in the Third World. It does not require government guarantees.

## International Monetary Fund (IMF)

an international financial institution proposed at the 1944 Bretton Woods Conference and established in 1946 that seeks to stabilise the international monetary system as a basis for the orderly expansion of international trade. Specifically, the IMF monitors exchange rate policies of member countries, lends them foreign exchange resources to support their adjustment policies when they experience balance-of-payments difficulties and provides them financial assistance through a special compensatory financing facility when they experience temporary shortfalls in commodity export earnings.

## International Telecommunications Union (ITU)

a United Nations organisation, headquartered in Geneva, Switzerland, within which governments and the private sector coordinate global telecommunication networks and services. Its work is performed through three groups or sectors: telecommunication standardisation, radio communication and telecommunication development.

## international trade

the business of buying and selling commodities beyond national borders.

## inventory

is the firm's position with the intent of quick resell or repurchase. Can refer to the open positions taken in the course of market making activities. This is opposed the Investment Account.

## inventory turnover ratio

is computed by dividing annual sales by inventories. It is usually desirable to have a relatively high inventory turnover ratio relative to competitors.

## inverse floater

is an instrument which the required interest payment, or coupon, will change inversely to rates prevailing at the time of the reset.

## inverted market

is the market condition whereby the deferred or more forward delivery months are at a progressive discount to the spot or nearby month. This condition is marked by premiums for immediate or nearby deliveries. This is also known as a backwardation market. This is opposite to a contango or carrying charge market.

■ **inverted yield curve**

is the market condition whereby the near-term interest rates are higher than long-term interest rates. For example, the two year rate is greater than the ten year rate; or, the spot (overnight) rate is higher than the thirty year rate. This inversion may be induced or result from changes in monetary policy, foreign exchange movements, immediate liquidity needs within the financial system, constrictions in money/credit and other financial forces.

■ **investment account**

is an account at a financial institution which is held for long term investment or capital purposes. This is opposed to the trading or inventory account.

■ **investment horizon**

is the actual or expected period that a financial position will be held. Some organisations and individuals use simple purchase-and-hold strategies, particularly for fixed income securities. For those parties, the investment horizon would be the time left to maturity. Other uses of the term are: day, short-term, intermediate- term and long-term holdings.

■ **invisible barriers to trade**

government regulations (national and local) and cultural conditions that do not directly restrict trade but hinder it with excessive and obscure requirements.

■ **invisible supply**

refers to uncounted or unverified, but known to exist, inventories of a commodity.

■ **invisible trade balance**

the balance of trade reflecting the import and export of services.

■ **invoice**

a written account or itemised statement, usually on a printed form with the name and address of the seller, listing merchandise sold or shipped to a purchaser, consignee, factor etc., showing their name and address and containing a description of the merchandise, the quantity, values or prices and charges and other significant details of the transaction such as the terms of sale and the currency of the purchase.

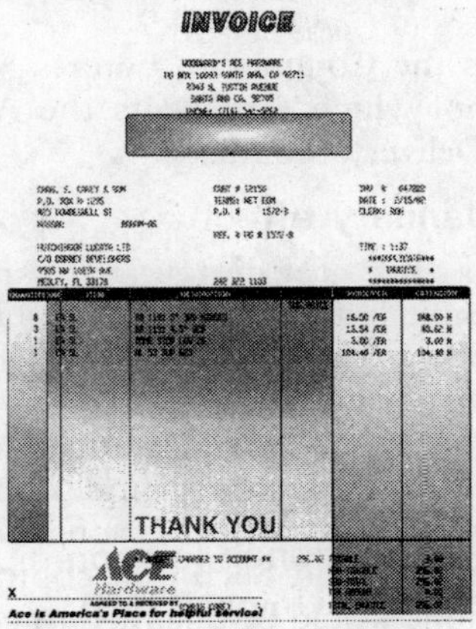


■ **irrevocable corporate purchase order**

a purchase order completed by a buyer on corporate letter head indicating type and quantity of products being ordered from a supplier.

■ **irrevocable letter of credit**

a letter of credit which cannot be amended or canceled without prior mutual consent of all parties to the credit.

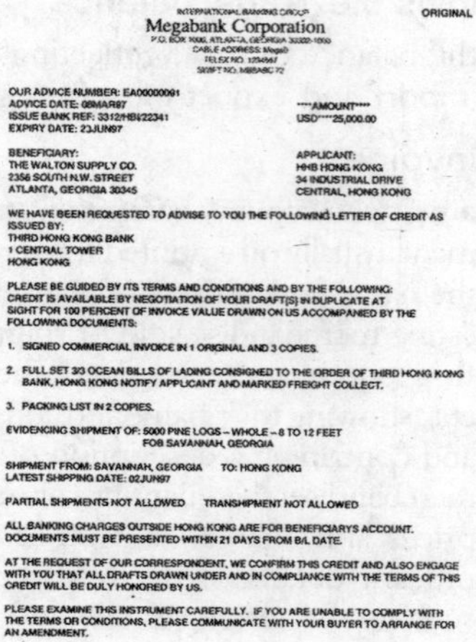

INTERNATIONAL BANKING GROUP
ORIGINAL
**Megabank Corporation**
P.O. BOX 1000, ATLANTA, GEORGIA 30302-1000
CABLE ADDRESS: MegaB
TELEX NO. 1234567
SWIFT NO. MBBABC 72

OUR ADVICE NUMBER: EA00000091
ADVICE DATE: 08MAR97
ISSUE BANK REF: 3312/HB/22341
EXPIRY DATE: 23JUN97

****AMOUNT****
USD****25,000.00

BENEFICIARY:
THE WALTON SUPPLY CO.
2356 SOUTH N.W. STREET
ATLANTA, GEORGIA 30345

APPLICANT:
HHB HONG KONG
34 INDUSTRIAL DRIVE
CENTRAL, HONG KONG

WE HAVE BEEN REQUESTED TO ADVISE TO YOU THE FOLLOWING LETTER OF CREDIT AS ISSUED BY:
THIRD HONG KONG BANK
1 CENTRAL TOWER
HONG KONG

PLEASE BE GUIDED BY ITS TERMS AND CONDITIONS AND BY THE FOLLOWING:
CREDIT IS AVAILABLE BY NEGOTIATION OF YOUR DRAFT(S) IN DUPLICATE AT SIGHT FOR 100 PERCENT OF INVOICE VALUE DRAWN ON US ACCOMPANIED BY THE FOLLOWING DOCUMENTS:

1. SIGNED COMMERCIAL INVOICE IN 1 ORIGINAL AND 3 COPIES.
2. FULL SET 3/3 OCEAN BILLS OF LADING CONSIGNED TO THE ORDER OF THIRD HONG KONG BANK, HONG KONG NOTIFY APPLICANT AND MARKED FREIGHT COLLECT.
3. PACKING LIST IN 2 COPIES.

EVIDENCING SHIPMENT OF: 5000 PINE LOGS – WHOLE – 8 TO 12 FEET
FOB SAVANNAH, GEORGIA

SHIPMENT FROM: SAVANNAH, GEORGIA TO: HONG KONG
LATEST SHIPPING DATE: 02JUN97

PARTIAL SHIPMENTS NOT ALLOWED TRANSHIPMENT NOT ALLOWED

ALL BANKING CHARGES OUTSIDE HONG KONG ARE FOR BENEFICIARYS ACCOUNT.
DOCUMENTS MUST BE PRESENTED WITHIN 21 DAYS FROM B/L DATE.

AT THE REQUEST OF OUR CORRESPONDENT, WE CONFIRM THIS CREDIT AND ALSO ENGAGE WITH YOU THAT ALL DRAFTS DRAWN UNDER AND IN COMPLIANCE WITH THE TERMS OF THIS CREDIT WILL BE DULY HONORED BY US.

PLEASE EXAMINE THIS INSTRUMENT CAREFULLY. IF YOU ARE UNABLE TO COMPLY WITH THE TERMS OR CONDITIONS, PLEASE COMMUNICATE WITH YOUR BUYER TO ARRANGE FOR AN AMENDMENT.

## ■ j

is the Commodity Futures Symbol which represents the April Delivery Month.

## ■ January effect

is the tendency for small capitalisation stocks to exhibit an upward bias in their price behavior. Some analysts believe that this may be partially attributable to the influence of index funds buying stocks for various retirement plans. Such new contributions would be qualified to commence in January. Also, the marginal impact of such purchases would be greater on smaller capitalisation issues as opposed to larger capitalisation stocks.

## ■ jetsam

articles from a ship or ship's cargo that were thrown overboard, (usually to lighten the load in times of emergency or distress.). The articles may sink or be washed ashore.

## ■ jettison

the act of throwing overboard at sea part of a vessel's paraphernalia or cargo or hull usually in hopes of saving the ship from sinking.

## ■ joint agent

a person having authority to transact business for two or more principals . In transportation it is a common occurrence.

## ■ joint and several liability

liability for damages imposed on two or more individuals or legal entities who are responsible together and individually, allowing the party harmed to seek full remedy against all or any number of the wrongdoers.

## ■ joint ownership

the ownership of property by two or more people, usually with the right of survivorship.

## ■ joint rate

a single freight rate on cargo moving via two or more carriers who then share the income..

## ■ joint stock company

an unincorporated business enterprise with ownership interests represented by shares of stock. Also a joint Stock Association.

## ■ joint tenancy

is a type of an account which has multiple owners.

## ■ joint tenants by the entirety

is a method of joint ownership. It is allowed for married couples only. There are issues relating to assets and liabilities. This form of ownership may offer some protection for the innocent spouse against creditor claims.

■ **joint tenants in common**

is a type of an account whereby the death of an owner sets aside the deceased's beneficial ownership for the estate. Surviving tenants do not necessarily acquire further interests in the account. Generally, the account ownership percentage is assumed to be pro rata. That is, if there are two owners of record each is assumed to own a 50 percent interest in the account. If there are five owners, then each is assumed to own a 20 percent interest in the account. However, the percentages do not have to be equal. In such cases written documentation is necessary to indicate unequal portions because the general assumption is equal shares.

■ **joint tenants with rights of survivorship**

is a type of account which permits multiple owners. In the event of death, the surviving holders acquire greater ownership interests until there is only one survivor who becomes the 100 percent beneficial owner. Generally, this type of an account is setup for spouses. There can be various interrelated estate planning issues.

■ **joint venture**

**a** combination of two or more individuals or legal entities who undertake together a transaction for mutual gain or to engage in a commercial enterprise together with mutual sharing of profits and losses.

■ **juice**

has many meanings. It can refer to power, such as, electrical, economic, financial, political or social.

■ **jump (diffusion process)**

is the phenomenon by which a market experiences a significant departure from a price level. This departure can be either higher or lower. It is thought that these occurrences support fat tails assumptions and methodologies. These fat tails alter the statistical expectations of normal curve procedures. The graphical appearance of this occurrence looks as a gap in the data or its chart.

■ **jump bonds**

are issues which are conditioned on an event or series of events. When the event such as breaking a prepayment collar occurs, it triggers a predetermined movement to another payment arrangement. This type of bond occurs in collateralised obligation structures.

■ **junk bonds**

refer to non-investment grade debt securities. Sometimes, these issues are called high yield securities. These securities have credit ratings below Baa/BBB-.

■ **jurat**

a statement signed by a person authorised to take oaths certifying to the authenticity of a document or affidavit.

■ **juristic act**

action intended to and capable of having, a legal effect, such as the creation, termination, or modification of a legal right.

■ **Just-In-Time (JIT)**

1. the principle of production and inventory control that prescribes precise controls for the movement of raw materials, component parts and work-in-progress. Goods are expected to arrive when needed for production rather than arriving prior to need and becoming inventory.

2. an in-bound manufacturing strategy that smoothes material flow into assembly and manufacturing plants. JIT minimises inventory investment by providing timely, sequential deliveries of product exactly where and when it is needed, from a multitude of suppliers. Traditionally an automotive strategy, it is being introduced into many other industries.

■ **jv**

refers to a Joint Venture.

■ **k**

is the Commodity Futures Symbol which represents the May Delivery Month.

■ **kappa**

is an option term sometimes used as a synonym for vega, lambda or sigma.

■ **karat**

is a measure of the purity of gold. Twenty-four karat (24K) is considered as pure gold.

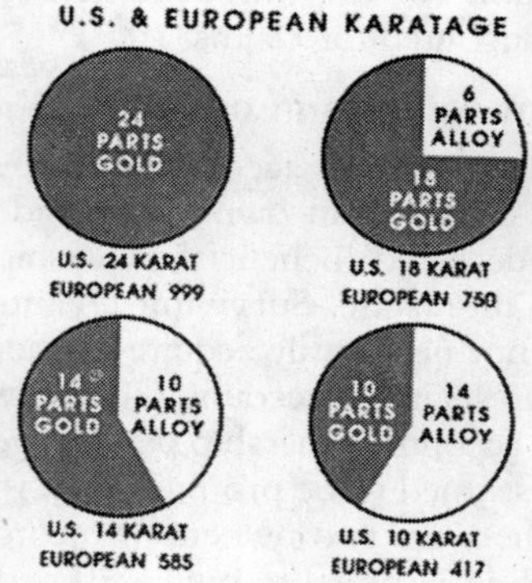


■ **keelage**

the charges paid by a ship entering or remaining in certain ports.

■ **key currency**

a major currency in the global economy. Key currencies include the U.S. dollar, the British pound sterling, the German mark, the Swiss franc, the French franc, the Dutch guilder, the Japanese yen and the Canadian dollar.

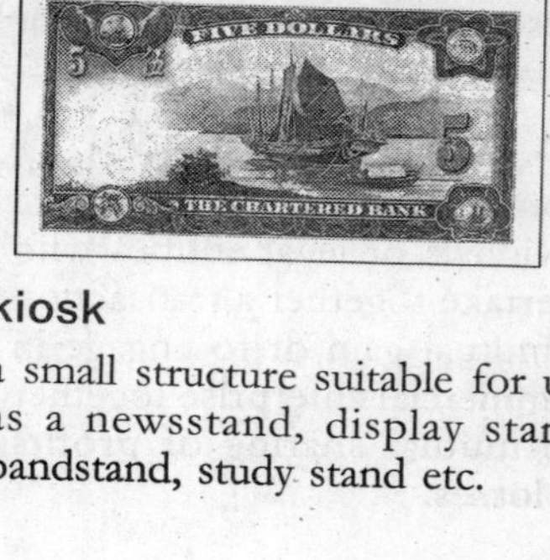


■ **kiosk**

a small structure suitable for use as a newsstand, display stand, bandstand, study stand etc.

■ **knocked down**

an article disassembled, or unassembled, or taken apart, or folded, or telescoped to reduce its bulk; subject to easy assembly. This is usually done to reduce the dimensions of the shipping package and thereby to save transportation and storage costs.

■ **knockin**

is an option feature which triggers the activation of an option contract.

■ **knockout**

is an option feature which triggers the cessation or kills an option contract.

■ **known loss**

1. loss discovered before or at the time of delivery of a shipment.
2. an evident loss (as opposed to a concealed loss or damage to contents within a package.)
3. a loss of which the insured and/or the insurer is aware at the time the insurance is effected.

■ **kurtosis**

is the statistic which describes the degree of peakedness or flatness of a probability distribution relative to the benchmark normal distribution.

■ **laissez-faire**

a term used to describe minimal governmental involvement in an economy, allowing market forces and individuals to make their own decisions, with little or no regulation.

■ **lambda**

is an option term sometimes used as a synonym for vega, kappa, or sigma.

■ **land bridge**

the movement of cargo (usually in containers) from one foreign country by vessel, transiting another country by rail or truck and then being loaded aboard another vessel for delivery to the destination country. The movement across the country from port to port is the land bridge portion of the transportation.

■ **landed cost**

total expense of receiving goods at place of retail sale, including retail purchase price and transportation charges.

■ **Last In, First Out (LIFO)**

accounting method of valuing inventory that assumes latest goods purchased are first goods used during accounting period.

■ **last notice day**

is the final day to indicate an intent to make a commodity delivery.

■ **last trading day**

is the final day of trading for a specific futures, options, or other derivative contract.

■ **lay order**

the period during which imported merchandise may remain at the place of unloading without some action being taken for its disposition.

■ **LBO**

is a Leveraged Buy Out. This transaction relies on borrowing funds. Often these borrowings are secured by various assets of the company which is targeted for acquisition.

■ **lead time**

that period of time needed to prepare for an action.

■ **leg**

is a part or piece of a transaction or position. For example, in futures trading there is a long leg and a short leg to a spread position.

■ **legal entity**

any individual, proprietorship, partnership, corporation, association, or other organisation that has, in the eyes of the law, the capacity to make a contract or an agreement and the ability to assume an obligation and to discharge an indebtedness.

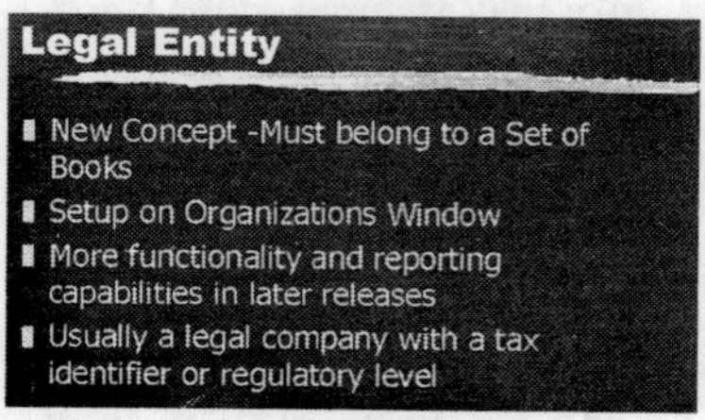


■ **legal list**

is the list of acceptable investments which can be made by banks, insurance companies and other specified financial institutions. Often these lists are compiled by states. These lists often indicate that investment grade securities are only permissible for investment purposes.

■ **legal tender**

any money that is recognised as being lawful for use by a debtor to pay a creditor, who must accept same in the discharge of a debt unless the contract between the parties specifically states that another type of money is to be used. It is that money which is lawful for the payment of all debts, public and private, public charges, taxes, duties and dues.

■ **legs**

refers to a security or a market which has the capacity to continue an underlying trend.

■ **lender**

a financial entity that makes funds

available to others to borrow.

## ■ lending

is the action of a creditor. The lending can be either funds or securities. When it is securities it is usually for short selling purposes. This short selling can be speculative or hedging oriented.

## ■ leptokurtic (Leptokurtosis)

describes the relatively peaked condition for a distribution. This condition is evaluated against the normal distribution and its attendant bell-shaped curve.

## ■ less than truckload

a shipment which does not completely fill a truck or which weighs less than the weight required for the application of the truck load freight rate (which is usually a lower freight rate than applied to less-than-truckload cargo.)

## ■ lessee

is the person who rents a property from its owner. These properties can be real estate, precious metals or other assets. When the asset is real estate the lessee is the tenant.

## ■ lessor

is the person who leases out a property to another person (lessee). The lessor either owns the property of holds a master lease which grants ownership-type powers. In the case of real estate, the lessor would be considered as the landlord.

## ■ letter of assignment

a document with which the assignor assigns its rights to a third party, the assignee.

## ■ Letter of Credit (L/C)

a method of paying for goods, where the buyer establishes credit with a local bank, clearly describing the goods to be purchased. Upon receipt of documentation, the bank is either paid by the buyer or takes title to goods and transfers funds to the seller.

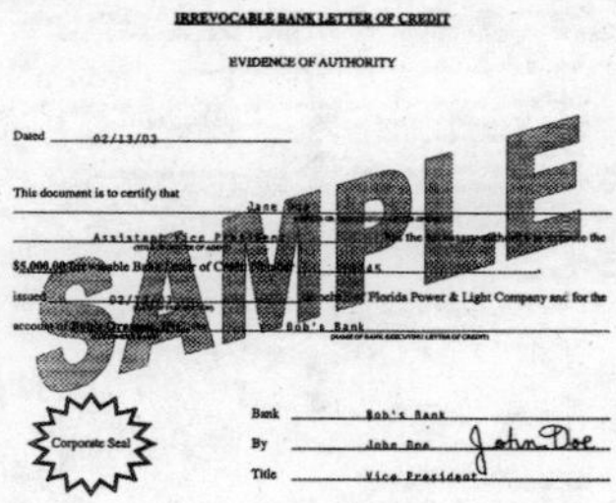
IRREVOCABLE BANK LETTER OF CREDIT

EVIDENCE OF AUTHORITY

Dated 02/13/03

This document is to certify that

Assistant Vice President

Florida Power & Light Company and for the

Bob's Bank

Corporate Seal

Bank Bob's Bank

By John Doe

Title Vice President

SAMPLE

## ■ letter of indemnity

a document which the writer issues to another party agreeing to protect them from liability for the performance of certain acts. In the case of international transportation when a negotiable bill of lading has been issued but is not available for surrender to the carrier when it is desired to take delivery of the shipment, a bank may issue a letter of indemnity to the carrier to persuade them to release the cargo. The bank will usually obtain a similar letter from its client to protect itself against the liability it assumes on behalf of the client. On export shipments, some carriers may permit shippers to issue letters of indemnity to the carriers in order to secure from them clean bills of lading in place of foul, or to replace lost original bills of lading.

■ **letter of intent**

a document that describes the preliminary understanding between parties who intend to make a contract or join together in another action.

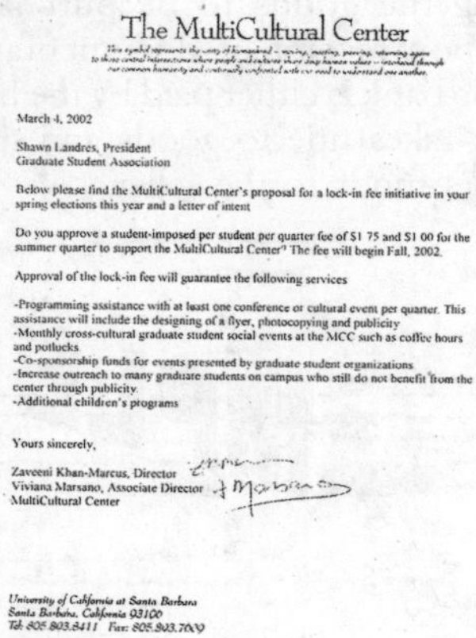
The MultiCultural Center

March 4, 2002

Shawn Landres, President
Graduate Student Association

Below please find the MultiCultural Center's proposal for a lock-in fee initiative in your spring elections this year and a letter of intent

Do you approve a student-imposed per student per quarter fee of $1 75 and $1 00 for the summer quarter to support the MultiCultural Center? The fee will begin Fall, 2002.

Approval of the lock-in fee will guarantee the following services

-Programming assistance with at least one conference or cultural event per quarter. This assistance will include the designing of a flyer, photocopying and publicity
-Monthly cross-cultural graduate student social events at the MCC such as coffee hours and potlucks
-Co-sponsorship funds for events presented by graduate student organizations
-Increase outreach to many graduate students on campus who still do not benefit from the center through publicity
-Additional children's programs

Yours sincerely,

Zaveeni Khan-Marcus, Director
Viviana Marsano, Associate Director
MultiCultural Center

University of California at Santa Barbara
Santa Barbara, California 93100
Tel: 805.803.8411 Fax: 805.803.7009

■ **leverage**

refers to the concept of increasing, multiplying, or magnifying the market impact of an investment. Leverage magnifies both the gains or the losses. In corporate finance, leverage often means the amount of debt to equity. Borrowing can enhance shareholder equity returns because the interest is deductible but the profits remain for the common share investors.
For derivative products, little or no margin is required for placing positions. Depending on the instrument, market, exchange and other factors, valuation swings may have to be satisfied by new margin or performance bond monies.

■ **licensed warehouses**

are facilities approved for the storage of a futures exchange traded commodity. Sometimes, the term is used specifically to refer to some commodities such as copper versus a precious metal.

■ **licensing agreement**

the issuance of a license permitting the use of patents, trademarks, or other technology.

■ **lien**

a legal claim against an asset that is used to secure a mortgage. To sell the property, the lien must be paid.

■ **life insurance trust**

a trust that has the proceeds of an individual's life insurance policy as its principal.

■ **life of contract**

is the time period which covers the commencement and cessation of trading for a specific futures contract. This is different from all time history, all-time high and all-time low.

■ **lift van**

a wooden or metal container used for packing household goods and personal effects.

## ■ light crude oil

is petroleum with a low specific gravity and a high API gravity. It has a relatively high proportion of light hydrocarbon products or fractions.

## ■ lighter

a barge towed by a tugboat and used mainly in harbors and inland waterways for the transport of cargo to and from ships. Some may be self-powered.

## ■ lighter aboard ship

some ships are constructed to carry special barges (lighters). These barges can go to smaller docks, go into inland waterways, load cargo at those places and then carry it back to the ship which lifts the barges aboard, with their cargo and transports them overseas. Discharge of cargo is accomplished in the same manner.

## ■ lighterage

the loading or unloading of a ship by means of a lighter (barge), especially when shallow waters prevent an ocean going vessel from approaching a berth, or if berths are unavailable.

## ■ limit

is an order which is to be filled at that stated price or better. Or better means a lower than the stated price for a buy or a higher than the stated price for a sale.

## ■ limitation period

a maximum period set by a statute within which a legal action can be brought or a right enforced.

## ■ line haul

the direct movement of freight between two major ports by a single ship.

## ■ line haul vessel

a vessel which is on a regularly defined schedule between ports,

## ■ liner

a vessel carrying passengers and cargo that operates with a fixed schedule on a particular route.

■ **liner terms**

conditions under which a shipping company will transport goods, including in the amount payable for freight the cost both for loading and discharge of the cargo from the vessel.

■ **liquidated damages**

a sum of money that a contracting party agrees to pay to the other party for breaching an agreement.

■ **liquidation**

1. the act or process of settling or making clear, fixed and determined.
2. the winding up of the financial affairs of a business.

■ **liquidation value**

is the expected or realised value of cash remaining after a complete liquidation occurs.

■ **liquidity**

1. the availability of liquid funds in an economy.
2. the status or condition of a person or business in terms of its ability to convert its assets into cash and to meet its obligations.
3. the capacity of a market in a particular security or commodity to withstand an unusual amount of buying or selling without affecting the market substantially.
4. is a characteristic of a market where size and speed of executions are sufficient to absorb many orders with little disturbance to price and in a timely manner.

■ **listed**

refers to securities which are approved for trading on a recognised exchange. Is a security or instrument which is traded on a recognised exchange.

■ **living trust**

a revocable trust established by a grantor during his or her lifetime in which the grantor transfers some or all of his or her property into the trust.

■ **living will**

a legal document directing that the maker's or signer's life is not to be artificially supported in the event of a terminal illness or accident.

■ **Lloyds of London**

an English association of insurance underwriters, the oldest of its kind in the world. Not in itself an insurance company.

■ **Lloyds registry**

an English society, independent of Lloyds of London, which surveys and classifies the ships of the world according to their description, condition, seaworthiness and compliance with codes and protocols. Also establishes standards for maintenance and construction. (Correct name is: Lloyds Register of Shipping.)

■ **long coupon**

refers to the initial coupon for a municipal security which reflects more than 6 months of accrued interest. The time of accrual is measure from the start of the Dated Date and continues until the end of the initial accrual period.

■ **long hedge**

refers to the status of the open

futures contract equivalent position. Here, it is understood that the hedger is long futures against a short actual position.

## ■ long the basis

refers to the status of the open cash or spot market position. Here, the hedger would be long the cash market and short the futures or forward market.

## ■ long ton

equivalent to 2,240 pounds or 20 long hundredweights. Also called gross ton.

## ■ longshoreman

a labourer who loads and unloads ships, handles cargo and containers at shipping terminals and loads and unloads containers at shipping terminals.

## ■ lookahead time

is the forward-looking time interval. Usually, it refers to one day but it can be more or less. For the calculation of SPAN® statistics it is usually set at one day, or from the present to the next day.

## ■ look back

is an option which permits the holder to effectively buy the low in the case of a call or sell the high in the case of a put. The time frame is defined as the term to expiration for the option.

## ■ lot

is one contract, car, or unit of trading in the commodities markets.

## ■ lot labels

labels attached to each piece of multiple lot shipment for identification purposes. Each lot label will carry the same number (the lot number) There may also be a consecutive number on each label to separately identify each package.

## ■ lower deck containers

carrier owned containers specially designed as an integral part of the aircraft to fit in the cargo compartments of a wide body aircraft. These compartments are on the lower deck of the aircraft below where the passengers sit.

## ■ m

is the Commodity Futures Symbol which represents the June Delivery Month.

## ■ macaroni defence

a tactic used by a corporation that is the target of a hostile takeover bid involving the issue of a large number of bonds that must be redeemed at a higher value if the company is taken over.

## ■ macaulay duration

is the present value of all cash flows, both principal and interest, weighted by time. It is a measurement expressed in years which is generally less than the stated maturity. An exception occurs for zero coupon bonds.

## ■ macro hedge

is an enterprise-wide, trading desk, or portfolio risk management offset aimed at the net risk of the aggregated position. Generally, these hedges are more efficient than micro hedges for complex portfolios.

■ **macro hedge funds**

are those which are more benchmark or index oriented. They tend to be top-down in approach rather than bottom-up. These Macro Hedge Funds employ strategies using actual securities, commodities, currencies, futures and derivatives. They also use various degrees of leverage to try to outperform the market or benchmark indices.

■ **macroeconomics**

the study of large scale economic factors affecting an economy as a whole.

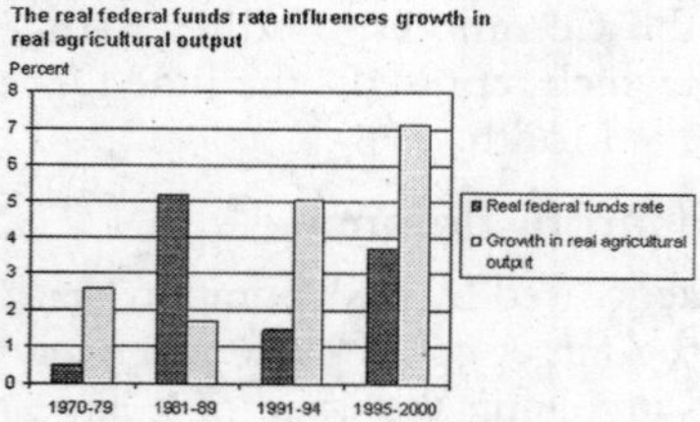


■ **magic of diversification**

the effective reduction of risk (variance) of a portfolio, achieved without reduction to expected returns through the combination of assets with low or negative correlations (covariances).

■ **mail entry**

a means of shipping and entering goods into a Customs Territory through the postal system.

■ **mail float**

time period that checks for payment spend in the postal system.

■ **maintenance call**

a call for additional money or securities when a margin account falls below its exchange-mandated required level.

■ **maintenance fee**

a yearly charge to maintain brokerage accounts, such as asset management accounts or IRAs.

■ **maintenance margin requirement**

a sum, usually smaller than but part of the original margin, that must be maintained on deposit at all times. If a customer's equity in any futures position drops to or below, the maintenance margin level, the broker must issue a margin call for the amount at money required to restore the customer's equity in the account to the original margin level. Related: Margin, margin call.

■ **maintenance requirement**

is the level of margin necessary to support open positions given adverse price movements. If the maintenance level is violated, a variation call is issued which would be equal to the amount to restore an account to the initial margin level.

■ **majority shareholder**

a shareholder who is part of a group that controls more than half the outstanding shares of a corporation.

■ **majority voting**

voting system under which corporate shareholders vote for each director separately.

■ **make a market**

dealers are said to make a market

when they quote bid and offer prices at which they stand ready to buy and sell.

## make whole provision

related to the lump-sum payments made when a loan or bond is called, equal to the NPV of future loan or coupon payments not paid because of the call. The payment can be significant and negate the attractiveness of a call.

## making delivery

refers to the seller's actually turning over to the buyer the assets agreed upon in a forward contract.

## mala fides

in bad faith. (A seller's representation that goods are usable for a particular purpose when in fact the seller knows that the goods are not.)

## managed account

an investment portfolio one or more clients entrusted to a manager who decides how to invest it.

## managed float

also known as dirty float, this is a system of floating exchange rates with central bank intervention to reduce currency fluctuations.

## management

the people who administer a company, create policies and provide the support necessary to implement the owners' business objectives.

## management buying

the acquisition of a controlling interest in a promising business by an outside investment group that retains existing management and places representatives on the board of directors.

## Management Buy Out (MBO)

leveraged buyout whereby the acquiring group is led by the firm's management.

## management fee

an investment advisory fee charged by the financial adviser to a fund typically on the basis of the fund's average assets, but sometimes determined on a sliding scale that declines as the dollar amount of the fund increases.

## management/closely held shares

percentage of shares held by persons closely related to a company, as defined by the Securities and Exchange Commission. Part of these percentages often are included in institutional holdings—making the combined total of these percentages over 100. There is overlap as institutions sometimes acquire enough stock to be considered by the SEC to be closely allied to the company.

## managerial decisions

decisions concerning the operation of the firm, such as the choice of firm sise, firm growth rates and employee compensation.

## managing underwriter

the leading firm in an underwriting group, which originates the deal and acts as an agent for the group.

■ **mandatory convertibles**

a debt instrument that is exchangeable at some point for equity in the form of common stock or a new issue.

**Mandatory convertibles**

Automatically be converted into stock at a specified time, unlike normal convertibles, which the holder has the right to convert at any time.

- As of Dec. 31, 1996, they represented 19.5 percent of total convertible market value, up from 9.8 percent in 1992.
- Holders of mandatory convertibles may have voting rights.
- They have the same downside risk as the underlying common stocks except for the yield advantage.

■ **mandatory redemption schedule**

schedule according to which bond sinking fund payments must be made.

■ **manifest**

1. a document listing and describing the cargo contents of a carrier, container or warehouse.
2. evident to the senses, especially to the sight, obvious to the understanding, evident to the mind, open, clear, visible, unmistakable, indubitable, indisputable, self-evident.
3. a control document used to list the contents (individual shipments) during loading and from which the contents are checked during unloading.

■ **manipulation**

dealing in a security to create a false appearance of active trading, in order to bring in more traders. Illegal.

■ **maple leaf**

a gold, silver, or platinum coin minted in Canada that usually trades at slightly more than its current bullion value.

■ **mapping**

refers to the presentation of financial positions. It is used in risk and portfolio management. It can be graphical or tabular.

■ **margin**

1. in commercial terms the difference between the cost of goods sold and the total net sales price.
2. the purchase of a stock or a commodity with payment of only part of the purchase price in cash (called the margin) and the balance by loan (usually made by the broker.)
3. is the amount required to open a position. This amount is different for each futures market depending on each contract. Also, the dollar amount varies for each security and option account because of the variations in holdings among all accounts.
4. allows investors to buy securities by borrowing money from a broker. The margin is the difference between the market value of a stock and the loan a broker makes. Related: Security deposit (initial).

■ **margin account (stocks)**

a leverageable account in which stocks can be purchased for a combination of cash and a loan. The loan in the margin account is collateralised by the stock; if the value of the stock drops sufficiently, the owner will be asked to either put in more cash, or sell a portion of the stock. Margin rules are federally regulated, but margin requirements and interest may vary among broker/dealers.

**■ margin agreement**

the agreement governing customers' margin accounts.

**■ margin call**

1. is the phrase used to represent a call for additional funds. This demand for more funds in either cash and/or securities is to restore an account to its initial margin requirement level. Generally, this occurs when the price action is adverse to the account holders positions. It can also reflect an increase in margin requirements.
2. a demand for additional funds because of adverse price movement. Maintenance margin requirement, security deposit maintenance.

**■ margin department**

the department in a brokerage firm that monitors customers' margin accounts, ensuring that all short sales, stock purchases and other positions are covered by the margin account balance.

**■ margin of profit**

gross profit divided by net sales. Used to measure a firm's operating efficiency and pricing policies in order to determine how competitive the firm is within the industry.

Operating margin and profit margin in distributive trades

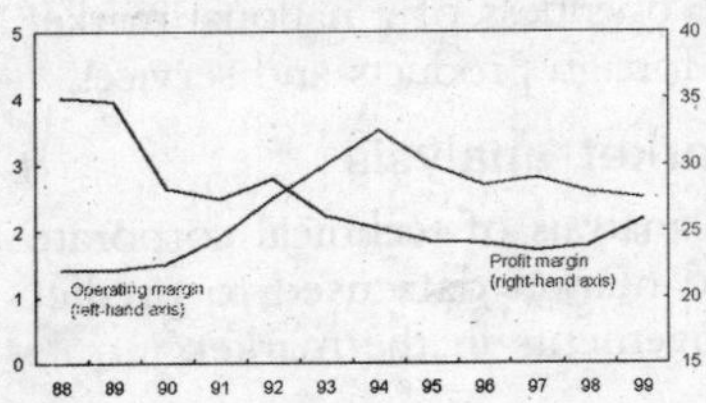


**■ margin of safety**

with respect to working capital management, the difference between the amount of long-term financing and the sum of fixed assets and the permanent component of current assets.

**■ margin requirement**

1. is the amount of funds necessary for a position or a portfolio's entire holdings.
2. the amount of cash an uncovered (naked) option writer is required to deposit and maintain to cover his daily position valuation and reasonably foreseeable intraday price changes.

**■ margin security**

a security that may be bought or sold in a margin account as defined in Regulation T.

**■ marginal**

incremental.

**■ marginal cost**

1. the increase in the total costs of a producer of producing one more unit of output, or the decrease in producing one less unit of output.
2. the increase or decrease in a firm's total cost of production as a result of changing production by one unit.

**■ marginal efficiency of capital**

the percentage yield earned on an additional unit of capital.

**■ marginal revenue**

the change in total revenue as a result of producing one additional unit of output.

■ **marginal tax rate**

the tax rate that would have to be paid on any additional dollars of taxable income earned.

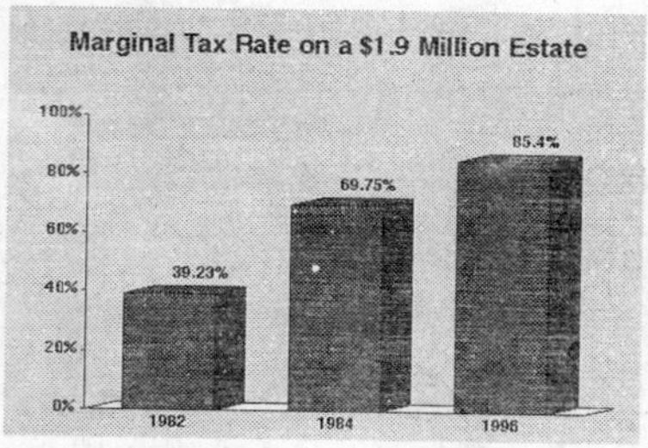


■ **marginal utility**

the change in total satisfaction as a result of consuming one additional unit of a specific good or service.

■ **marital deduction**

1. a deduction allowing for the unlimited transfer of any or all property from one spouse to the other generally free of estate and gift tax.
2. a tax deduction that allow spouses to transfer unlimited amounts of property to one another.

■ **maritime**

business pertaining to commerce or navigation by sea.

■ **mark down**

refers to the amount of spread or transaction fee subtracted from a security for purchase by a dealer from a client. There are various guidelines provided by regulatory and industry groups. Excessive mark downs are prohibited.

■ **mark up**

refers to the amount of spread or transaction fee added to a security for sale by a dealer to a client. There are various guidelines provided by regulatory and industry groups. Excessive mark ups are prohibited.

■ **markdown**

the amount subtracted from the selling price of securities when they are sold to a dealer in the OTC market. Also, the discounted price of municipal bonds after the market has shown little interest in the issue at the original price.

■ **marked-to-market**

an arrangement whereby the profits or losses on a futures contract are settled each day.

■ **market**

1. is an order to buy or sell an instrument at the prevailing price (bids and offers). In the case of a buy order it means taking the offers whereas for a sell order it means hitting the bids.
2. usually refers to the equity market. The market went down today means that the value of the stock market dropped that day.

■ **market access**

the openness of a national market to foreign products and services.

■ **market analysis**

an analysis of technical corporate and market data used to predict movements in the market.

## market cap or market capitalisation

is a value placed on a company. It is computed by multiplying the number of outstanding shares by the current share price.

## market capitalisation

the total value of all outstanding shares. Computed as shares times current market price. Capitalisation is a measure of corporate sise.

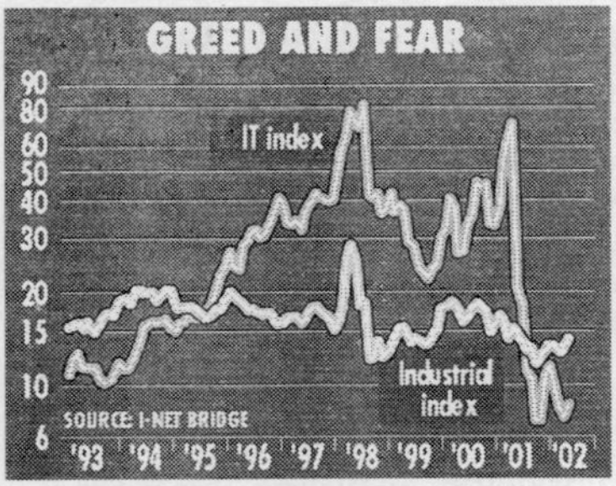


## market capitalisation rate

expected return on a security. The market-consensus estimate of the appropriate discount rate for a firm's cash flow.

## market clearing

total demand for loans by borrowers equals total supply of loans from lenders. The market, any market, clears at the equilibrium rate of interest or price.

## market conversion price

also called conversion parity price, the price that an investor effectively pays for common stock by purchasing a convertible security and then exercising the conversion option. This price is equal to the market price of the convertible security divided by the conversion ratio.

## market cycle

the period between the two latest highs or lows of the S&P 500, showing net performance of a fund through both an up and a down market. A market cycle is complete when the S&P is 15% below the highest point or 15% above the lowest point (ending a down market).

## market disruption

a situation where a surge of imports of a certain product causes a sharp decline in the domestic sales of that product and creates a hardship for domestic producers.

## market economy

an economic system where resources are allocated and production of goods determined by market forces rather than by government decree.

## market efficiency hypotheses

refer to theories which try to explain financial market behavior. Some hypotheses state that the markets are rigorously efficient and operate by an immediate discounting of perfect information. Other theories state that the markets are relatively inefficient, particularly when socially-oriented goals are also to be considered. Other hypotheses state that information is good or even very good but not perfect. Also, not all market participants believe or simultaneously act on new data or information. The latter theorists believe that the markets try to attain pure efficiency. However, they also recognise that competition breeds asymmetrical change and this influences the discounting and adaption processes. A simple example will highlight this view. While improvements in technology are reducing costs and communication times, not everyone updates their systems given each and every change in chip speeds and processing power. To do so would be too expensive and this creates one of example of a marketplace paradox.

### ■ market eye

a financial information service based in the U.K. sponsored by the ISE (International Stock Exchange of the U.K. and the Republic of Ireland) that provides current market and statistical information.

### ■ market if touched

is an order that becomes market action when a price is hit. Buy Market if Touched orders are activated when the market price declines to the stated level. Then the broker is authorised to buy to satisfy the quantity. This is different than a limit order where all the quantity must be executed at the stated price or better.

### ■ market impact costs

the result of a bid/ask spread and a dealer's price concession. Also called price impact costs.

### ■ market index

market measure that consists of weighted values of the components that make up certain list of companies. A stock market tracks the performance of certain stocks by weighting them according to their prices and the number of outstanding shares by a particular formula.

### ■ market jitters

anxiety among many investors, causing them to sell stocks and bonds, pushing prices down.

### ■ market letter

a newsletter analysing the market that is written by an SEC-registered investment adviser who sells the letter to subscribers.

### ■ market maker

1. is a party who is prepared to buy and sell securities from all parties at the market maker's bid and offer.
2. used in the context of general equities. One who maintains firm bid and offer prices in a given security by standing ready to buy or sell round lots at publicly quoted prices.

### ■ market model

The market model says that the return on a security depends on the return on the market portfolio and the extent of the security's responsiveness as measured by beta. The return also depends on conditions that are unique to the firm. The market model can be graphed as a line fitted to a plot of asset returns against returns on the market portfolio. This relationship is sometimes called the single-index model.

■ **market on close**

is an order to buy or sell on the close of a market. Typically, there is a brief period prior to the day's cessation of trading which is defined as the close. This period varies from market-to-market and exchange-to-exchange.

■ **market on opening**

is an order to buy or sell on the opening of a market. Typically, there is a brief period at the commencement of the day's trading which is defined as the opening. This period varies from market-to-market and exchange-to-exchange.

■ **market opening**

the start of formal trading on an exchange.

■ **market price**

the last reported price at which a security was traded on an exchange.

■ **market price of risk**

a measure of the extra return, or risk premium, that investors demand to bear risk. The reward-to-risk ratio of the market portfolio.

■ **market prices**

the amount of money that a willing buyer pays to acquire something from a willing seller, when a buyer and seller are independent and when such an exchange is motivated by only commercial consideration.

■ **market rent**

the best rent at which a property might reasonably be expected to be let with vacant possession in the open market, with a willing landlord and tenant, taking full account of all terms of the tenancy offered.

■ **market research**

a technical analysis of factors such as volume, price trends and market breadth that are used to predict price movement.

■ **market return**

the return on the market portfolio.

■ **market risk**

risk that cannot be diversified away. Related: Systematic risk

■ **market sectors**

the classifications of bonds by issuer characteristics, such as state government, corporate, or utility.

■ **market segmentation theory or preferred habitat theory**

a biased expectations theory that asserts that the shape of the yield curve is determined by the supply of and demand for securities within each maturity sector.

■ **market share**

the percentage of total industry

sales that a particular company controls.

■ **market sweep**

a second offering following a tender offer, allowing institutional investors to obtain a controlling interest at a price higher than the original offer.

■ **market timer**

a money manager who assumes he or she can forecast when the stock market will go up and down.

■ **market timing**

asset allocation in which investment in the equity market is increased if one forecasts that the equity market will outperform T-bills and is decreased when the market is anticipated to underperform.

■ **market timing costs**

costs that arise from price movement of a stock during a transaction period but attributable to other activity in the stock.

■ **market tone**

the general state of well-being of a securities market, based mostly on trading activity.

■ **market value**

is the value of an open position. It is determined by multiplying the known or implied prevailing price by the quantity.

■ **market value**

1. the price at which a security is trading and could presumably be purchased or sold.
2. what investors believe a firm is worth; calculated by multiplying the number of shares outstanding by the current market price of a firm's shares.

■ **market value ratios**

ratios that relate the market price of the firm's common stock to selected financial statement items.

■ **market value-weighted index**

an index of a group of securities computed by calculating a weighted average of the returns on each security in the index, where the weights are proportional to outstanding market value.

■ **marketability**

a negotiable security is said to have good marketability if there is an active secondary market in which it can easily be resold.

■ **marketable securities**

securities that are easily convertible to cash because there is high demand allowing them to be sold quickly.

■ **marketable title**

a clear, reasonably incontestable title to a piece of real estate that is good for transaction purposes.

■ **market-book ratio**

market price of a share divided by book value per share.

■ **marketed claims**

claims that can be bought and sold in financial markets, such as those of stockholders and bondholders.

■ **market-if-touched (MIT)**

a price order, below market if a buy or above market if a sell, that automatically becomes a market order if the specified price is reached.

■ **Market-On-Close (MOC) order**

an order to trade stocks, options, or futures as close as possible to the market close.

■ **marketplace price efficiency**

the degree to which the prices of assets reflect the available marketplace information. Marketplace price efficiency is sometimes estimated as the difficulty faced by active management of earning a greater return than passive management would, after adjusting for the risk associated with a strategy and the transactions costs associated with implementing a strategy.

■ **marking up or down**

the amount by which a securities dealer raises or lowers the price of a stock or bond due to changes in demand and supply.

■ **marking: country of origin**

the physical markings on a product that indicate the country of origin where the article was produced. (With very few exceptions, the U.S. requires every imported article to be so marked.)

■ **markowits diversification**

a strategy that seeks to combine in a portfolio assets with returns that are less than perfectly positively correlated, in an effort to lower portfolio risk (variance) without sacrificing return. Related: Naive diversification.

■ **marks**

identification placed on the outer surface of shipping containers or packages. At one time it consisted of pictures, letters and numbers. With the advent of computers, pictures are no longer used. Instructions on the packages for their proper handling, such as This side up may also be considered part of the marks. Also the weight and measurements of the packages.

■ **mark-to-market**

is the valuation process which provides an indication of reasonable prices for positions on a daily basis or some other proscribed time frame.

■ **mark-to-market**

adjustment of the book value or collateral value of a security to reflect current market value.

■ **marriage penalty**

a tax that has the effect of penalising a married couple because they pay more tax on a joint tax return than they would if they file tax returns individually.

■ **marriage value**

latent value which the merger of two or more interests in land would release.

■ **married put**

1. is the purchase of a put and its underlying stock at the same time. Effectively, it behaves like a synthetic long call but can have different of special tax implications.
2. a put option bought at the same time as its underlying securities in

order to hedge the price paid for the securities.

**Master Limited Partnership (MLP)**

a publicly traded limited partnership.

**matador bond**

bond issued on the Spanish market by an obligor who is not domiciled in Spain.

**matador market**

the foreign market in Spain.

**matched and lost**

the outcome of the flip of a coin used to determine which of two brokers who are locked in competition for equal trades may actually execute the trades.

**matched book**

a bank runs a matched book when the of maturities of its assets and liabilities is distribution equal.

**matched funding**

is an asset and liability management technique which offsets fund sources to fund uses.

**matched maturities**

the coordination by a financial institution of the maturities of its assets (loans) and liabilities (deposits) in order to enable it to meet its obligations at the required times.

**matched orders**

used for listed equity securities. Participate in equal amounts of a trade at a certain price, particularly when two parties have the same level of priority on the exchange floor (this requires standing in the trading crowd).

**maximum capital gains mutual fund**

a mutual fund whose objective is to produce capital gains by investing in small or risky rapid-growth companies.

**maximum price fluctuation**

the greatest amount by which the contract price can change, up or down, during one trading session, as fixed by exchange rules in the contract specification. Related: Limit price.

**May day**

the date of May 1, 1975, after which brokers were allowed to charge any brokerage commission, rather than a mandatory rate.

**May expand**

used in the context of general equities. Warning that the size of the order/total may be increased.

**meals and entertainment expense**

a tax deduction allowed for meals and entertainment expenses incurred in the course of business.

**mean**

1. is often considered as the simple arithmetic average of the sum of the observed values divided by the number of observations. The simple unweighted mean of the listed four observations: 8,12, 10 and 14 is 11. This statistic is computed by (8+12+10+14=44) 44 divided by 4.

The geometric mean of the same four observations is 10.77. It is computed by multiplying each observed value and then deriving the $n^{th}$ root of that number. The geometric mean can only be equal to or less than the comparable arithmetic mean.
2. the expected value of a random variable. Arithmetic average of a sample.

■ **mean of the sample**
the arithmetic average; that is, the sum of the observations divided by the number of observations.

■ **mean reversion**
is the postulate that short term rates or volatilities will move toward longer term averages.

■ **mean-variance analysis**
evaluation of risky prospects based on the expected value and variance of possible outcomes.

■ **mean-variance criterion**
the selection of portfolios based on the means and variances of their returns. The choice of the higher expected return portfolio for a given level of variance or the lower variance portfolio for a given expected return.

■ **measurement cargo**
a cargo on which the transportation charge is assessed on the basis of size or dimensions, instead of upon the gross weight.

■ **measurement error**
errors in measuring an explanatory variable in a regression, which leads to biases in estimated parameters.

■ **medium of exchange**
anything which is widely accepted in payment for goods and services and in settlement of debts. Its acceptability is based upon the fact that it can provide a common basis of measurement of the value of things.

■ **medium-term bond**
a bond maturing in two to ten years.

■ **medium-term note**
a corporate debt instrument that is continuously offered to investors over a period of time by an agent of the issuer. Investors can select from maturity bands of: 9 months to 1 year, more than 1 year to 18 months, more than 18 months to 2 years, etc., up to 30 years.

■ **melt down or meltdown**
is a sudden decline or collapse in financial values. Tends to be used for broader indicators such as market indices or asset classes.

■ **melt up or melt up**
is a sudden advance or increase in financial values. Tends to be used for broader indicators such as market indices or asset classes.

■ **member bank**
a national- or state-chartered bank that is a member of the Federal Reserve System.

■ **member firm**
used for listed equity securities. Brokerage firm that has at least

one membership on a major stock exchange even though, by exchange rules, the membership is in the name of an employee and not the firm itself.

## microbridge

an intermodal movement of cargo which involves a vessel leg to a port and then a movement via another transportation mode, truck or rail, to an inland point where the movement terminates. In the reverse direction, the cargo is picked up at a point inland for transport via truck or rail to a port where a vessel loads the cargo and transports it to an overseas port. The land portion of the two intermodal moves described is the microbridge.

## microeconomics

analysis of the behaviour of individual economic units such as companies, industries, or households.

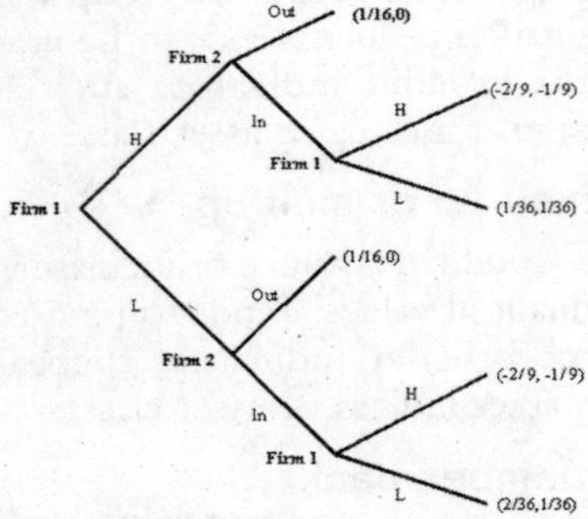


## middle office

is the area or function which relates to risk management. This area measures, monitors and occasionally proactively manages the firm's exposure. This proactive dimension is gradually being implemented in the industry.

## Milan stock exchange

the largest regional stock exchange in Italy, facilitating more than 90% of the country's trading volume.

## Miller, Merton

Nobel laureate and co-author of the famous Miller-Modigliani theorems. Finance professor at the University of Chicago.

## mimic

an imitation that sends a false signal.

## minibridge

an intermodal movement of cargo involving a vessel leg from one country to a port in another country and then a movement via truck or rail to another port in that country and there the voyage is terminated. The traversing of the land in the second country from discharge port to destination port is the minibridge portion of the movement. There could be a similar but opposite combined minibridge movement in the other direction.

## mini-manipulation

trading in the underwriting security of an option contract in order to manipulate its price so that the options will become in the money.

## minimum charge

the lowest amount that will be charged regardless of the amount of service rendered.

**minimum maintenance**

the lowest required equity level that must be held with a broker in a margin account.

**minimum price fluctuation**

smallest increment of price movement possible in trading a given contract. Also called point or tick.

**minimum purchases**

for mutual funds, the amount required to open a new account (minimum initial purchase) or to deposit into an existing account (minimum additional purchase). These minimums may be reduced for buyers participating in an automatic purchase plan

**minimum-variance frontier**

graph of the lowest possible portfolio variance that is attainable for a given portfolio expected return.

**minimum-variance portfolio**

the portfolio of risky assets with lowest variance.

**minority interest**

an outside ownership interest in a subsidiary that is consolidated with the parent for financial reporting purposes.

**minus**

the symbol (-) that precedes the change figure in a stock table to indicate a closing sale lower than that of the previous day.

**misery index**

an index that sums the unemployment and inflation rates, used as a political rating or measure of consumer confidence.

**mismatch bond**

floating-rate note whose interest rate is reset at more frequent intervals than the rollover period (e.g., a note whose payments are set quarterly on the basis of the one-year interest rate).

**mixed account**

a brokerage account holding both long and short positioned securities.

**mixed bag**

used in the context of general equities. Group of stocks including some that are up, some down and some neutral.

**mln**

refers to a million. Sometimes it is described as MM. At times, some use M to refer to a million. However, this can be confusing as M is often used to refer to a thousand.

**mob spread**

the yield spread between a tax-free municipal bond and a Treasury bond with the same maturity.

**mock trading**

the simulated trading of securities used as a learning device in training investors and brokers.

**modelling**

the process of creating a depiction of reality, such as a graph, picture, or mathematical representation.

**modern portfolio theory**

principles underlying the analysis and evaluation of rational portfolio choices based on risk-return trade-offs and efficient diversification.

**■ modified pass-throughs**

agency pass-throughs that guarantee (1) timely interest payments and (2) principal payments as collected, but no later than a specified time after they are due. Related: Fully modified pass-throughs.

**■ momentum**

the amount of acceleration of an economic, price, or volume movement. A trader who follows a movement strategy will purchase stocks that have recently risen in price.

**■ momentum indicators**

indicators used in market analysis to quantify the momentum of upward and downward price movements.

**■ monetarist**

an economist who believes that changes in the money supply are the most important determinants of economic activity and economic cycles.

**■ monetary gold**

gold held by government authorities as a financial asset.

**■ monetary indicators**

economic indicators of the effects of monetary policy, such as the condition of the credit market.

**■ monetary/nonmonetary method**

under this translation method, monetary items (e.g. cash, accounts payable and receivable and long-term debt) are represented at the current rate, while nonmonetary items (e.g., inventory, fixed assets and long-term investments) are represented at historical rates.

**■ monetise the debt**

financing the national debt by printing new money, which causes inflation as a result of a larger money supply.

**■ money**

1. any denomination of coin or paper currency of legal tender that passes freely as a medium of exchange.
2. currency and coin that are guaranteed as legal tender by the government.

**■ money base**

composed of currency and coins outside the banking system plus liabilities to the deposit money banks.

**■ money centre banks**

banks that raise most of their funds from the domestic and international money markets, relying less on depositors for funds.

**■ money creation**

the increase in money supply by the central or commercial banks.

**■ monopoly**

market characterised by absolute control of all sales and distribution in the market by one firm, due to some barrier to entry of other firms, allowing the firm to sell at a higher price than the societally optimal price.

**■ monopsony**

market characterised by the existence of only one buyer in a market, forcing sellers to accept a lower price than the societally optimal price.

**■ Monte Carlo simulation**

an analytical technique for solving a problem by performing a large number of trial runs, called simulations and deducing a solution from the collective results of the trial runs. Method for calculating the probability distribution of possible outcomes.

**■ moor**

to secure a vessel to an anchor, buoy, or pier.

**■ moorage**

charges assessed for mooring a vessel to a pier or wharf.

**■ moral hazard**

the risk that the existence of a contract will change the behavior of one or both parties to the contract, e.g., an insured firm will take fewer fire precautions.

**■ moral obligation bond**

a tax-exempt bond issued by a municipality or a state financial intermediary that is backed by the moral, but not legal, obligation of a state government to appropriate funds in case of default.

**■ more behind it**

used in the context of general equities. More stock exists to be bought or sold by the same buyer or seller, respectively. Often, the buyer or seller does not disclose the full sise of its buy or sell interest as not to affect the market adversely.

**■ mortgage**

1. is a pledge of real property in order to obtain a loan: It is not the note itself. The loan instrument is a note or bond. However, these two terms are frequently used synonymously.
2. a loan secured by the collateral of some specified real estate property that obliges the borrower to make a predetermined series of payments.

**■ mortgage life insurance**

a life insurance policy that pays off the remaining balance of the insured person's mortgage at death.

**■ mortgage pass-through security**

also called a pass-through, a security created when one or more mortgage holders form a collection (pool) of mortgages and sells shares or participation certificates in the pool. The cash flow from the collateral pool is passed through to the securityholder as monthly payments of principal, interest and prepayments. This is the predominant type of MBS traded in the secondary market.

**mortgage pipeline**

the period from the taking of applications from prospective mortgage borrowers to the marketing of the loans.

**mortgage pipeline risk**

the risk associated with taking applications from prospective mortgage borrowers who may opt to decline to accept a quoted mortgage rate within a certain grace period.

**mortgage pool**

a group of mortgages with similar class, interest rate and maturity characteristics.

**mortgage rate**

the interest rate on a mortgage loan.

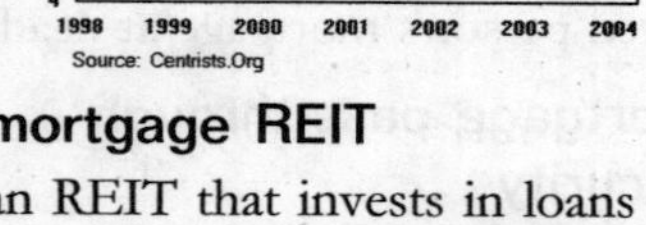


**mortgage REIT**

an REIT that invests in loans secured by real estate that derives income from mortgage interest and fees.

**mortgage servicing**

the collection of monthly payments and penalties, record keeping, payment of insurance and taxes and possible settlement of default, involved with a mortgage loan.

**mortgage tax**

is a tax which is assessed against a new mortgage. It is usually paid by the borrower.

**Mortgage-Backed Securities (MBS)**

investment instruments backed by a pool of mortgage loans.

**Mortgage-Backed Securities Clearing Corporation (MBSCC)**

a wholly owned subsidiary of the Midwest Stock Exchange that operates a clearing service for the comparison, netting and margining of agency-guaranteed MBS transacted for forward delivery.

**mortgagee**

1. is the lending party in a mortgage transaction.
2. the lender of a loan secured by property.

**mortgager**

the borrower of a loan secured by property.

**mortgagor**

is the borrowing party in a mortgage transaction.

**Moscow Interbank Currency Exchange (MICEX)**

Established in 1992, the most liquid and best organised financial exchange in Russia.

**most active list**

the stocks with the highest volume of trading on a certain day.

**■ most distant futures contract**

when several futures contracts are considered, the contract settling last. Related: Nearby futures contract.

**■ most favoured nation**

a trade policy commitment on the part of one nation to extend to another nation tariff rates as low as applies to any other most favoured nations and to treat imports from that nation without discrimination.

**■ moving average**

used in charts and technical analysis, the average of security or commodity prices constructed in a period as short as a few days or as long as several years and showing trends for the latest interval. As each new variable is included in calculating the average, the last variable of the series is deleted.

**■ multicurrency clause**

an agreement in the case of a Euro loan that permits the borrower to switch from one currency to another currency on a rollover date.

**■ multicurrency loans**

give the borrower the flexibility of drawing a loan in different currencies.

**■ multimodal transport**

transportation which includes at least two modes of transport, such as shipping by rail and by sea.

**■ Multinational Corporation (MNC)**

a firm that operates in more than one country.

**■ multioption financing facility**

a syndicated confirmed credit line with attached options.

**■ multiperiod immunisation**

creating a portfolio that will be capable of satisfying more than one predetermined future liability regardless of interest rate changes.

**■ multiple listing**

an agreement used by a broker who is a member of a multiple-listing organisation, providing the exclusive right to sell, with the additional authority and obligation to distribute the listing to the other brokers in a multiple listing organisation.

**■ multiple listing service**

is a network or system which provides detailed listing information to its members.

**■ multiple peril insurance**

insurance policy that covers a wide variety of property damage.

**■ multiple rates of return**

more than one rate of return from the same project that makes the net present value of the project equal to zero. This situation arises when the IRR method is used for a project in which negative cash flows follow positive cash flows. For each sign change in the cash flows, there is a different rate of return.

**■ multiple regression**

the estimated relationship between

a dependent variable and more than one explanatory variable.

## multiples

another name for price-earnings ratios.

## multiplier

1. is a factor which can increase the leverage of an instrument such as a floater or inverse floater. While sometimes the multiplier is less than 1.0, it is usually greater than 1.0. Multipliers are often seen in structured financings such as CMOs and Over-the-Counter derivatives.
2. in the case of an investment a factor that quantifies the overall effects of investment spending on total income. In the case of deposit, a factor that shows the effects of a change in bank deposits on the total amount of outstanding credit and the money supply.

## multirule system

a technical trading strategy that combines mechanical rules, such as the CRISMA (cumulative volume, relative strength, moving average) with other trading systems.

## mutilated security

a certificate on which the name of the issue, the issuer, or some other identifying detail cannot be read.

## mutual association

a savings and loan association organised as a cooperative. Members purchase shares, vote on association affairs and receive income in the form of dividends.

## mutual company

a corporation that is owned by a group of members and that distributes income in proportion to the amount of business that members do with the company.

## mutual fund

1. is an investment company of which the number of shares outstanding varies according to demand. If investors seek to own more shares, the fund will sell new ones. If existing shareholders seek to reduce their holdings then the fund will purchase them at the Net Asset Value. In recent years, there have been new provisions which can slow down the redemption process. It had been the case that fund shares were to be redeemed immediately on demand. This type of investment company is also known as an Open End Fund because the number of shares outstanding can vary widely from day-to-day.
2. mutual funds are pools of money that are managed by an investment company and regulated by the Investment Company Act of 1940. They offer investors a variety of goals, depending on the fund and its investment charter. Some funds seek to generate income on a regular basis. Others seek to preserve an investor's money. Still others seek to invest in companies that are growing at a rapid pace. Funds can impose a sales charge, or load, on investors when they buy or sell shares. No-load funds impose no sales charge. Related: Open-end fund, closed-end fund.

**mutual savings bank**

a state-chartered savings bank that is owned by its depositors and managed by a fiduciary board of trustees.

**mutually exclusive investment decisions**

investment decisions in which the acceptance of a project precludes the acceptance of one or more alternative projects.

**MV**

is the Market Value.

**n**

is the Commodity Futures Symbol which represents the July Delivery Month.

**NAFTA**

North American Free Trade Agreement.

**naked option**

is an open option position which is not covered or hedged. Frequently, it is used in the context of a sold option position.

**narrowing**

is the movement towards convergence between the cash and futures market or the cash and forwards market. Here, the price or interest rate differentials are becoming smaller over time between the comparative delivery dates.

**national treatment**

national treatment affords foreign individuals and firms the same competitive opportunities, including market access, as are available to domestic parties.

**nationalisation**

takeover by a government of a public or private activity.

**natural hedge**

is the occurrence when a firm's or investor's holdings are such that some components directly offset others.

**negative amortisation**

is the increment to principal over time. This feature reflects the inadequacy of the periodic payment to service both principal and interest. It usually is the result of the addition of interest to the outstanding loan balance.

**negative carry**

is the condition whereby a portfolio after financing considerations generates a negative income stream or loss.

**negative leverage**

is a concept which states that there is an opportunity cost loss associated with the purchase of an option on a future. This is due to the fact that futures can be initially margined with certain approved securities whereby the client continues to collect interest.

**negotiable**

legally capable of being transferred by endorsement or delivery.

**negotiable bill of lading**

a bill of lading transferable by endorsement by virtue of its terms which make the goods which it covers deliverable to bearer, or to the order of a named party, or to the assigns.

## negotiated issues

are new security issues where the issuer selects an underwriter or underwriting group. This compares to a competitive offering where different underwriters compete for the intended business.

## nest egg

refers to savings. Often this savings is for retirement.

## nested

packed one within another; for example the way paper cups are stacked as a way of saving space.

## net

is the difference between long and short positions or the bottom line impact of a transaction.

## net asset value

refers to the value of a share or unit of investment. It is computed by adjusting the market value of all investments by the liabilities. Then this net dollar amount is divided by the number of shares or units outstanding. Unless there are additional charges to be imposed upon redemption, the Net Asset Value becomes the bid and transaction market price. Most open end funds only calculate transactional net asset values once a day based on the closing and settlement prices.

## net cash

payment for goods sold without any deduction allowed from the price.

## net coupon

is the coupon or interest payment made to the investor of a mortgage backed security. It is lower than the gross coupon of the collateral by an amount equal to the servicing, guarantee and other applicable fees.

## net interest margin

is the difference between the interest revenue and the interest expense. Sometimes, it is referred to as the spread.

## net national product

the total amount of goods and services produced in a nation in a given period of time less the quantity of goods and services needed for its production.

## net position

is the difference between longs and comparable shorts. It can also refer to the rupee difference for the combined market values of all long and short positions. Often it refers to the net trading exposure on a market directional basis. However, some firms use different definitions depending on whether the analysis is originating from accounting or trading.

## net present value

is one of the building block processes for finance. It provides a methodology for evaluating and pricing securities and projects. In a simple case it is the discount mechanism for a zero coupon security. Here, there is one payment predicated either on interest or principal. By knowing the time left to maturity, assuming no option features and knowing the discount rate, one can price or evaluate the zero coupon. Pricing bonds is an extension of this process. Now, instead of evaluating, one payment, there is an entire interest and principal payment stream. For equities, the process evaluates expected cash or dividend flows and the residual value of the enterprise. Complexity arises when there are multiple discount rates (bids and offers), yield curve shapes and credit differences. Even the selection of discrete, compounding or accretion modelling can make a substantial impact on the value of a simple zero coupon bond.

## ■ net price

price after all deductions, discounts, rebates, etc have been taken.

## ■ net weight

1. the weight of goods without packaging. The weight of the contents of a package.
2. weight of article without packing and container.
3. weight of entire contents of vehicle.

## ■ netting

is a process used by institutions and clearinghouses to determine the marginal risks and demands for funds.

## ■ network

a group of providers that have agreed to accept the payment offered by the insurance company.

## ■ neutral spreads

is a term used to describe various positions. It can refer to a position that attempts to capitalise on flat or stable market price conditions, to be relatively immune to market swings, or to benefit from volatility. In these cases, the spread tries to minimise the impact of adverse price, duration, or volatility movements.

## ■ no show

freight that has been booked for shipment on a carrier, but has not physically arrived in time to be loaded before departure of the carrier. This term is also applied to passengers who do not arrive for a departure

## ■ nominal

is used in the sense of an indication. For example, a security may have a nominal price, nominal bid, or nominal offer. This not reflects a broker or dealer's willingness to execute at that price, for that security and at that time. It shows a level or point from which subsequent price discovery may evolve.

## ■ non-discretionary account

is an account through which the client makes all the trading decisions. However, the client may give very limited discretion to the broker or account executive. This limited discretion is in terms of price or time. However, an order as to whether to buy or sell, quantity and exact instrument is required to be given.

Summary of Initial General Account Outlays, FY 1995-FY 1996

(in billions of yen)

| | Initial FY 1995 | Initial FY 1996 | Change |
|---|---|---|---|
| Discretionary Items | | | |
| Social Security | ¥13,924.4 | ¥14,287.9 | |
| 2.6% | | | |
| Education and Science | 6,076.5 | 6,227.0 | 2.5 |
| Pensions | 1,726.6 | 1,659.0 | -3.9 |
| Defense | 4,723.6 | 4,845.5 | 2.6 |
| Economic Cooperation | 1,035.1 | 1,071.5 | 3.5 |
| Public Works | 9,171.5 | 9,550.1 | 4.1 |
| Disaster Reconstruction | 68.2 | 68.2 | 0.0 |
| Small Business Measures | 185.7 | 185.5 | -0.1 |
| Food Control Programs | 272.3 | 270.5 | -0.7 |
| Energy Measures | 681.9 | 692.3 | 1.5 |
| Administration and Operations | 5,053.4 | 5,061.8 | 0.2 |
| Transfer to Industrial Investment Special Account | 1,281.2 | 171.5 | -86.6 |
| Emergency Financial Institution Stabilization Funds | — | 685.0 | n.a. |
| Reserves | 350.0 | 350.0 | 0.0 |
| Subtotal | 44,550.4 | 45,125.9 | 1.3 |
| Nondiscretionary Items | | | |
| Transfers to Local Governments | 13,215.4 | 13,603.8 | 2.9 |
| Debt Service | 13,221.3 | 16,375.2 | 23.9 |
| Subtotal | 26,436.7 | 29,979.0 | 13.4 |
| Total | 70,987.1 | 75,104.9 | 5.8 |

Source: Ministry of Finance

## ■ nonstationary

refers to a time series or time series process which has no natural mean. This condition is an accurate representation of many financial time series such as stocks or volatilities.

## ■ normal market

is the typical activity for an instrument or exchange. It is also a pricing term structure which exhibits appropriate financing and storage costs over time. In its general form it shows prices to be progressively higher as delivery dates are further away from the current or spot market.

## ■ not held

is an instruction which qualifies an order. It states that the client will not hold the broker liable in the event of failing to execute or complete a transaction. Also, the order can give a degree of latitude, pricing or time, to the broker in order to more favourably execute a transaction.

## ■ notary public

a person commissioned by a state for a stipulated period to administer certain oaths and to attest and certify documents. In some countries, the authority of a notary public is much more extensive.

## ■ note

is the instrument which represents the actual indebtedness. However, the term mortgage is often used as a synonym for the note.

## ■ notice of arrival

on arrival of freight at destination, notice is sent promptly to the consignee showing number of packages, description of articles, route, rate, weight, etc.

## ■ notice of sale

refers to the advertisement placed by a municipality. This notice includes the municipality's intention to sell new securities and invites underwriters to bid for the new issues.

## ■ notify address

address of the party mentioned in the transport document to which the carrier is to give notice about the arrival of the shipment.

## ■ notify party

name and address of a party indicated in the transport document to be notified by the shipping company of the arrival of a shipment.

## ■ notional

is the stipulated principal amount for a swap transaction. There is no transfer of ownership in the principal for a swap; but there is an exchange in the cash flows for the designated coupons.

■ **offering circular**

is comparable to a prospectus.

■ **office of management and budget**

an executive office of the President which evaluates, formulates and coordinates management procedures and program objectives within and among central departments and agencies. It also controls the administration of the central budget.

■ **off-route points**

points located off regular route highways of line-haul carriers, generally served only on irregular schedules.

■ **offshore bank**

a bank located in a country other than the bank which owns it. The owning bank is usually in a major country and the offshore bank in a smaller country.

■ **offshore banking centre**

a financial centre where many of the financial institutions have little connection with that country's financial system, but have located themselves there to benefit from less regulation and/or lower taxes.

■ **off-the-run**

are previously issued treasury securities which are not generally used for benchmark or pricing purposes. They tend to be somewhat less active and liquid than the most recent issuances, particularly in respect for time remaining to maturity.

■ **on-balance-volume**

is an analytical technique which creates a time series to determine whether a stock or futures contract is subject to Accumulation or Distribution. The basic rule is straightforward. If the instrument was up on the day, then the entire volume is assigned a plus sign and is positively interpreted. If the instrument was down on the day, then the entire volume is assigned a minus sign and is negatively interpreted. These pluses and minuses are summed on a cumulative sequential basis. The analysis assumes that if the instrument is trading at the same price over time and the On-Balance-Volume (OBV) series is increasing, then the instrument is being accumulated and is poised for an upside move. Conversely, if the instrument is trading at the same price over time and the OBV series is decreasing, then the instrument is being distributed and is poised for a downside move. There are many variations of this theme. Some use each transaction while others use only large or block trades.

■ **one cancels the other**

is an order whereby one set of instructions replaces a previous set of instructions. In the process, the previous set of instructions is to be cancelled.

■ **one-tail test**

is a statistical test which focuses on only one side of a probability distribution. Often this side is the one related to extraordinary losses and not extraordinary gains.

**on-line trading**

is the investment activity which takes place over the internet without the physical inclusion of a broker. Orders are entered via terminals and reports are returned to the investor in a similar fashion. Confirmations remain a part of the investment or trading process.

**on-the-runs**

are recently issued treasury securities. These are often used as the benchmarks for indices, baskets and pricing purposes.

**open account**

credit extended that is not supported by a note, mortgage, or other formal written evidence of indebtedness.

**open conference**

a shipping conference in which there are no restrictions upon membership other than ability and willingness to serve the trade and abide by the rules of the conference.

**open economy**

an economy free of trade restrictions.

**open end investment company**

is a mutual fund that offers and redeems its shares on a daily basis. These funds can be no-load funds which do not charge fees for the initial investment or redemption. These funds can be load funds which do charge fees for investment or redemption according to a published schedule.

**open interest**

is the amount of open contracts for the futures and options markets. This amount can fluctuate throughout the day and day-by-day. It represents the quantity of contracts which are subject to offset by either liquidation of long positions, covering of short positions or making and taking delivery. Sometimes referred to as commitment or open commitment.

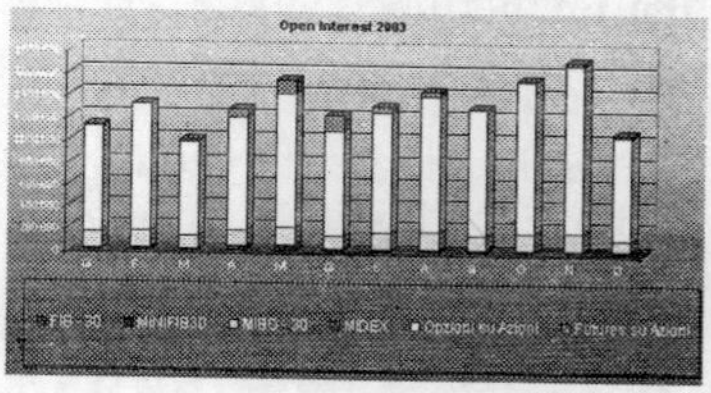


**open market rent review**

where the rent review clause provides that the rent on review should be based on the open market prevailing for new lettings.

**open order**

is an order that is or remains live or in effect until it is filled or canceled.

**open outcry**

is the announcement of bids and offers on the floor of an exchange. This compares to Electronic or Computerised Trading and negotiated transactions.

**open-end contract**

an agreement by which the buyer may purchase an unspecified amount of goods from a seller over a certain period of time without changes in the price or the contract terms.

## ■ opening transaction

is the initial purchase or sale of an option contract position. This transaction creates an open position.

## ■ option adjusted duration

refers to the measurement of duration which is targeted for the stated first option (put or call) feature. This reduces the duration statistic from its ordinary measurement. For embedded option securities such as mortgages or other prepayable loans, an estimate is calculated for the expected time of the first option exercise.

## ■ option adjusted spread model

is an approach whereby securities are evaluated by considering the implied option characteristics. Two key variables are interest rate and prepayment rate behaviour. These models incorporate the average spread of the Mortgage Backed Security or CMO tranche to the treasury yield curve. The usual reason for differences in evaluations is due to assumptions and modelling efforts for prepayments.

## ■ options clearing corporation

is the entity through which various securities exchanges clear options transactions. This clearing activity consists of serving as the buyer to all sellers and the seller to all buyers in terms of guaranteeing contractual performance.

## ■ order

1. a request to deliver, sell, receive or purchase goods or services.
2. an instruction, command or direction authoritatively given.
3. a designation of the person to whom a bill of exchange is to be paid, or delivery of goods made, or a bill of lading consigned (A key word which makes a document negotiable.)
4. a rank, class or division of men.

## ■ order bill

a bill of lading that states that goods are consigned to the order of the person named, or simply to order (of no one in particular.) Such a bill of lading is a negotiable document.

*The Coffee Roasting Company*

**Sales Order** 987 Campus Lane, Corvallis, OR 9733 No: 402

Sold To: New Wave Cafe
33 Sartre Ave
Euqene, OR 97440

| Customer Code | Date of Order | Delivery Date | Contact Person and Phone |
|---|---|---|---|
| NewWav | 04-Apr-95 | 05-Apr-95 | F. Smith (503) 294-6789 |

| Mix Code | Mix Name | Mix Type | Quantity Ordered | Price per Pound | Extended Price |
|---|---|---|---|---|---|
| MC-3 | Mexican Calm | Blend | 250 | $7.60 | $1,900.00 |
| VR-3 | Vienna Roast | Reg | 400 | $6.60 | $2,640.00 |

## ■ order book official

is the book of public orders held for execution by the Chicago Board Options Exchange (CBOE).

## ■ order notify

a bill of lading which is negotiable because it is consigned to order with no entity named; but it does have a named party indicated to whom the carrier is expected to send a notice of arrival.

## ■ orderly

refers to trading or markets which behave in a smooth, rational manner.

## ■ ordinary dividend

is a payment declared or paid by a corporation. It reflects the recently established or declared amount. It is not expected to be a one-time or special declaration.

**original issue discount**

is a bond which is sold at a discount to par. It can also be a zero coupon bond. This designation refers to either corporate or treasury bonds. The accretion on these bonds can be subject to taxation even though there is no periodic cash flow.

**origination fee**

is the cost for initiating a mortgage. Some use the term more broadly. Here, it would refer to the process of considering a mortgage application.

**outliers**

are probabilistically remote events. Often viewed as statistically independent as well. Various techniques can test if actual data differ in a statistically significant manner from the benchmark or normal distribution. Also, independence assumptions can be tested to see if they are accurate representations of the underlying processes.

**outright**

free from reserve or restraint, direct, positive, downright, altogether, entirely, openly.

**outstanding principal**

the amount borrowed from the lender that remains unpaid (this excludes interest outstanding).

**over the counter**

securities trading which takes place outside the normal Security Exchanges.

**overnight**

the period in which settlement is required on a transaction such as a currency trade or a swap on the next business day after the transaction.

**overnight repos**

are Repurchase Agreements which are negotiated or renegotiated (rolled over) for 1 day periods. They are a form of borrowing/lending.

**over-renting**

this occurs when the rent passing exceeds the current open market rent

**overriding lease**

an intermediate lease which the landlord grants to another party for a term longer than that of an existing lease, thereby creating a landlord and tenant, but not a contractual, relationship between the new and old lessee.

**overwrites**

is the option activity whereby a party grants or sells more than one option relative to the underlying instrument. In the event of sudden adverse price movement, in terms of the option position, the delta equivalency can be in excess of 1 to 1.

**owner's risk**

when owner of goods remains responsible during shipping, relieving carrier of part of risk.

■ **owner-operators**

drivers who own or operate their own trucks. May lease rig/driver to another carrier.

■ **pallet loader**

a device employing a vertical lift platform for the mechanical loading or unloading of pallets of freight at plane side.

■ **pallet transporter**

a vehicle for the movement of loaded pallets from one place to another.

■ **palletisation**

system for shipping goods on lightweight, double-decked wooden platforms called pallets. Permits shipment of multiple units as one large unit.

■ **palletising**

the loading and securing of a number of sacks, bags, boxes or drums on a pallet base.

■ **paper loss**

is an unrealised loss. When trading commodities, futures and options on futures, the mark-to-market process effectively equates these losses to realised losses. This is not necessarily the case for securities transactions.

■ **paper profit**

is an unrealised gain. When trading commodities, futures and options on futures, the mark-to-market process effectively equates these gains to realised gains. This is not necessarily the case for securities transactions.

■ **par**

equal. An equality between the face value of a bill of exchange, share of stock etc. and its actual market value. If it can be sold for more, it is above par; if for less, it is below par.

■ **par exchange rate**

the free market price of one country's money in terms of the currency of another.

■ **par of exchange**

the precise equivalency of a given sum of money of one country with the like sum of money of another country into which it is to be exchanged.

■ **par value**

1. the official fixed exchange rate between two currencies or between a currency and a specific weight of gold.
2. par value of a currency is its official rate of exchange.
3. par value of a share of stock is the value declared on its face.
4. as to a mortgage or a trust deed, it is the balance owing, without discount.

■ **par value (stocks)**

is the accounting term for the capitalisation of the equity. It is usually arbitrary.

■ **parent bank**

a bank in one country that has a subsidiary in another country.

■ **parity**

1. equality in amount or value.
2. equivalence of prices of goods

or services in different markets.
3. the relationship between two currencies such that they are exchangeable for each other at par or at the official rate of exchange.
4. equivalence of prices of farm products (or farm income) to those existing at a former time, or to the general cost of living.
5. is the point where a convertible security equals the converted value of the underlying instrument.

### parole contract

a contract that is oral only as distinguished from one that is written.

### partial fill

is the result where only a portion of an order was filled. For example, less than the indicated amount was bought or sold at a stipulated price limit.

### partial hedge

is a risk management concept whereby some, but not all, of the risk of a combined position is managed away. This can occur by choice or market action. For the latter it is considered due to exogenous factors.

### participating provider

a doctor, hospital or lab that has agreed to participate or accept an insurance company's payment schedule. When you use these providers, because they charge less, you will also end up paying less.

### participation

occurs when an investor receives a portion of the profits, appreciation, or increased cash flow. This term tends to occur in the fixed income or real estate markets.

### patent

a grant by law of a privilege, property, or authority, to one or more individuals including the grant to an inventor of the right to exclude others from making, using or selling the invention for a term of years.

### path

is the route that market prices followed or are expected to follow.

### path dependent

is a strategy and/or derivative which is predicated on a particular occurrence or direction in price movement.

### path independent

is a strategy and/or derivative which is not predicated on a particular occurrence or direction in price movement.

### payable in exchange

a negotiable instrument conspicuously marked on its face Exchange and naming a payee, is considered to be negotiable and payable to the order or assigns of the designated payee.

### payee

1. the person or organisation to whose order a cheque or draft or note is made payable.
2. one to whom money is paid or is to be paid.

### payer

is a mortgage back securities term which refers to a tranche currently paying both interest and principal.

■ **penalties**

1. punishment, corporeal or pecuniary, or civil or criminal, although its meaning is generally confined to pecuniary punishment for doing an act that is prohibited or failing to do one which is required.
2. the sum of money which the obligor of a bond undertakes to pay in the event of his failure to perform his obligations under the conditions of the bond.

■ **penalty bid**

refers to a syndicate's effort to support or stabilise the price of the newly issued security. This activity is executed at or below the initial offering price.

■ **per diem**

Latin term meaning by the day. Daily charge for use of railcars.

■ **performance**

the proper fulfillment of a contract or obligation according to its terms.

■ **peril point**

an estimated limit beyond which a reduction in tariff protection would cause material injury to a domestic industry.

■ **period certain**

refers to an annuity which guarantees a minimum number of periodic payments.

■ **perishable freight**

1. goods subject to decay or deterioration during shipment.
2. commodities subject to rapid deterioration or decay, which require special protective services such as refrigeration or heating.

■ **permanent financing**

consists of stock or long-term bonds. While most bonds have maturities they are still considered a type of permanent financing.

■ **personal finance**

refers to income, savings, investments, insurances, speculations, loans, mortgages, budgets, spending and other financial affairs on an individual basis.

■ **petrodollars**

hard currency, principally U.S. Dollars, earned by developing nations through the production and sale of petroleum.

■ **phantom income**

is a taxable event even though no cash flow was generated during the year other than an accounting accretion which represented interest.

■ **phytosanitary inspections**

a certificate issued by the agency of a national government indicating that an export shipment has been inspected and is free from harmful pests and plant diseases.

■ **pickup**

is the enhancement in yield or income relative to a comparable treasury instrument.

■ **pickup and delivery service**

an optional additional service for the transport of shipments from shipper's door to originating carrier's terminal and from the terminal of destination to receiver's door, offered by some airlines, railroads and sometimes by other shipping modes. With some transportation services such as the postal and small package express services, it is a standard service rather than optional.

■ **pickup order**

an order to a carrier to pick up freight at a location.

■ **pier-to-pier**

shipment of cargo with carrier responsibility from origin pier to discharge pier.

■ **piggyback**

1. the transportation of truck trailers and containers on specially equipped railroad flat-cars.
2. a form of intermodal transportation where trailers/containers are carried on railcars.

■ **pilferage**

taking of property by stealth or clandestine theft, usually in small quantities.

■ **pilot**

1. a person who flies an aeroplane.
2. a person whose occupation is to guide ships, particularly along a coast, or into and out of a harbour.

■ **pin**

is the at-the-money strike price, particularly at an option's expiration.

■ **pin risk**

is the uncertainty that an option position may be exercised into the underlying instrument. It is risky because it often refers to markets flirting with the prevailing at-the-money level. At such times, the gamma on a position is very erratic and difficult to hedge. Also, there are doubts about the exercise or assignment process. A trader can experience significant changes in net positions due to option exercises.

■ **pink sheets**

is the daily report which lists interdealer quotes for over-the-counter stocks.

■ **pipeline**

is a type of risk often associated with mortgages. It occurs from the time an application is accepted to the sale of the asset. Some analysts partition this process into two parts: production and inventory. Production starts at the time of the application and continues until the closing of the mortgage. Inventory risk starts at the closing and continues until the product is hedged or sold. Different hedging techniques are suggested for the two partitions.

■ **pit**

is the area on the floor of an exchange where trading occurs. It is also known as the ring.

■ **planned amortisation class**

is a security which is structured to have a reasonable life expectancy provided the prepayment speeds stay within the defined ranges. The scheduled interest and principal payments tend to be more stable for these tranches relative to the other parts of the deal.

■ **platykurtic (platykurtosis)**

describes the relatively flat condition for a distribution. This condition is evaluated against the normal distribution and its attendant bell-shaped curve.

■ **plimsoll mark**

the horizontal line on the outside of a ship which represents the depth to which a vessel may be safely loaded.

■ **point**

is one percent of the principal amount.

■ **point of origin**

1. the location in which a good is manufactured or produced.
2. the location at which a shipment is received by a transportation line from the shipper.
3. the station at which a shipment is received from the shipper by a transportation line.

■ **pool**

is a term used in several ways. From a futures trading perspective, it refers to the amount or size of unfilled orders. This inability to fill orders can occur at a limit up or limit down market condition. For mortgages or other loans, it refers to the individual collateral underlying the security. For securitised mortgages, it can refer to information such as the issuer's name, year of origination, geographic distribution, WAC, WAM and the maturity date.

■ **pooling**

is the combining of different loans into standardised or predefined units for trading purposes. This activity increases the homogenisation of the underlying collateral. A key benefit of pooling is a diverse, generic security.

■ **pooling agreement**

the dividing of revenue/business among two or more carriers in accordance with previous contracts/agreements.

■ **port**

1. a place intended for loading and unloading the cargo or passengers of vessels
2. it may be within a natural harbour on a coast, or on a river, or within sheltered water produced by artificial jetties.
3. a place where customs officers are stationed for the collection of duties and the control of imports and exports.

■ **port charge**

a charge made for various services performed at ports.

■ **port of discharge**

the port at which a shipment is off

loaded by a transportation line.

■ **port of entry**

a place designated by law at which Customs is stationed and carriers from foreign ports, foreign goods and persons are permitted to arrive.

■ **port of export**

a place where Customs is stationed to control departures of carriers, passengers and goods to foreign countries.

■ **portfolio**

is the holding of a collection of investments. For some individuals and institutions it is the entire holdings consisting of both assets and liabilities.

■ **portfolio analysis**

is the methodology which quantified systematic and nonsystematic risk for investment holdings. Harry Markowits is considered the primary influence in this field.

■ **portfolio insurance**

is a form of hedging equity products, although others include credit instruments as well. Sometimes, this process is called dynamic hedging because it requires quick adjustments in the hedge. Initially, futures were used at various stop points to serve as synthetic put options. However, rapid and abrupt price moves can cause serious imbalances in the hedging mix.

■ **portfolio investment**

in investment, the collective term for all the securities held by one person or institution.

■ **portfolio theory**

evaluates the reduction of nonsystematic or diversifiable risks through the selection of securities or other instruments into a composite holding or efficient portfolio. This efficiency means that a portfolio would offer lower risks or more stable returns for a targeted return level. Instruments that have independent returns lower nonsystematic risks. Also, instruments that are inversely related on a return basis reduce the diversifiable risks. The basic theory assumes that returns are independent, investor expectations are homogeneous and that the normalised probability distributions are stable.

■ **positive carry**

is the condition whereby a portfolio after financing considerations still generates a positive income.

■ **postdated cheque**

a cheque delivered prior to its date, generally payable on or after the day of its date.

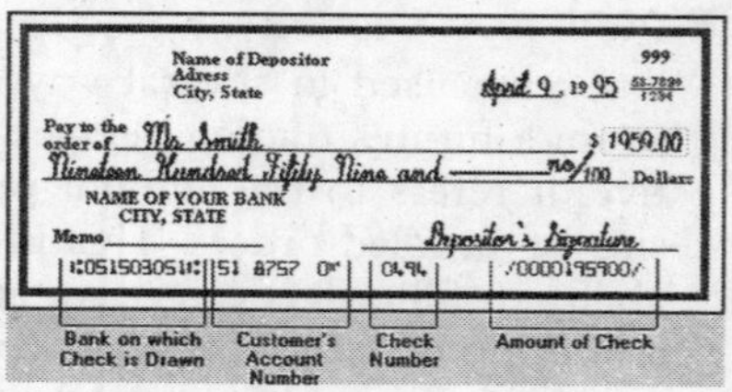


■ **power cap**

is a derivative that pays off from the long's perspective in an exponential manner. If the current market price of the benchmark is greater than the strike, then the long receives payment. The payment is determined by raising to the predetermined power the difference between the current price and the strike price. For the case of a 2 power cap, or raised to the second power, the difference between the current market and the strike is squared. For a cubed power cap, the payoff would be the difference between the current price less the strike raised to the third power. The powers can be whatever is agreed upon. It should be noted that the risk profiles show abrupt and accelerating movements.

## ■ power of attorney

1. is the granting of decision making authorisation by one party to another. Here, it would be the client to the money manager or account executive. The Power of Attorney may be limited or full. When it is limited, the limitation is to trading or investing decisions only. When it is full it expands to cash and other decisions as well. The usual arrangement for trading, investing or speculating is a Limited Power of Attorney Arrangement.
2. a written legal document that gives an individual the authority to act for another.

## ■ powers of appointment

a right given to another in a written instrument, such as a will or trust that allows the other to decide how to distribute the property. The power of appointment is general if it places no restrictions on who the distributees may be. A power is limited or special if it limits the eventual distributee.

## ■ precious metals

refers to Gold, Palladium, Platinum and Silver from a futures or bullion trading perspective.

## ■ precious metals lease

is a vehicle or technique used to finance precious metals inventories. It is related to the term structure of precious metals prices.

## ■ preference

1. a creditor's right to be paid before other creditors of the same debtor.
2. a trade preference is the granting of a preferred status to some or all of the goods of a preferred country, such as lower rates of duty or admissibility of goods in quantities over and above those normally permitted.

## ■ preferential tariff

a tariff which imposes lower rates of duty on goods imported from some countries.

## ■ preferred country

a country which has lower rates of duty imposed on its goods or is given other preferential trade treatment by another country.

## ■ preferred stock

is an equity security which has a priority relative to ordinary common shares for dividends and return of par amount in the event of a corporate dissolution. Often, preferred shares are nonvoting equity interests. However, a default in the payment of that issue's preferred dividend or other covenant breach may temporarily give the preferred holders voting powers. Preferred shares can have convertible, cumulative, participating, voting, or other special features.

### ■ premium

1. is used in several ways. It can refer to the value of an option, the amount that a credit instrument is trading over par, or the price differential due to quality or location characteristics of commodities.
2. the price an actual or prospective lessee pays to a lessor, usually in return for the rent being reduced to below what otherwise would be payable. Or a sum paid at the outset of the purchase of a lease.

### ■ premium for bonds

is the amount of price above par for Mortgage Backed Securities, Corporate Bonds and Government Bonds. For convertibles, it is the amount that the convertible security is trading over the converted out value of the underlying instrument.

### ■ prepaid

1. a notation on a shipping document indicating that shipping charges have already been paid by the shipper to the carrier, or it is an expression of the intention that payment is to be made by the shipper.
2. an expense paid before it is currently due.
3. a service or good paid for before it is delivered.

### ■ prepaid charges

in transportation, this term may mean that all charges, including freight, are to be paid by the shipper. Or, it may mean that only those charges designated as prepaid are to be paid by the shipper with other charges to be collected from the receiver. Which charges are which are generally decided by prior agreement.

### ■ prepayment

is an additional principal amount in excess of the required amount paid by the mortgagor to reduce the open mortgage balance.

### ■ prepayment penalty

refers to a cost which may be charged against a borrower in the event of a prepayment.

### ■ prepayment risk

is the potential loss related to an early retirement of debt. The risk tends to be more common in declining interest rate environments.

### ■ prequalification

is an informal assessment of the creditworthiness of a potential borrower. Often it is a quick view of income versus existing obligations and expected obligations. For real estate transactions, it estimates the prospect's potential borrowing and buying capacity.

### ■ price discovery

is the process which reflects the interaction of buyers and sellers, supply and demand and creates a record of transactions. The financial markets are classic examples of this behavior. Securities and commodities quickly reflect the relative desirability of ownership.

**■ price support**

subsidy or financial aid offered to specific growers, producers, or distributors, in accordance with governmental regulations to keep market prices from dropping below a certain minimum level.

**■ price to earnings ratio**

is the relationship between the current price of an equity and its earnings stream.

**■ price-to-book ratio**

is computed by dividing the current share price by the book value per share. Book value per share is determined by dividing assets less the liabilities (the book value) by the number of shares outstanding.

**■ prime covenant**

the best quality of investment, represented by prime property.

**■ prime location**

the most desirable or sought after location.

**■ prime property**

a term used to define property of particular interest to investors. Broadly, prime property is likely to be a modern or recently refurbished building, finished to a high specification, well situated in a commercially strong geographical location and let to a good tenant.

**■ principal**

the amount borrowed from the lender.

**■ priority air freight**

reserved air freight or air express service wherein certain shipments by special arrangement, at extra cost, have a priority after mail and the small package services.

**■ private corporation**

a business corporation with shares that are not traded among the general public.

**■ privity of contract**

the principle in English common law that landlord and tenant continue to have obligations under the lease despite subsequent assignment. Privity of contract was abolished for new leases coming into force from 1 January 1996. Leases entered into before then are still subject to privity, but landlords wishing to sue previous tenants still bound by privity have to serve notice within six months of rent or service charges becoming due. The current legislation enables landlords in certain circumstances to require the outgoing tenant to guarantee the performance of the incoming tenant, until there is a further assignment.

**■ pro number**

any progressive or serial number applied for identification to freight bills, bills of lading, etc.

**■ probability distribution**

is the mechanism which generates occurrences, observations, events, returns and variability of returns or risk. A famous distribution is the Normal Distribution with its often cited bell-shaped curve. It should be noted that many other distributions have bell-shaped curve appearances but do not necessarily behave in a normal manner. There are several statistical tests to compare and differentiate between seemingly similar curves but significantly different processes. Some probability distributions are: Bernoulli, Beta, Binomial, Cauchy, Chi Square, Exponential, F, Gamma, Geometric, Lognormal, Negative Binomial, Normal, Pascal, Poisson, t and Uniform.

## procurement

the act of obtaining, attainment, acquisition, purchasing, buying.

## product groups

classification of products into groups for various purposes: statistics, export control, import quotas etc.

## production

is the amount of revenue generated by a broker or account executive.

## productivity

a measurement of the efficiency of production.

## profit and loss statement

is the report which shows a client's, trader's, desk's, operating line's or firm's profitability. It can refer to one trade or some designated accounting period. In the gross form, these reports only indicate trading impacts. Depending on the reporting purposes, the reports can take into account other income and expenses.

Report: Profit and Loss

| Account Name | Type | Profit and Loss (subaccounts) | Balance |
|---|---|---|---|
| Income | Income | | $8,500.00 |
| Income: Articles | Income | $1,000.00 | |
| Income: Books | Income | $2,500.00 | |
| Income: Consulting | Income | $5,000.00 | |
| Expenses | Expense | | –$3,650.83 |
| Expenses: Hardware | Expense | –$1,500.00 | |
| Expenses: Internet Access | Expense | –$250.00 | |
| Expenses: Software | Expense | –$79.95 | |
| Expenses: Subscriptions | Expense | –$59.99 | |
| Expenses: Telephone | Expense | –$114.99 | |
| Expenses: Travel | Expense | –$1,645.90 | |
| | | Net | $4,849.17 |

## programme trading

is the activity which uses computers and algorithms to initiate and close transactions. One popular form is index arbitrage and another is the use of programs to buy or sell entire baskets or portfolios via different access systems.

## proof of delivery

1. evidence that one party has turned over something (cargo) to another. Commonly, in transportation, a signed, dated acknowledgement of receipt.
2. copy of way bill signed by consignee at time of delivery as receipt.

## proportional weight

lower than normal rate on segment of through movement to encourage traffic or capture competitive traffic. May be percentage of standard rate or flat rate that is lower between given points.

■ **proprietor**

a person who has an exclusive right or interest in property or in a business (the owner.)

■ **proprietorship**

a business, usually unincorporated, owned and controlled by one person (sole proprietorship.)

■ **prospectus**

is the formal or official document which presents financial condition, key employees and management and the purpose of the organisation. It accompanies an Initial Public Offering or Mutual Funds transactions.

■ **protectionism**

the deliberate use or encouragement of restrictions on imports to enable relatively inefficient domestic producers to compete successfully with foreign producers, or to protect and preserve those industries and producers considered of critical national interest.

■ **protective service**

some airlines offer a protective service where shippers can arrange to have their shipments under carrier surveillance at each stage of transit.

■ **protective tariff**

a duty or tax on imported products to make them more expensive in comparison to domestic products.

■ **proxy**

is the written authorisation by the shareholder to another party to vote the shares as the shareholder designates or to vote the shares as the proxy holder deems fit.

■ **public corporation**

1. a business corporation with shares traded among the general public, such as through a stock exchange.
2. also, an instrumentality of the state, founded and owned by the public interest, supported by public funds and governed by those deriving their authority from the state.

■ **public warehouse**

storage place renting space to anyone desiring it.

■ **published rate**

1. the freight charges for a particular class and quantity of cargo as published in a carrier's tariff.
2. the service charges of many kinds of public utilities (usually government regulated enterprises) which are published in tariffs for public information.

■ **pull to par**

is the phenomenon that as time passes, the price of a credit instrument in good standing moves towards its par value. The nearer to maturity the greater the influence because the security will only pay out the stated principal amount.

■ **pump and dump**

refers to actions by brokers or market makers to attract new buyers. Here, the brokers create the illusion of high trading volume by inflating or pumping up the market for the security. This engineers a brief period of inflated prices. These activities may prompt investors to purchase the targeted securities only to have the broker dump many shares on the market place at the momentarily higher prices. This triggers a rapid decline in values and unnerves the recent investors.

■ **purchase and sale**

is a report which lists a sale and a purchase of the same security, option, futures, derivatives, or currency. It shows dates, quantities, prices and instrument identification. Other information may also be included.

■ **purchase order**

1. a purchaser's written offer to a supplier formally stating all terms and conditions of a proposed transaction.
2. form buyer uses when placing order for merchandise.

■ **purchased call**

is a bullish strategy. It confers the right but not the obligation to exercise the contract into a long position in underlying instrument. The risk is limited to the premium paid and the reward is theoretically considered to be unlimited.

■ **purchased put**

is a bearish strategy. It confers the right but not the obligation to exercise the contract into a short position in the underlying instrument. The risk is limited to the premium paid and the reward is theoretically considered to be limited to the difference between the strike less a zero market price.

■ **put option**

is a derivative contract which grants to the purchaser the right but not the obligation to exercise. In the case of stocks, the put holder or owner would transfer 100 shares of stock upon exercise to the seller of the put at the stipulated strike price. In the case of futures, the holder or owner of the put would effectively receive a short position in the market which would be priced at the strike. The seller of the put would receive the corresponding long futures position.

■ **pyramiding or to pyramid**

occurs when a position grows significantly and is funded by current profits, particulary open profits.

■ **q**

is the Commodity Futures Symbol which represents the August Delivery Month.

■ **QPP**

Qualified Pension Plan.

■ **qualified plan**

is a retirement account or plan that meets tax law requirements which permit the deferment of tax and the tax-free accumulation or appreciation of assets held within the plan.

■ **quant**

is a person who is mathematical by training or inclination and applies various numerical approaches in analysing or trading securities or markets.

■ **quantitative analysis**

is the practice of using numerical techniques in researching securities, markets, strategies and structures.

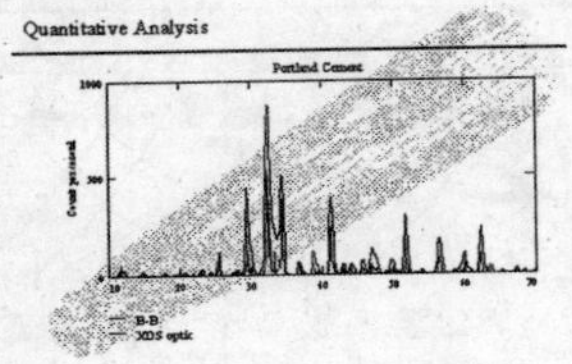


■ **quantitative restrictions**

explicit limits, or quotas, on the physical amounts of particular commodities that can be imported or exported during a specified time period, usually measured by volume but sometimes by value. The quota may be applied on a selective basis, with varying limits set according to the country of origin or destination, or on a quantitative global basis that only specifies the total limit and thus tends to benefit more efficient suppliers.

■ **quanto**

is an option feature which removes foreign currency risk from a derivative transaction from the investor's viewpoint. It is built into the structure. Quantos are also known as Guaranteed Exchange Rate Contracts. The purpose is hedge or lock in a known currency exchange rate.

■ **quarantine**

1. the term during which an arriving ship or airplane, including its passengers, crew and cargo, suspected of carrying a contagious disease, is held in isolation to prevent the possible spread of the disease.
2. the place in which a person or carrier under quarantine is held.

■ **quay**

a structure built for the purpose of mooring a vessel; also called a pier.

■ **queue**

a line of people, vehicles etc., especially a waiting line as before a ticket window or a toll booth.

■ **quick asset ratio**

refers to the ratio of cash, cash equivalents and accounts receivable relative to the total current liabilities. It is also known as the acid test ratio. This measure of liquidity is more rigorous than the current ratio.

■ **quick assets**

refer to current assets which are readily convertible into cash. These quick assets are often defined as current assets minus inventory values.

■ **quid pro quo**

1. a mutual consideration; securing an advantage or receiving a

concession in return for a similar favour.

2. a mutual consideration which passes between the parties to a contract and which renders it valid and binding.

■ **quiet enjoyment**

most leases contain a covenant for quiet enjoyment, entitling the tenant to enjoy his lease without lawful entry, eviction or interruption.

■ **quota**

a limitation on the quantity of goods that may be imported into a country from all countries or from specific countries during a set period of time. Export quotas have similar parameters.

■ **random**

is a condition in finance or economics whereby changes occur on a probabilistic basis. The underlying probability function may be known or unknown.

■ **random walk**

is the financial theory that asserts that changes in price or rate time series are unpredictable. However, the theory recognises that there is a statistical interdependency between the data. This non-random stickiness is sometimes referred to as autocorrelation or serial correlation.

■ **range**

is the difference between the high and the low for a time series for a stated period. For example, it can refer to the daily, weekly, monthly, yearly or lifetime range in prices, interest rates or other economic indicator.

■ **rate basis**

formula of specific factors/elements that control making of rate.

■ **rate of exchange**

the price at which the money of one country can be exchanged for the money of another country.

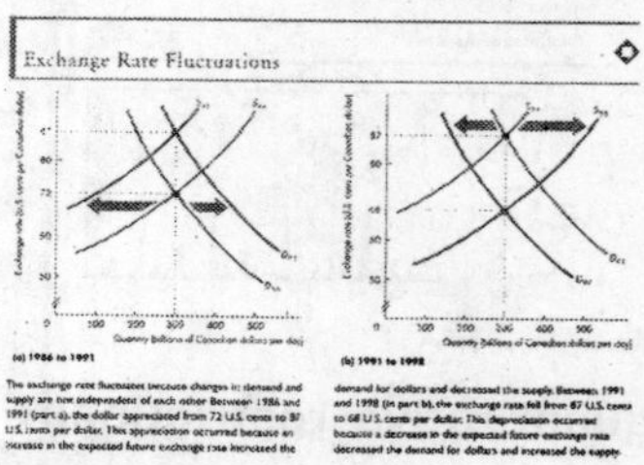


■ **rate war**

when carriers cut rates in an effort to secure tonnage. Can occur in all commodities.

■ **ratio writes**

refers to writing options against the underlying instrument in a greater- or less-than one-to-one relationship. Typically, it refers to writing multiple options against a position. Sometimes, this activity is explained as being delta neutral and at other times it is a more aggressive posture.

■ **real rights**

rights in real estate or in items attached to real estate.

■ **realignment of currencies**

simultaneous and mutually coordinated revaluation and devaluation of the currencies of several countries.

■ **rebate**

unlawful practice in which carrier returns part of transportation charge to shipper. Done to encourage shipper to use same carrier again.

■ **receipt**

1. any written acknowledgment of value received. It is a mere admission of a fact without containing any affirmative obligation.
2. receipt of goods means taking possession of goods.

■ **received for shipment bill of lading**

a bill of lading which confirms the receipt of goods by the carrier for transportation on a particular vessel, but not their actual loading on board the vessel nor their actual shipment.

■ **receiving papers**

in transportation, paperwork that accompanies a shipment when it is brought to a carrier.

■ **reciprocal trade agreement**

an international agreement between two or more countries to establish mutual trade concessions that are expected to be of equal value.

■ **reciprocity**

1. an exchange of rights. In motor transportation, may involve granting equal rights to vehicles of several states in which reciprocity agreements are in effect.
2. to give preference in buying to vendors who are customers of buying company.
3. the process by which governments extend similar concessions to each other.

■ **reconsignment**

in transportation, a change in the name of the consignee; a change in the place of delivery; or relinquishment of the shipment by the carrier at the point of origin.

■ **recourse mortgage**

a mortgage for which another company (usually the parent) is responsible for payments if the original borrower defaults on the mortgage.

■ **redemption fee**

is a charge assessed against an investor for redeeming shares or interests in a fund. Often this charge is used for early or premature withdrawals. This feature is more common for funds investing in illiquid securities or emerging market funds and annuity products.

■ **reefer**

slang term for a refrigerated trailer that hauls perishables.

■ **reefer container**

a controlled temperature shipping container (usually refrigerated with a self-contained refrigeration unit).

■ **re-entry**

a landlord may exercise his right to regain possession of premises by peaceable re-entry where there has been a breach of a condition by the tenant, or a breach of a covenant of a lease with a forfeiture clause.

**reexport**

the export of imported goods without appreciable added value.

**reflate**

is the economic and financial process whereby the monetary and fiscal authorities act to stabilise or reverse a downward trend in general price levels. Monetarists would view this activity as increasing the money supply.

**refund**

1. to repay or restore. To return money in restitution or repayment. To return overpaid charges.
2. that which is refunded. The amount returned.
3. to fund again or renew; specifically to borrow in order to pay off an existing loan with the proceeds.

**registered options principal**

is a person deemed qualified to provide suggestions or recommendations regarding options to the public. Also, Branch Managers are required to be Registered Options Principals. This person is Securities Series 4 licensed.

**registrar**

is typically a bank or trust company hired by a corporation to maintain a record of ownership for the company's securities. Its other key responsibility is to account for the shares outstanding and avoid the issuance of new shares in excess of the authorised limit.

**regulatory capital**

is the amount of capital available for trading or position taking purposes by financial institutions. The total capital base is adjusted for memberships, various fixed assets, type and/or maturity of securities as well as other factors.

**reinvestment risk**

is the situation whereby prepaid principal amounts will be reinvested in lower yielding securities.

**rejection**

is the refusal to accept securities. These securities did not conform to good delivery standards.

**relative value**

is the comparative analysis between two or more assets. It is also a form of spread trading.

**relay**

in marine transportation, a procedure in which a shipment is shipped to an intermediate port and transferred to another vessel for delivery to the ultimate destination port.

**rental value**

the rent that a property might reasonably be expected to command in the open market at a given time, subject to the terms of the lease.

**repayment schedule**

a listing of the amount of principal and interest, due dates and balance after payment for a given mortgage.

**replevin**

a legal action for the recovery of property brought by the owner or party entitled to repossess the property against a party who has wrongfully kept it.

## ■ reporting level or reporting position level

is the thresshold at which an account must formally document the size of open positions. There are different limits for each contract and exchange.

## ■ request for quotation

a negotiating approach whereby the buyer asks for a price quotation from a potential seller for specific goods.

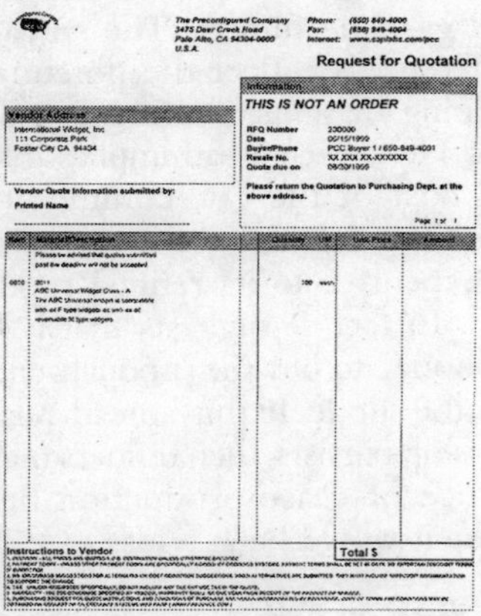

The Preconfigured Company
3475 Deer Creek Road
Palo Alto, CA 94304-0000
U.S.A.

Phone: (650) 849-4000
Fax: (650) 849-4004

**Request for Quotation**

Information

*THIS IS NOT AN ORDER*

RFQ Number 230000
Date 05/15/1999
Buyer/Phone PCC Buyer 1 / 650-849-4001
Resale No. XX XXX XX-XXXXXX

Please return the Quotation to Purchasing Dept. at the above address.

Vendor Address

International Widget, Inc
111 Corporate Park
Foster City CA 94404

Vendor Quote Information submitted by:

Printed Name

| Item | Material/Description | Quantity | UM | Unit Price | Amount |
|---|---|---|---|---|---|
| | Please be advised that quotes submitted past the deadline will not be accepted | | | | |
| 0010 | ABC Universal Widget Class - A | | | | |

Instructions to Vendor

Total $

## ■ rescind

to abrogate, annul, avoid, cancel a contract; declare it void in its inception and put an end to it as though it never were.

## ■ reserved freight space

a service by some carriers (airlines and ship lines) enabling shippers to reserve freight space on designated voyages.

## ■ reset

is the process which defines the benchmark, spread, timing, new coupon and other characteristics of a variable security.

## ■ reset date

is the designated time for the reset event to occur. This timing feature can be monthly, quarterly, yearly or whatever is designed for the structure.

## ■ reset options or reprice options

are options which have the terms such as price reset to different levels. Often this technique has been used to grant new and more favourable terms to the holder. For example, in a declining market for a company's stock, some executives or employees may have their options effectively repriced to lower strikes. Critics claim that this defeats the purpose of performance based options.

## ■ resistance

is a price level where stocks, bonds, currencies and commodities are expected to receive sell orders. At its simplest application it is the ask or offer side of a quote. On a more complex level it refers to the upper boundary of some described trading range.

## ■ restrictive covenant

a covenant in a lease restricting the tenant in some respect, eg a covenant in a shop lease providing that only a particular type of trade may be carried out at the premises. More generally, an obligation in a deed whereby the covenantor undertakes to refrain from some act affecting the land of the covenantee.

**retaliation**

1. the return of evil for evil.
2. action taken by a country to restrain its imports from a country that has increased a tariff or imposed other m easures that adversely affect its exports.

**revaluation**

1. the restoration of the value of a nation's currency that had once been devalued in terms of the currency of another nation.
2. the restoration of purchasing power to an inflated currency.
3. restoration of the value of a currency
4. currencies of countries undergoing inflation are more often devalued, meaning that either by market forces or by declaration of the issuing government, a greater number of units of its currency are required to purchase other currencies. When the reverse occurs, usually in an attempt to restore the purchasing power of an inflated currency, this is called revaluation.

**revenue anticipation note**

is a security issued by a municipality against expected revenues. It has a maximum maturity of one year and is used as a cash management tool.

**reversals**

are changes in direction for a time series for markets, such as, commodity, stock, currency or interest rates. Often these events are abrupt as prices suddenly change direction or trend.

**reverse conversion**

is a strategy which consists of a long synthetic position and a short underlying position. In the futures markets, a trader would be synthetically long and actually short the underlying futures. It is essentially used for arbitrage purposes.

**reverse crack**

is the sale of crude oil against the purchase of the refined products. In futures trading, it is the simultaneous sale of crude oil futures versus the purchase of heating oil and gasoline futures. The spread differentials reflect the potential refining margins, profitability, or loss. Here, the spread implies that the cost of the raw commodity input, crude oil, is relatively rich or expensive to its refined products. In fact, it suggests that it is economic to buy the products and sell the input. If this spread relationship persists, then refiners may reduce or cease production because it would be at a loss.

**reverse crush**

is the sale of soybeans against the purchase of the processed products. In futures trading, it is the simultaneous sale of soybean futures versus the purchase of soybean oil and soybean meal futures. The spread differentials reflect the potential processing margins, profitability, or loss. Here, the spread implies that the cost of the raw commodity input, soybeans, is relatively rich or expensive to its processed products. In fact, it suggests that it is economic to buy the products and sell the input. If this spread relationship persists, then crushers or processors may reduce or cease production because it would be at a loss.

■ **reverse preferences**

tariff advantages offered by developing countries to imports from certain developed countries that had granted them trade preferences in the past.(This practice has generally ceased) .

■ **reverse premium**

on assignment, the payment of a sum of money by the assignor to the assignee to reflect the unfavourable lease terms, e.g., where there is over-renting.

■ **reverse split**

occurs when a corporation reduces the number of shares outstanding by reorganising its capitalisation structure. Here, fewer shares may be an effort to have a higher unit share price. One motivation for this is that some exchanges have listing/delisting criteria of which share price is a factor. The proportional ownership of the shareholders does not change but the shares held do change.

■ **reversion**

the return of property to the landlord on the expiry of a lease.

■ **revolving letter of credit**

a letter of credit which when drawn upon is automatically restored to its full amount, periodically, or after a particular event prescribed in the credit.

■ **rho**

is the interest rate sensitivity of an option relative to a change in the interest rate option pricing variable. It measures an option's change in value for a given change in the interest rate.

■ **rich**

is a term used in relative value analysis. The cash flow characteristics, when analysed against a benchmark or comparison bond, suggest an over-valued security. This implies that the former security has arbitrage potential against the comparative security.

■ **right**

is the security which allows current shareholders to maintain their percentage of ownership in the corporation. Often the terms are such that one or more rights are required to purchase one share of common at a particular price. This price is at a discount to the current market. The time to expiration for a right or rights offering tends to be brief. It is related to a warrant, however the warrant tends to have a longer time to expiration.

■ **ring**

is the area on the floor of an exchange where trading occurs. It is also known as the pit.

■ **risk**

is the variability inherent in investment, speculative or trading activities. The greater the variability, the higher the risk. Risk can be attributed to many factors. As such, the specification of a risk can described with the use of an associated qualifying term. These terms include but are not limited to credit, counterparty, liquidity, market, fraud, currency, roll, agency, coupon, event, corporate and country.

## ■ risk arbitrage

is a form of trading whereby the risk arbitrageur attempts to profit from issues involved in merger/ acquisitions. The underlying rationale is that the current price after the announcement is still below the bid price. Also, the company may find itself subject to other bids for its stock in excess of the initial announced bid. These price differentials are the arbitrage part. The risk is that other bids do not materialise or the initial announcement fails due to other considerations.

## ■ risk position

the condition of an asset or liability which is exposed to fluctuations in value (on the international markets this would include changes in exchange rates or interest rates as well as changes in market value)

## ■ risk transformation

is the result of an effective hedge. Here, price, interest, or currency level risk is transformed into the more manageable and less volatile, basis risk. This volatility is measured in terms of comparative rupee value swings.

## ■ RMDs

refer to Required Minimum Distributions from retirement accounts/plans. The rules governing these distributions are complex and subject to changes, new interpretations or even definitions. This subject matter becomes more complicated in the event of a death. Given those few caveats, RMDs are those distributions which must be made each period by the owner of the retirement account. Depending on the type of account factors such as life expectancy, over-funding, new contributions, actual age and its relationship to a statutory limit affect the calculation of Required Minimum Distributions.

## ■ ROA

Return on Assets. It is calculated by dividing income by the total assets.

## ■ road waybill

transport document is used to control shipments of goods via truck. It contains the same information as an inland bill of lading, with freight and other charges and routing.

## ■ ROE

is the Return on Equity. It is calculated by dividing income by the equity.

## ■ rogue trader

is a person who operates outside the limits of his authority. There may or may not be criminal intent. Often these rogues try to hide losses but in the process incur even greater ones. Often these traders take on larger positions which are not authorised in order to recoup open losses.

### ROI
is the Return on Investment. It is calculated by dividing income by the total investment.

### roll down
is the movement out of a higher coupon or option strike price into a lower coupon or option strike price. It can also describe the movement down a yield curve from a relatively longer maturity security into a relatively shorter maturity security.

### roll on, roll off
a category of ships designed to load and discharge cargo which rolls on wheels and as the name says is driven onto the decks of the vessel and driven off.

### roll up
is the movement out of a lower coupon or option strike price into a higher coupon or option strike price. It can also describe the movement up a yield curve from a relatively shorter maturity security into a relatively longer maturity security.

### rollover
is the transfer of a position into a different delivery month.

### rollover credit
short term notes or loans which may be extended after the initial due date.

### rotation
refers to the movement or flow of investments. Usually, it describes the flow into one sector of stocks and the reduction of positions in another stock sector.

### roundturn
is a term used in the futures industry to reflect the commissions for a completed purchase and sale of a futures contract. Half of a roundturn represents the commission for either the purchase or the sale of a contract. Generally, it is important to specify that options will be charged a half of a roundturn because they may expire worthless or be exercises. Depending on the arrangement with the FCM, a customer may be charged for the roundturn immediately even though only a purchase or sale was transacted.

### route
1. a customary or regular line of passage or travel.
2. the course or direction that a particular shipment moves.
3. to direct the routing of a shipment (and whose services shall be employed).

### routing
1. process of determining how shipment will move between origin and destination. Routing information includes designation of carrier(s) involved, actual route of carrier and estimated time en route.
2. right of shipper to determine carriers, routes and points for transfer on TL and CL shipments.

### royalties
1. refers to income or payments derived from intellectual property or certain depletable assets such as oil and gas. Sometimes, there may

be preferential income tax treatment.

**2.** compensation for the use of property, usually copyrighted or patented material or natural resources, based on an agreed percentage of the income arising from its use or an amount per unit produced.

### ■ sacred cow

is an asset, position, or project which is considered protected by management. Often this investment is presented as off-limits or non-negotiable.

### ■ sale and leaseback

an arrangement whereby a property is sold, with the vendor simultaneously being granted a lease on the property by the purchaser, generally either at rack rent or at some lesser rent related to the price paid.

### ■ sales agreement

a written document (a contract) by which a seller agrees to convey property to a buyer for a stipulated price under specified conditions.

### ■ sales tax

a tax placed by a state on items at the time of their sale, usually a percentage of the purchase price.

The Sales Tax

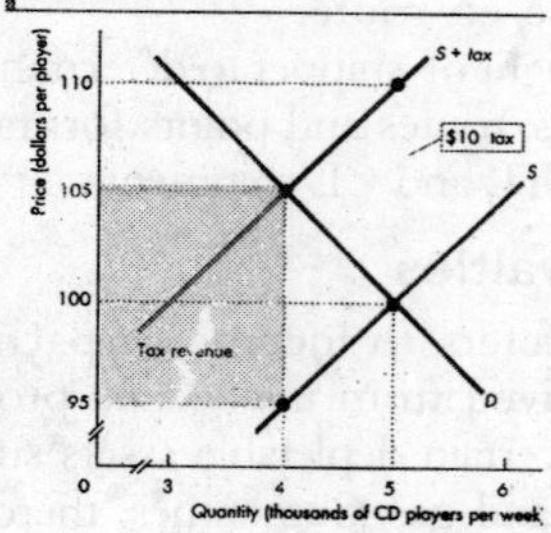


### ■ salvage

1. compensation paid for the rescue of a ship, its cargo or passengers from the perils of the sea.
2. the act of saving a ship or its cargo from possible loss.
3. property saved from a wreck or fire.

### ■ salvage value

is the amount remaining after a depreciated useful life. It refers to the residual or recoverable value of a depreciated asset. It should be noted that the gross salvage value may be adjusted by a removal or disposal cost. This adjustment would lower the gross salvage value.

### ■ samurai bond

bond issued on the Japanese market in yen for non-Japanese borrowers.

### ■ sanction

1. a punitive act taken by one or more nations against another nation which has violated a treaty or international law.
2. a provisc in a law to secure its enforcement by imposing a penalty for its violation or offering a reward for its observance.

### ■ satellite

1 local servicing terminal. Also called city, group, or end-of-the-line terminals.
2 accounting designation for a specific service area; not a regular freight terminal location.

### ■ SBIC

is a Small Business Investment Company.

■ **scenarios**

are hypothetical outcomes or path dependent behavior for trading, hedging or analytical purposes.

■ **seal**

a mark or sign that is used to attest the execution of an instrument, contract, or other document.

■ **seasonal**

refers to a recurring process. Often data are deseasonalised to smooth out spikes and provide a better basis for analytical purposes. Examples of this would be sales of heating oil, gasoline, retail employment statistics and other economic and financial time series.

■ **seasoned**

is a mortgage industry term that describes the aging process underlying collateral. It refers to mortgages, which are at least 30 months old and are expected to have relatively stable prepayment rates.

■ **seat**

refers to membership on an exchange. A seat can be purchased or leased.
Some exchanges offer different types of membership or trading privileges. These can be full membership, associate membership, time-limited membership and product-limited membership.

■ **secondary property**

a term used for property which is defective in one (or possibly two) of the characteristics of prime property.

■ **secured**

1. is a credit instrument which has priority of claim against a specific asset or portfolio of assets.
2. guaranteed as to payment by the pledge of something valuable as security or collateral.

■ **securitisation**

1. the conversion of assets into tradeable securities.
2. is the process of homogeni-sing and packaging financial instruments into a new fungible one. Acquisition, classification, collateralisation, composition, pooling and distribution are functions within this process. One common advantage of securitisation is the enhancement of liquidity relative to the underlying collateral or financial instrument. Another benefit is the movement towards standardisation of unit specifications.

■ **security**

1. property pledged as collateral to a debt.
2. protection; assurance; indemnification.
3. a document that indicates evidence of indebtedness or of equity interest
including notes, bonds, debentures, stocks, certificate of interest, etc. which may be traded on an exchange.

■ **seed**

is the initial value or piece of data which is used to initiate an algorithm or process. In commodities, it refers to the part of the crop or crop inventory which is set aside for subsequent planting purposes.

■ **seisure**

the act of taking possession of property.

■ **sell on close**

is an order to sell at the close. It can be at the market or at a limit.

■ **sell on opening**

is an order to sell at the opening. It can be at the market or at a limit.

■ **seller's market**

1. refers to a situation when a holder of assets has greater flexibility and influence in receiving improved bids or proposals. Often the number of potential buyers is greater and the prices higher than those previously transacted.
2. exists when goods are in short supply compared to the demand, at which point the economic forces of business tend to cause goods to be priced at the vendor's estimate of value.

■ **seller's option**

is the contractual latitude or choice of the seller in a transaction to pick the date, grade, coupon, or maturity of a deliverable commodity or actual security. The degree of latitude varies according to the different exchanges and markets.

■ **selling rate**

rate at which a bank is willing to sell foreign exchange or to lend money.

■ **sellside or sell-side**

refers to the brokerage industry which originates, presents, or sells securities to investors such as money managers and mutual funds.

■ **semi**

slang term for semi-trailer. Also used loosely in referring to tractor-trailer combination.

■ **sequential**

is a class of bonds often described as short or long-term. It is critical to analyse the relationship of these bonds relative to the underlying collateral coupon. One version of these bonds is vulnerable to extension risk whereas another version is vulnerable to call risk.

■ **sequential analysis**

is a small sample, nonparametric method. It does not presuppose sample sizes or probability distributions. It is an effective technique to use when analysing or monitoring hedge or trading programmes. The approach uses Type I and Type II Error frameworks.

■ **serial bonds**

is an issuance of bonds which have different maturity dates for the principal. Often these bonds are issued on a year-by-year basis but there can be maturity gaps as well.

■ **serial correlation**

is the statistical dependency of items between two or more times series. However, this term is sometimes used as a synonym for autocorrelation.

## series

can refer to a sequential or chronological arrangement of bonds. This arrangement is sometimes referred to as Tranches or Serial Bonds. The term also refers to the financial industry test and associated license.

## service charge

the amount a tenant pays for services his landlord provides.

## settlement date

1. is the date of the financial satisfaction of a transaction. This satisfaction can include payment and delivery of securities. In recent years, there has been progress towards closing the gap between trade date and settlement date. Many back office systems are primarily focused on settlements whereas front office systems are primarily focused on trades or transactions. Here, too the gaps are narrowing with the implementation of middle office software.
2. the date on which payment for a transaction must be made.

## settlement for real estate

is often synonymous with the Closing. It refers to the concluding financial transactions required to satisfy the deal.

## share equivalency

is a term used in convertible trading and hedging which indicates the number of common shares that the convertible instruments could be exercised into.

## share repurchase

occurs when a company buys its own shares on the open market. Sometimes, it is done to bolster value, at other times it is executed to acquire shares for option or other incentive plans. When the rationale is the former, it is often considered preferable to use available to reinvest in the business than make other less apparently attractive investments or dividend distributions.
These activities reduce the number of shares outstanding and therefore increase the earnings per share statistic.

## shipment

1. delivery of cargo to a carrier for transportation.
2. the transportation of goods.
3. the property which is the subject of transportation.

## shipped on deck

goods shipped on the deck of a vessel. The bill of lading covering goods shipped on deck must be annotated to that effect.

## shipper

1. one who transports goods for a charge. In normal usage, such a person would be called a carrier, but carriers are also called shippers
2. one who tenders goods to a carrier for transportation.
3. the sender of goods to be transported as distinct from the receiver or the consignee.

## shipping order

instructions from a shipper to a

carrier for the transportation of goods.

■ **ship's manifest**

a list of the individual shipments constituting the ship's cargo.

■ **ship's papers**

the documents a ship must carry to meet the safety, health, immigration, commercial and customs requirements of a port of call or of international law.

■ **ship's stores**

the food, medical supplies, spare parts and other provisions carried for the day-to-day running of a vessel.

■ **short**

is the position opposite that of a long. Some who is short the market.

■ **short form bill of lading**

a bill of lading on which the detailed conditions of transportation are not listed in full, but instead there is a statement which declares them to be incorporated by reference and states the place where they are available.

■ **short hedge**

refers to the status of the open futures contract equivalent position. Here, it is understood that the hedger is short futures against a long actual position.

■ **short of exchange**

the position of a foreign exchange trader who has sold more foreign currency of a particular country than he has in possession to cover sales.

■ **short option minimum charge**

is the amount charged for short positions in extremely deep-out-of-the-money options. This amount is the greater of the actual risk weighted statistic or the stated exchange or clearing house minimum.

■ **short position**

refers to several concepts. It can refer to market directional positions. For example, the sale of a call or the purchase of a put are bearish in nature. These trades have a negative market bias. Short position can also refer to the actual short sale of a derivative. Here, a short sale of a put is viewed as bullish or market directional positive but categorised by the short sale event.

■ **short selling**

is the act by which a speculator or risk manager sells an instrument at a high price with the intent of purchasing it lower. This is particularly the case for the speculator. The risk manager would generally be selling short against a specific or global exposure. There are technical differences in selling short on the futures and securities markets. Also, the purchase of puts or other derivative strategies can serve as a substitute for being short. There are different rules which apply to short sellers on securities markets. The key differences are between market makers and market participants.

■ **short shipment**

piece of freight missing from shipment as stipulated by documents on hand.

■ **short the basis**

refers to the status of the open cash or spot market position. Here, the hedger would be short the cash market and long the futures or forward market.

■ **short weight**

any shipment found to weigh less than the documents indicate, be it a bill of lading, a dock receipt, a warehouse receipt, an inspection certificate, or a weight tally.

■ **shortage**

a deficiency in quantity shipped, stored, or received.

■ **shortening**

is the reduction of the held duration for assets or liabilities. It can be intentional or the result of prepayments, events, or exercised options.

■ **shrink wrap**

a plastic wrap used by shippers to secure cartons on a pallet.

■ **side agreement**

terms agreed separately by landlord and tenant, or by buyer and seller, which do not form part of the lease or contract of sale.

■ **side of the market**

refers to the underlying market-driven or market directional position. For example, a long stock position is considered as a long side-of-the-market position. Similarly, a purchased call on the same security is viewed as long the same-side-of-the-market. A sold or short put position in the same security is considered as long the same-side-of-the-market. However, a purchased put is viewed as short or short side of the market. This term enables firms, exchanges and clearinghouses to quantify positions as to market-side or market direction. This is very useful when evaluating complex positions.

■ **skewness**

occurs when a distribution is not symmetrical about its mean. A distribution is symmetrical when its median, mean and mode are equal. A positively skewed distribution occurs when the mean exceeds the median. A negatively skewed distribution occurs when the mean is less than the median. These conditions are also known as skewed to the right and skewed to the left, respectively.

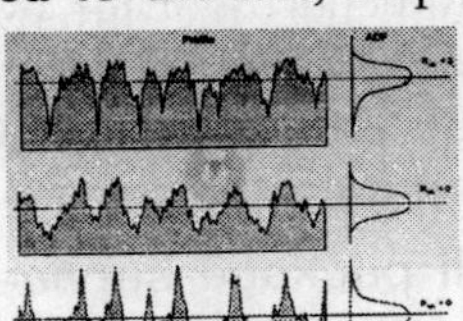

■ **skid**

a wooden platform upon which freight is stacked for transportation.

■ **sleeper**

tractor with a sleeping compartment in the cab.

■ **sling**

a contrivance into which freight is placed to be hoisted into or out of a ship.

■ **slip**

a vessel's berth between two piers.

■ **slippage**

refers to the commissions, fees and other costs of executing a transaction. The other dominant cost is the spread between the bid and offer and price adjustments for size. Sometimes, there are additional expenses in trading odd lots or very large blocks.

■ **slugs**

are State and Local Government Series securities used for escrow for advanced refunding. The image of these securities became marred when they were a focus point for yield burning cases.

■ **SMA**

is the Special Memorandum Account. It refers to the amount of withdrawable cash from a margin account. It is the difference between the Account Equity and the Margin Requirement at Current Market Values.

■ **small package service**

a specialised service to guarantee the delivery of small parcels within specified express time limits.

■ **smuggling**

moving goods across a customs frontier in a clandestine manner, evading customs control. It may be goods on which duty and taxes have been avoided, or it may be goods which are not permitted to be imported or exported.

■ **SOES**

Small Order Execution System.

■ **soft**

refers to weak price or basis behaviour. It is a market which weakens on selling. Buyers are not aggressive.

■ **soft currency**

the currency of a country that is not readily accepted by other countries and is not readily converted into currencies which are readily acceptable (hard currencies).

■ **soft loan**

a loan made with easy or generous terms such as low or no interest and long payback.

■ **sold call**

is a bearish strategy. It requires the grantor of the option to fulfill the contract by accepting a short position in the underlying instrument upon exercise. The risk is unlimited and the reward is limited to the premium received.

■ **sold put**

is a bullish strategy. It requires the grantor of the option to fulfill the contract by accepting a long position in the underlying instrument upon exercise. The risk is considered unlimited, though bounded by a zero price and the reward is limited to the premium received.

**■ sovereign credit**

a direct borrowing or a borrowing guaranteed by the government of a sovereign state.

**■ sovereign risk**

1. the risk to a lender that the government of a sovereign state may default on its financial obligations.
2. also, the risk to a lender that unfavourable changes in the borrowers overall currency exchange position might imperil the payment of a loan.
3. also, the risk to a lender that unfavourable political events in the country of the debtor might imperil repayment.

**■ soybean complex**

refers to the commodity futures market for soybeans, soybean oil (soyoil) and soybean meal.

**■ special purpose vehicle**

is an organisation constructed with a limited purpose or life. Frequently, these Special Purpose Vehicles serve as conduits or pass through organisations or corporations. They are created for various mortgage backed, real estate, or loan transactions.

**■ special rates**

rates that apply to cargo traffic under special conditions and usually to and from a limited number of points.

**■ specialist**

is a person on the floor of an exchange who is supposed to buy when others are selling and sell when others are buying so as to maintain an orderly market. In doing so, specialists run risks and they are compensated by the spreads.

**■ specific commodity rate**

with reference to freight rates, it is a favourable freight rate usually applicable to certain classes of commodities which move in large volume shipments.

**■ spillover effects**

occurs when conditions or behaviour in some markets or sectors pour over into other markets or securities. For example, selling in stocks may trigger margin selling which may be satisfied by selling other assets such as bonds to raise cash to meet the calls.

**■ spinoff**

is a company or division which is separated from the parent. Here, the parent's shareholders receive pro rata ownership shares in the newly free standing organisation..

**■ spot cash**

immediate cash payment on a transaction.

**■ spot exchange**

the purchase and sale of foreign exchange for delivery and payment at the time of the transaction.

**■ spot exchange rate**

the price of one currency expressed in terms of another currency at a given moment in time.

■ **spot market**

the market for a commodity or foreign exchange available for immediate delivery.

■ **spot operations**

foreign exchange dealings and commodity trading in which settlement of the mutual delivery and payment commitment is made immediately.

■ **spot price**

1. the selling of goods or commodities for immediate delivery.
2. the rate (price per unit) for purchase or sale of a commodity or foreign exchange for immediate delivery.

■ **spotting**

the placing (or parking) of a container in the place where required, to be loaded or unloaded or held for further action.

■ **spread**

is the simultaneous purchase and sale of two related instruments. This strategy tries to transform outright price risk into a basis or relationship risk position. It is also viewed as the difference between the bid and the offer or the profit margin.

■ **stack**

is a position which is focused on a particular delivery or expiration date. For example, a futures position which comprises 12 contracts all of which are established for December delivery.

■ **stagflation**

is the economic and financial phenomenon which represents a relatively high rate of unemployment coupled with a relatively moderate to high rate of inflation.

■ **standard deviation**

this is a measure of volatility, risk, or statistical dispersion. The standard deviation is calculated by: computing the mean of the series, then taking the deviation by subtracting the mean from each observation, squaring the differences or deviations for each observation, dividing the sum of the squared deviations by the number of observations, then calculating the positive square root of the sum of squared deviations. In other words, the standard deviation is the positive square root of the variance.

■ **standby commitment**

a bank commitment to loan money up to a specified amount for a specific period, to be used only in a certain contingency.

■ **standby letter of credit**

a letter of credit which a bank issues on behalf of its customer to serve as a guarantee to the beneficiary of the letter of credit that the bank's customer will perform a specified contract with the beneficiary. If the customer defaults, the beneficiary may draw funds against the letter of credit as penalties or as payments, whichever the terms of the credit provide.

■ **stationary**

refers to a time series or time series process which has a natural mean or tendency towards one. Over time and given larger samples, some economic time series tend to converge towards a natural level with stable volatilities.

■ **statistical analysis**

is a mathematical approach which quantifies market action. In its general form, it is reliant on large sample statistics and linear analysis. It assumes independence. Its popular terms are: the mean, variance, standard deviation, alpha and beta.

■ **steamship (or steamer)**

vessels powered by steam engines. However, the term is often used to describe powered vessels in general and companies who operate ocean going cargo vessels are often called steamship companies despite the fact that the use of steam power for ocean going vessels is obsolete, the modern standard being diesel engines fuelled by oil.

■ **steamship indemnity**

a contract of indemnity issued by a bank to an ocean carrier indemnifying the carrier for any loss incurred for release of goods without surrender of the original bill of lading properly endorsed.

■ **stevedore**

1. a person having charge of the loading and unloading of ships in port.
2. sometimes used to indicate those labourers who actually perform the physical work of loading and unloading a ship (usually called longshoremen.)

■ **stochastic**

is a condition in finance or economics whereby changes occur on a more abrupt basis than those expected to be normally encountered. In some ways stochastic has infinite variance and/or non-converging means implications.

■ **stocks and bonds hedge funds**

are combinations which are analogous to Balanced Mutual Funds but, depending on the underlying charter, can use higher degrees of leverage or derivatives.

■ **stop**

is an order that becomes market executable when a stated level is hit or crossed. Sell stops become market activated when the market declines to the stated stop price or lower. Then the order requires the instrument to be sold at prevailing market prices. Buy stops become market activated when the market advances to the stated stop price or higher. Then this order requires the instrument to be purchased at the prevailing market prices. A variation of the Limit Order is the Stop Limit Order.

**■ stop limit**

is a combination of a Stop and Limit order. In the case of a Sell Stop Limit, a Stop Price is given and the same or lower Limit Price is given. The market must decline down to this price or range for the order to become executable. In the case of a Buy Stop Limit, a Stop Price is given and the same or higher Limit Price is given. The market must advance up to this price or range to become executable. Therefore, this type of order can only be executed at one price or a range of prices. Typically, this range is rather narrow.

**■ storage**

the keeping of goods in a warehouse or other repository.

**■ storage demurrage**

a storage charge made on property remaining on the dock or terminal past the permitted free-time period.

**■ storage in transit**

the stopping of freight traffic at a point located between the point of origin and destination to be stored and reforwarded at a later date.

**■ store-door delivery**

the movement of goods to the consignee's place of business, customarily applied to movement by truck.

**■ stowage**

the arranging and packing of cargo in a vessel for shipment.

**■ stowage instructions**

specific instructions given by the shipper or his agent concerning the way in which cargo is to be handled or stowed. It may refer to the location in the hold, whether a particular side is to be on top, the kind of other cargo it may not be near, the number of pieces which may be stacked, what implements may not be used to move it, such as use no hooks on bales, etc.

**■ stowplan**

a diagram showing where cargo has been placed in a vessel (also known as a stowage plan.)

**■ straddle**

is an option strategy where the near- or at-the-money put and call are combined to form a position. The straddle can be long (purchased) or short (sold).

**■ straight bill of lading**

1. a nonnegotiable bill of lading that designates a consignee who is to receive the goods and obligates the carrier to deliver the goods to that consignee only.
2. non-negotiable document provides that shipment is to be delivered direct to party whose name is shown as consignee. Carrier does not require its surrender upon delivery except when needed to identify consignee.

**■ straight-line depreciation**

is an accounting procedure

whereby each year's depreciation is equal to the other years. If an asset has an expected useful life of 5 years then 20 percent of its adjusted cost is charged against revenues each year. If the asset has an expected useful life of 10 years, then 10 percent of its adjusted cost is charged against revenues each year.

■ **strangle**

is related to the straddle. It is an option strategy where the put and call are out-of-the-money. The strangle can be long (purchased) or short (sold).

■ **strengthening**

is a hedging or risk management term used to describe the relative gain of value between the underlying market and the hedge vehicle. It suggests that the cash or spot commodity or market is becoming more valuable relative to the futures or forward as defined by the basis.

■ **stretching**

is the increase of the held duration for assets or liabilities. It can be intentional or the result of slowdowns in prepayments, events, or exercised options.

■ **strike clause**

an insurance clause which may be included in policies to cover against losses as a result of strikes, riots and civil commotions.

■ **strike price**

is the stipulated price of an option at which level the underlying security, futures, or commodity will be priced or valued upon exercise.

■ **strip**

is a term in the commodity markets which refers to the placement of contracts in different delivery months. For example, the simultaneous placement of 12 contracts in the January through December calendar months would be a strip.

■ **stripping**

emptying truck of cargo and arranging shipments by destination.

■ **structuring**

is a term which is used several ways. It can refer to arranging a deal.

Structuring can refer to rearrange the cash flow components, both interest and principal, into new streams or structures.

Structuring is the name for breaking down currency payments below treasury department reporting limits. The usual motivation for this is avoidance of income taxes or cloaking ownership. Here, cash and postal money orders are considered as currency.

■ **stuffing**

the loading of cargo into a container.

■ **subletting**

where the tenant lets part or all of the premises to a subtenant, as permitted by the terms of the lease. It differs from assignment in that the head lessee remains responsible to the landlord for the payment of rent and fulfilment of other obligations.

■ **subordinated**

is a class of securities which have lower priority or claim against a borrower. Typically, these are unsecured obligations. They are also called Junior notes and bonds.

■ **subsidiary**

any organisation more than 50 percent of whose voting stock is owned by another firm.

■ **subsidy**

a grant paid by a government to producers or exporters of goods to strengthen their competitive position.

■ **substitute cash or dividend payment**

occurs when there has been a short sale. The lender of the security is entitled to a substitute dividend or cash payment. The party who buys the actual security is entitled to the actual dividend as well as voting rights, if any.

■ **super floater**

is a floating rate instrument which has its coupon set as a multiple of a benchmark. It exhibits greater movement than an ordinary floater.

■ **super PAC**

is Planned Amortisation Class security that has broader prepayment protection due to its wider collar or prepayment band.

■ **supply access**

assurances sought by importing countries that they will, in the future, have fair and equitable access at reasonable prices to supplies of raw materials and other essential imports.

■ **supply chain management**

designing and implementing complex distribution systems that begin with the sourcing of raw materials and end with delivery of goods to the consumer and back, if necessary. This includes the operation of technologically superior smart warehouses, managing orders and returns and packaging products for distribution.

■ **support for prices**

is a price level where stocks, bonds, currencies and commodities are expected to receive buy orders. At its simplest application it is the bid side of a quote. On a more complex level it refers to the lower boundary of some described trading range.

■ **surcharge**

a charge or tax above the usual or customary charge.

■ **surety**

a bond or other security that protects a person, corporation, or other legal entity in case of another's default in the payment of a given obligation, improper performance of a given contract, malfeasance of office, etc. The one who undertakes to be the surety is primarily liable in case of the default.

■ **survey**

1. to examine and report on the

condition of a vessel for purposes of establishing seaworthiness, value, or dimensions.
2. to examine and report on the condition of goods or a structure.
3. to examine and report on the condition of goods or property after a casualty to determine the extent of the loss and the probable cause. (Often to support an insurance claim, although there may be a claim without insurance being involved.)
4. the reports described above, generally conducted by an independent third party, called a surveyor.

## ■ swap

is a customised financial transaction between two or more counterparties. However, banks or brokerage firms often act as intermediaries or assume some of the risk of the total transaction as well. A swap is engineered between counterparties who agree to make periodic payments or adjusts to one another. Swaps cover interest rate, equity, commodity and currency products. They can be simple floating for fixed exchanges or complex hybrid products with multiple option features. Swaps are not exclusively OTC transactions because listed instruments are often include in the risk management of the position. Often managers evaluate the relative merits of conducting a swap (OTC) or a hedge predicated on listed instruments. The interaction between these two markets promotes greater financial efficiencies.

## ■ swap (transactions)

a kind of financial transaction which has many variations, usually highly complex. They generally involve a simultaneous exchange of assets (the swap) by counterparties for other different assets of comparable value. The assets may be commodities or they may be financial instruments involving interest rates, cash flows, foreign exchange, debts or equities. In addition to financial profits, the swaps have many purposes such as limiting risks, overcoming restrictions in certain markets, or balancing portfolios.

## ■ sweetener

is an added incentive to purchase a security. One example of this would be the coupling of warrants with a convertible bond issue. Here, the warrants would be viewed as the sweetener.

## ■ switch

is the trading process whereby an open contract position is closed and another contract month is opened. This activity is sometimes called a spread or a rollover.

## ■ switch arrangements

a form of countertrade in which the seller sells on credit and then transfers the credit to a third party at a discount. Or, in another type of switch, the rights to purchase certain goods, resulting from a countertrade operation, are sold to a third party at a discount.

## ■ synthetic futures

is a position constructed with options which have the same strike price and same expiration. It can be either long or short. A long synthetic futures position consists of a purchased a call and a sold a put. A short synthetic futures position consists of a sold call and a purchased put. It is a part of the conversion and reverse conversion strategies.

■ **synthetic long call**

is a long position in the underlying instrument or futures combined with a long or purchased put.

■ **synthetic long put**

is a short position in the underlying instrument or futures combined with a long or purchased call.

■ **synthetic long straddle**

is constructed by the purchase of a futures contract or underlying instrument coupled with the purchase of two at-the-money puts. Since the purchase of the underlying with the purchase of one at-the-money put is a synthetic long call, then the purchase of the second put completes this synthetic option strategy. This synthetic long straddle position can also be constructed by the short sale of the futures or underlying coupled with the purchase of two at-the-money calls. Here, the short sale of the underlying and the purchase of the put create a synthetic long put position. The purchase of the second call completes this synthetic option strategy. Note that in both cases, the buyer is paying a premium or purchasing time value which makes the position synthetically long.

■ **synthetic short call**

is a short position in the underlying instrument or futures combined with a short put position.

■ **synthetic short put**

is a long position in the underlying combined with a short call. Is sometimes referred to as a covered call write position.

■ **synthetic short straddle**

is constructed by the purchase of a futures contract or underlying instrument coupled with the sale of two at-the-money calls. Since the purchase of the underlying with the sale of one at-the-money call is a synthetic short put, then the sale of the second call completes this synthetic option strategy.

This synthetic short straddle position can also be constructed by the short sale of the futures or underlying coupled with the sale of two at-the-money puts. Here, the short sale of the underlying and the short sale of the put create a synthetic short call position. The sale of the second put completes this synthetic option strategy. Note that in both cases, the trader is collecting a premium or receiving time value which makes the position synthetically short.

■ **tanktainer**

tank built into standard container frame and used to transport liquids.

■ **tare weight**

the weight of a container and/or packing materials, but without the goods being shipped. The gross weight of a shipment less the net weight of the goods being shipped. (In other words, the weight of the packing.)

■ **target funds**

are mutual funds which invest in specified categories, such as, average maturities or durations.

■ **tariff**

1. a comprehensive list or schedule of merchandise with applicable duty rates to be paid or charged for each listed article; together with governing rules and regulations.(A customs Tariff.)
2. a schedule of rates and charges applied by a business, especially a common carrier, together with a description of the services offered and the rules and regulations applicable.
3. the printed price list issued by a carrier showing transportation charges.

■ **tariff anomaly**

in a customs tariff, a tariff anomaly exists when the tariff on raw materials or semi-manufactured goods is higher than the tariff on the finished product.

■ **tariff escalation**

in a customs tariff, a situation in which duties on raw materials are nonexistent or very low; duties on semi-processed goods are moderate; and duties on manufactured goods are relatively high.

■ **tariff rate quotas**

(Customs) application of a higher duty rate to imported goods after a specified quantity of the item has entered the country at a lower prevailing rate.

■ **tariff schedule**

(Customs) a comprehensive list of the goods which may be imported into a country and the import duties applicable to each product.

■ **tariff war**

(Customs) when one nation increases the tariffs on goods imported from, or exported to another country and that country then follows by raising tariffs itself in a retaliatory manner.

■ **tax anticipation note**

is a security issued by a municipality against expected tax collections. It has a maximum maturity of one year. It is used for cash management purposes.

■ **tax efficient portfolios**

are investment holdings which have both trading profits and tax minimisation impact as goals. These portfolios recognise that the subsequent payment of taxes reduces the investor's after tax returns. When holdings are held by pension plans or tax deferred accounts, there is no immediate tax liability on realised gains. However, an investor holding mutual funds which have high rates of security turnover and significant realised gains are subject to immediate tax year liabilities.

## tax haven

a nation offering low tax rates and other incentives for individuals and businesses of other countries to locate there.

## technical analysis

is the study of market behaviour which tries to discern patterns which enhance position taking. Among some of the tools and indicators used are: charts, volume, open interest, put to call ratios, moving averages and oscillators.

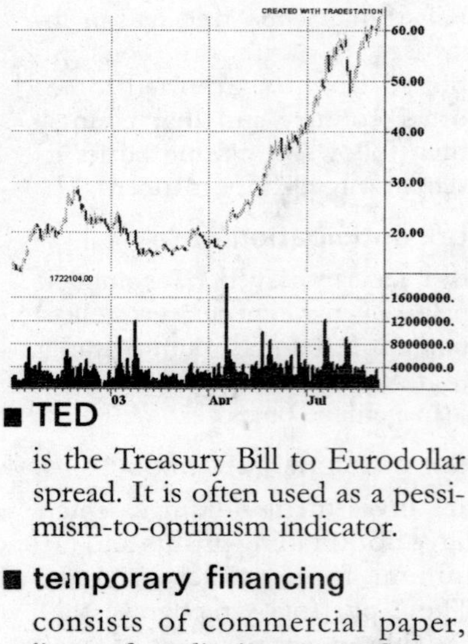


## TED

is the Treasury Bill to Eurodollar spread. It is often used as a pessimism-to-optimism indicator.

## temporary financing

consists of commercial paper, lines of credit, inventory financing and bridge loans. These obligations have to be satisfied within a relatively short timeframe.

## temporary importation (admission temporaire)

a customs procedure under which certain goods can be brought into a customs territory temporarily, conditionally relieved from the payment of import duties and taxes; such goods must be imported for a permitted purpose and must be intended for exportation within the permitted period.

## tender

1. a small vessel which serves a larger vessel in a port for the purpose of supplying provisions and carrying passengers to and from ship to shore.
2. an offer of money. An offer to supply something. An offer to present something.
3. to satisfy a claim, an unconditional offer to perform coupled with a manifest ability to carry out the offer.
4. a car connected behind a steam railroad locomotive to carry coal and water. (Almost obsolete).
5. an offer of goods for transportation by a shipper, or an offer of delivery by a carrier.

## tenor

the term fixed for the payment of a draft or debt.

## term repos

are repurchase agreements which are negotiated or renegotiated (rolled over) for more than 1 day periods. These periods can be for multiple days, weeks, or sometimes, months. They are a form of borrowing/lending.

## term structure of interest rates and volatility

refers to the variability of short-term rates relative to longer-term rates. It has been documented that short-term rates exhibit greater variability or volatility than long-term rates. However, longer-term instruments experience greater price sensitivity than short-term instruments for a given change in the underlying rate. A quick measure of this price sensitivity is provided by duration. Typically, debt instruments without option features, explicit or implicit, have greater duration with longer maturities. Zero coupon securities tend to have the greater price sensitivity relative to coupon paying securities.

■ **terminal**

an facility which is used by a rail, ship, air, or truck line as a place for receiving and delivering cargo; loading; unloading; transferring; temporarily storing; and similarly handling freight; and repairing and servicing equipment..

■ **terminal charge**

a charge made for services performed at transportation terminals.

■ **terminal value**

refers to the financial remainder, residual amount, or end-of-process (life) valuation. Some examples are the remaining value of an expired option or hedge position. It may also refer to a non-discounted or discounted financial value for an investment.

■ **termination**

the coming or bringing to an end of a lease, by mutual agreement, by the effluxion of time, or by the exercise of a right of one of the parties.

■ **terms**

the specific condition and details of an agreement or contract.

■ **terms of trade**

the ratio of the index of export prices to the index of import prices. (Note the difference from Trade Terms

■ **testamentary trust**

a trust that is created upon death by the terms of a person's will.

■ **testator**

an individual who dies leaving a will or testament in force.

■ **the GATT agreement**

a multilateral trade agreement among autonomous economic entities (not limited to countries) aimed at expanding international trade as a means of raising world welfare. The GATT was signed in 1947 as an interim agreement providing the rules for a multilateral trading system. This version is now referred to as GATT 1947. Provisions of the GATT agreement were applied reciprocally among its contracting parties to reduce uncertainty in connection with commercial transactions across national borders. The cornerstone of the GATT was traditionally the most-favored-nation clause (Article 1 of the General Agreement), but in the 1970s and 1980s, regional and other trade preference systems became pervasive, weakening the role of GATT in ensuring equal market access among GATT members. Prior to the establishment of the WTO, the

GATT was the principal point of reference for the conduct of U.S. trade policy. U.S. association with the GATT was implemented through or by an executive order and was not a treaty obligation. U.S. observance of GATT provisions depended on congressional approval of implementing legislation, as well as the policy orientation of the president.

### ■ theory of hedging

refers to economically reasonable techniques that generate compensatory offsets relative to inventory, portfolio or other course of business positions and transactions. It is predicated on the understanding that the resultant basis series between the actual position and the hedge position is financially more stable and has a lower monetary amplitude than the unhedged series. Often this definition refers to verisimilar items in terms of the position to be hedged and the hedge vehicle.

### ■ theta

is the sensitivity of an option premium or price relative to changes in time. This characteristic tends be viewed on an instantaneous basis in financial literature and on a daily change basis in practice.

### ■ theta risk

refers to the time value exposure for an option. Academic literature tends to view it on an instantaneous basis whereas practioners tend to view it on a daily basis. For the later it can calculate the time value difference between 6.7.00 and 6.8.00 all other things being held constant. Then the amounts would be expressed in rupees or other designated currency.

### ■ thin tails

describes the appearance of a probability curve which has a lower-than-normally-expected occurrence of observations in the remote areas, or tails, away from the mean.

### ■ third market

is when a listed security is traded over-the-counter by non-exchange member brokers.

### ■ third world countries

developing countries, especially in Asia, Africa and Latin America.

### ■ through bill of lading

a single bill of lading covering receipt of cargo at a point of origin for delivery to an ultimate consignee, usually involving multiple carriers and multiple modes of transport.

### ■ through bill of lading

this document covers goods moving from point of origin to final destination, even if transfers are made to different carriers in transit.

### ■ through rate

a shipping rate applicable to transportation from point of origin to destination where multiple carriers and multiple modes of transport may be involved.

### ■ ticket

is the physical record of an order. Tickets are time stamped and show quantity, price or market pending price, type of order and customer. If additional information is required to minimise errors such as type of order, market location, commission or spread, broker taking the order and so forth then that should be entered at the time of order acceptance. In some firms tickets are generated from the Trading Blotter.

## ■ tied loan

a loan made by a government that requires a foreign borrower to spend the proceeds in the lender's country.

## ■ time

is the element which quantifies investment horizons, time remaining to maturity, time remaining to expiration, or time of holding period. It measures the distance between chronological points. Its definition can be complex even when determining the remaining period for an option until its expiration. This is because some practitioners use only business days, others use calendar days, still others base their years on 252, 253, 360, 365 or 366 days (leap years). Also, for modelling purposes some analysts view time discretely while others view it continuously. At the simplest level, this is evident between the difference of simple interest calculations and continuous compounding interest calculations.

## ■ time is of the essence

is a clause which asserts that there will not be any change in the settlement or timing of a transaction.

## ■ time value

has two general meanings. The first is the value or amount of a sum of money adjusted by an interest rate for a given time period. The second common usage is in the context of options. Here, it defines the amount of premium attributed to the remaining term of the option after factoring out any in-the-money component. Is multiplicative factor which is dependent on the time remaining to expiration and the attendant volatility. However, time value is not proportional but tends to more nearly approximate a square root function.

## ■ title

1. is a document indicates ownership of a specific property such as a motor vehicle, boat, or real estate.
2. document that confers on holder right of ownership/possession/transfer of merchandise specified, e.g., bills of lading and warehouse receipts.

## ■ title insurance

is insurance coverage which protects against defects in title. Most lenders require its purchase. Unlike insurances, it is purchased by a one-time premium payment.

## ■ title search

is the examination of a property's filed document history. This would include verification of title/ownership, tax records, judgments, liens and other items which could encumber the title.

■ **to be announced**

is the generic forward market for mortgage backed securities. A coupon, par quantity, agency, maturity and coupon characteristics are indicated but the exact details, such as specific pools, are to be formalised at a later time. This subsequent specification is to be done within the rules governing deliveries.

■ **to leg**

is the non-simultaneous execution of a spread, rollover, or modification of a complex position. It entails the separate execution of component parts of the entire position.

■ **to order**

a term on a financial instrument or title document indicating that it is negotiable and transferable.

■ **tombstone ad or advertisement**

is a published announcement of a new issue by the underwriters after the fact.

■ **total return or total rate of return**

refers to the change in asset value plus income. For a stock it would refer to the change in the adjusted stock price plus and dividends and other distributions, if any. For a bond it would reflect the change in bond price plus any interest received or accrued. It more completely measures the overall perform of an investment.

■ **toxic waste**

is a security which has been severely value impaired due to events or triggers of implicit option features.

■ **toxic waste swap**

is a transaction whereby two traders agree to exchange toxic waste or deeply underwater securities with one another with a swap transaction. Here, the traders can hide the losses associated with the initial losing position. Nevertheless, both parties continue to hold positions in securities which are inherently overvalued for trading or investment purposes. Upon discovery these positions will be subject to severe mark downs in price.

■ **TPA or TPAS**

refer to Third Party Administrators.

■ **tracer**

a request upon a transportation line to trace a shipment for the purpose of locating its whereabouts, expediting its movement or establishing delivery.

■ **tracking**

a carrier's system of recording movements of shipments from origin to destination.

■ **trade acceptance**

a draft drawn by the seller of goods upon the buyer who agrees to pay by signing accepted on the draft.

■ **trade date**

is the date of the transaction.

■ **trade deficit**

a nation's excess of imports over exports over a period of time.

■ **trade house**

is a company which deals in the actual or physical commodities. These firms may also do an important amount of futures or options related business.

■ **trade name**

the name under which an organisation conducts business, or by which the business or its goods and services are identified.

■ **trade promotion**

encouragement of the progress, growth, or acceptance of trade. (Note: Some would define it solely as the encouragement of exports.)'

■ **trade restrictions**

are taxes, tariffs, capital constraints, multiple currency rates dependent on type of transaction, quotas and other impediments or requirements to execute an exchange of goods, services or financial transactions.

■ **trade surplus**

a nation's excess of exports over imports over a period of time.

■ **trade terms**

the setting of responsibilities of the buyer and seller in a sale including sale price, the payment of costs such as shipping, insurance and customs; the arranging of the performance of these activities; and the determination of when title passes. (Note the difference from Terms of Trade)

■ **trailer**

a vehicle without motor power designed to be drawn by another vehicle.

■ **tramp**

vessel that does not operate along definite route on fixed schedule, but calls at any port where cargo is available.

■ **tramp line**

a transportation line operating tramp steamers in waterborne commerce.

■ **tramp steamer**

a vessel which does not operate under any regular schedule from one port to another, but calls at any port where cargo may be obtained and charges a negotiated amount of freight. Usually they transport breakbulk or bulk cargo.

■ **tranche**

is the piece, portion or slice of a deal or structured financing. The so called A to S securities of a CMO offering of a partitioned MBS portfolio. It can also refer to segments which are offered domestically and internationally. Tranches have distinctive features which for economic or legal purposes must be financially engineered or structured in order to conform to prevailing requirements.

■ **transfer agent**

is the party that maintains a record of each registered shareholder. This record includes the name and address of the shareholder, the number of shares held by each and is responsible for issuing and cancelling security certificates. The last procedure occurs when there is a change in ownership.

■ **transfer of technology**

the movement of modern or scientific methods of production or distribution from one enterprise or country to another.

■ **transfers (mail, wire, cable)**

a transfer is the remittance of a sum of money to a party in another place. This may be accomplished by mailing cash or drafts or using the services of a commercial bank or a wire transfer company for a fee.

■ **transit zone**

an area in a port of entry in a coastal country that is established as a storage and distribution centre for the convenience of a neighbouring country which lacks adequate port facilities or access to the sea.

■ **transmittal letter**

in international commerce, a letter from the shipper or their agent transmitting documents relative to a shipment. Usually there will be included a list of the documents enclosed and details covering the transportation of the shipment such as the name of the carrier, date of departure etc.

■ **transparency**

1. refers to the presentation or announcement of positions. In portfolio and risk management it focuses on positions and the associated risk profiles.

While strides can be made in depicting greater transparency, reports by their very nature are historic. Many financial institutions experience continuous change in assets, liabilities and equity. Positions during the day may significantly be greater than end-of-day positions.

Nevertheless, explanations or realistic descriptions of intraday, end-of-day and intraperiod and end-

of-period positions and risks is useful. This transparency activity reduces the mystery of financial positions. Often substantial off-balance sheet items such as forwards, futures, swaps and unsettled transactions could have a material impact on an organisation's finances.
2. the extent to which laws, regulations, agreements and practices affecting international trade are open, clear, measurable and verifiable.

### ■ transport documents

all types of documents evidencing acceptance, receipt and shipment of goods.

### ■ trans-ship

1. to transfer goods from one transportation line to another, or from one ship to another, or from one airline to another in order to complete a delivery.
2. to ship to one country and then to re-export to another. (Sometimes the second exporting country may be incorrectly represented as the country of origin.)

### ■ traveller

one who passes from place to place, whether for pleasure, instruction, business or health.

### ■ traveller's cheques

cheques designed for business travellers and tourists, issued by a financial institution of sufficient importance that it will be readily accepted or cashed by businesses and banks. For safety it is often designed to be countersigned twice by the traveller in order to be valid, once at issuance and once upon being cashed.

### ■ treasury stock

is the amount of stock held by a corporation after its issuance. When it is held by the corporation, it is nonvoting and no dividends are paid. These shares may be reissued subsequently for various purposes. At that time, they regain their voting rights and dividend status. These shares may also be permanently retired.

### ■ triangular trade

trade between three countries which creates a more favourable flow of trade for each than would exist between only two of them dealing directly with each other.

### ■ trigger

is a point, threshold, or event which precipitates an action, exercise, or change in behaviour. The occurrence is often viewed as the catalyst of an important condition.

### ■ trustee

the individual or institution entrusted with the duty of managing property placed in the trust. A co-trustee serves as trustee with another. A contingent trustee becomes trustee upon the occurrence of a specified future event.

### ■ turnkey

a term for a method of construction whereby the contractor assumes total responsibility from design through completion of the product and release to the client in a stage so complete that the buyer need only turn the key to open the door and walk into a facility that is ready to operate.

■ **turnkey contract**

an agreement under which a contractor agrees to complete a product so that it is ready for use when delivered to the other contracting party.

■ **turnover rent**

where part or all of a rent, especially of retail premises, is based on a specified proportion of the tenant's turnover.

■ **two-tail test**

is a statistical test which evaluates both extreme sides, or tails, of a probability distribution. It considers both high rates of return and high rates of loss.

■ **two-tier market**

an exchange rate regime employed in some countries with managed currency exchange rates where the more favourable rates are maintained for selected activities..

■ **u**

is the Commodity Futures Symbol which represents the September Delivery Month.

■ **ullage**

empty space present when container is not full.

■ **ultimate consignee**

the person who is the true party in interest, receiving goods for the designated end use.

■ **unable**

is an indication report that the order, as given or when given, was unable to be executed. This can happen on a limit order where the market continues to trade at the limit price but there were other orders ahead of it on a time basis.

■ **uncertainty**

usually refers to risk or volatility.

■ **unconfirmed letter of credit**

a type of letter of credit bearing the obligation of the issuing bank only, not of any other bank.

■ **unconscionable**

unreasonable; outrageous. Courts in many countries may refuse to enforce contracts which they deem to be unconscionable.

■ **underdeveloped Country**

a nation which, comparative to others, lacks industrialisation, infrastructure, developed agriculture and developed natural resources and suffers from a low per capita income as a result.

■ **underlying**

is the actual or physical security, commodity, futures, index or basket underlying a derivative product. It is the benchmark for pricing and evaluation purposes.

■ **underwater**

is an investment which is losing money or an unprofitable project.

■ **undivided account**

refers to a new issue underwriting whereby each member is responsible to distribute her allocated portion of the deal. After the member sells her portion, her liability remains with regard to the syndicate if there is remaining inventory.

■ **unfair trade practice**

unusual government support to firms, ranging from export subsidies to anti- competitive practices by the firms themselves, such as dumping, boycotts or discriminatory shipping arrangements, that result in competitive advantages in international trade for the benefiting firms.

■ **unit**

is a bundled securities position. One example is the combination of stock warrants with a convertible bond. These two combined positions, particularly, in the context of a new offering are considered as a unit.

■ **unit investment trust**

is an investment vehicle which is funded at the beginning and once investments are acquired acts like a liquidating investment. For example, corporate bonds, sovereign bonds, or mortgage backed securities would be acquired. The interest, principal repayments and accelerated payments would be passed on to the investors. These funds would not be retained by the fund for further investment. It is more nearly analogous to a closed-end fund and different from an open-ended fund.

■ **unit load**

various cargo carrying devices, or sizes of containers, which carry several smaller shipping packages, including the banding together of a number of individual packages on a pallet to create a single unit.

■ **unit load device**

term commonly used when referring to containers and pallets and similar devices which consolidate packages of freight for mechanical handling.

■ **united nations conference on trade and development**

a part of the UN General Assembly which promotes international trade and seeks to increase trade between developing countries and countries with different social and economic systems.

■ **united nations industrial development organisation**

established in 1967, under the UN Secretariat, UNIDO serves as a specialised agency to foster industrial development in lesser developed countries through offering technical assistance in the form of expert services, supplying equipment and/or training.

■ **unitisation**

the practice or technique of consolidating many small pieces of freight into a single unit for easier handling.

### universal copyright convention

an international agreement that affords copyright protection to literary and artistic works in all countries that voluntarily agree to be bound by the Convention terms.

### unloading

1. the physical removal of cargo from a vessel, a truck, an aeroplane, a railroad car.
2. the physical removal of cargo from a container; also called devanning.

### unrestricted letter of credit

a letter of credit which may be negotiated through any bank of the beneficiary's choice.

### unsecured

is a credit instrument which a lower priority of claim against a borrower.

### unwind

is the activity which reverses a position. If an investor was long an option spread then he would sell the position to close it. If the investor had a butterfly position in bonds, then she would have to offset each leg or wing to remove the trade. Unwind can refer to long liquidation or short covering activities.

### up tick

is a positive change in price after a sequence of flat or down changes. It can also be another positive change in price in a long series of plus changes. It is important for some program trading operations as well as short selling activities in the securities markets.

### up-and-in

is an option feature by which a derivative contract becomes active when an indicator, such as price, goes through an upside trigger point or threshold. Related topics are Down-and-Out, Down-and-In and Up-and-Out.

### up-and-out

is an option feature by which a derivative contract dies or ceases to be active when an indicator, such as price, goes through an upside trigger point or threshold. Related topics are Down-and-Out, Down-and-In and Up-and-In.

### upgrade

is the raising, increase, or positive change in an company's or country's credit rating. Often it can refer to one or more issues.

### upstairs trader

is an institutional trader or money manager who is not on the floor of an exchange.

**upward only rent reviews**

clauses in leases providing for regular reviews, at which the rent will be fixed at either the current rent passing or the open market level, whichever the higher.

**Uruguay round**

the eighth round of multilateral trade negotiations under the General Agreement on Tariffs and Trade (GATT). The Uruguay Round (so named because meetings began in Punta de Este, Uruguay in 1987) concluded in December, 1993 after seven years of talks between 117 member nations. From these negotiations the World Trade Organisation came into being.

**usance**

the common period fixed for payment by usage, custom, or habit of dealings between the country where a bill of exchange is drawn and that where it is payable. It varies according to the countries involved.

**v**

is the Commodity Futures Symbol which represents the October Delivery Month.

**VADM**

is the Very Accurately Defined Maturity security. It is an accretion based or directed bond. The degree of call risk for a VADM is dependent on the bond structure to which they are linked.

**valuation**

the act of ascertaining the worth of a thing. The estimated worth of a thing.

**valuation charges**

transportation charges assessed shippers who declare for carriage a value of goods higher than the carriers' limits of liability. They may be in lieu of or in addition to regular freight charges.

**valuation, actual**

the actual value of goods shown on a bill of lading by the shipper when the rate to be applied depends on the value of those goods.

**value added**

the amount by which the value of an article is increased at each stage of its production, exclusive of initial costs.

**value added tax**

an indirect tax on consumption that is assessed on the increased value of goods at each discrete point in the chain of production and distribution, from the raw material stage to final consumption. The tax on processors or merchants is levied on the amount by which they increase the value of items they purchase and resell.

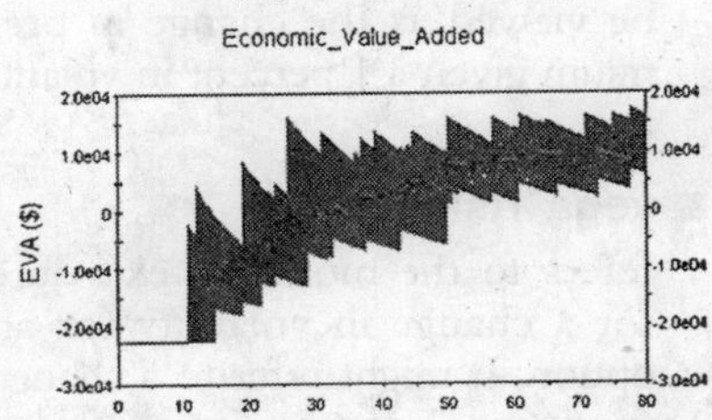


**value at risk**

is the methodology which measures the sensitivity of a portfolio or firm's position with parametric statistical techniques. It uses historical information to estimate the impact of various standard deviation events upon the value of the holdings and the associated impact on earnings.

## ■ value funds

are mutual or hedge funds which invest in apparently undervalued companies. These companies on a quantitative basis may exhibit lower-than-average ratios, such as price/earnings, price/sales, or book value. Nevertheless, these stocks are viewed by participants as being bargain priced or value attractive.

## ■ variable rate

the interest rate (i.e. the percentage) applied on the outstanding principal amount fluctuates from period to period.

## ■ vega

is the measure of change in an option given a change in the volatility. Theoretically, it measures the instantaneous change in premium to the instantaneous change in volatility. In practice, it tends to be viewed as the change in premium given a 1 percent in volatility.

## ■ vega risk

refers to the monetary exposure for a change in volatility for an option. It might refer to a change from 6 to 7 or 6 to 5 percent depending on whether a party is short or long the option. Some participants breakdown the vega risks into finer gradients or decimals.

## ■ vendor

a company or individual that sells goods or services. A merchant, a retail dealer; a supplier; one who buys to sell.

## ■ verbal

is the oral report or order given between the parties in a transaction. Verbal fills or order executions must be followed by written documentation of the transaction. This documentation is the confirmation.

## ■ versus purchase

is the specific identification of securities to be paired as completed transactions for tax purposes. If securities are not identified as specifically purchased and sold, then the transaction defaults to First-In First-Out (FIFO).

## ■ vessel ton

a unit of measurement of vessels which provides that 100 cubic feet of vessel volume equals one ton.

## ■ visa

a stamp, seal or endorsement on a document validating it for a particular use such as on a passport admitting the holder to a country, or on a license issued by the government of an exporting country for the export to a specific importing country of a certain quantity of a quota controlled commodity subject to a voluntary export restriction or a voluntary restraint agreement.

## ■ volatility

is the annualised standard deviation of the natural logarithms of asset returns.

## ■ volume

is the quantity of trading activity. Generally, it is viewed from the sell-side. This aspect is connected to the transaction reporting obligation being on the part of the seller. Some observers consider NASDAQ activity as being double counted, whereas other do not. Here, market activity occurs with market makers. Often they will purchase a position for immediate resale to another buyer. Therefore, the 100 shares of stock will be viewed as a total volume of 200 shares. The first 100 is when the stock went into the market maker's inventory and the second 100 is when it went into the (second) client's portfolio.

## ■ volume rate

a freight rate assessed in connection with a specified volume of freight based upon the premise that it will be substantial in total over a period of time. It is generally a lower rate than normally assessed for smaller lots of cargo.

## ■ voluntary export restriction

an understanding between trading partners in which the exporting nation, in order to reduce trade friction, agrees to limit exports of a particular good to the other partner.

## ■ voluntary restraint agreements

informal bilateral or multilateral arrangements through which the exporting nations voluntarily restrain certain exports, usually through export quotas, to avoid economic dislocation in an importing country and to avert the possible imposition of mandatory import restrictions by the importing country.

## ■ voyage charter

engaging services of cargo ship for specified trip from one port to another at established tonnage rate.

## ■ vulture funds

are investment vehicles which focus on acquiring properties which may be available due to financial distress. The properties themselves may not be damaged but the principal owners may be in immediate need of cash. Usually, the term describes investment activities in real estate or closely held companies which may not enjoy the liquidity benefits of an exchange listing.

## ■ waiver

the act of voluntarily giving up, or intentionally relinquishing, a claim, benefit or interest. A landlord waives his right of forfeiture, when a tenant is in breach of covenant, if he knows of the breach and accepts or demands rent or unequivocally recognises the continued existence of the lease.

## ■ war clause

a marine insurance provision excluding the liability of an insurer if a loss is caused by war or hostile action. Bills of Lading and charter parties may contain a War Clause giving the vessel options to maintain it's safety in case of hostilities.

## ■ war risk

the risk to a vessel, its cargo and passengers by aggressive actions of a hostile nation or group.

## ■ war risk insurance

insurance covering loss or damage caused by war or other hostile actions. Usually a separate policy from a marine insurance policy, or a special attachment to it.

## ■ warehouse

place for receiving/storing goods and merchandise for hire. Warehouseman is bound to use ordinary diligence in preserving goods.

## ■ warehouse receipt

is another form of documentation indicating ownership of a commodity at an approved warehouse or storage facility.

## ■ warrant

1. is used differently by the securities and commodities industries. In the securities industry, it refers to a derivative instrument which has an expiration date and strike price and other exercise conditions. In the commodities industry, it refers to a receipt indicating ownership of a specific lot of a commodity.

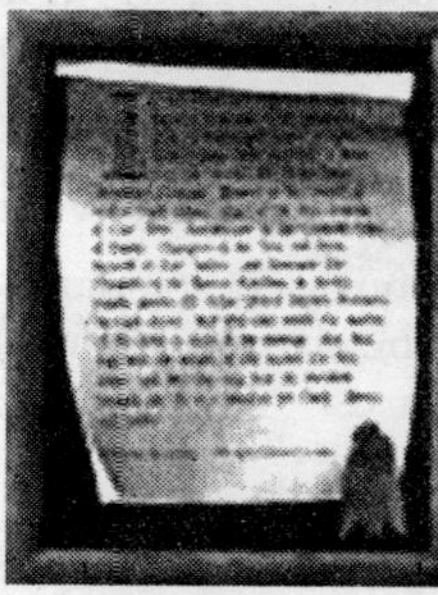

2. a promise by a contracting party that the other party can rely on certain facts or representations as being true.

## ■ Warsaw convention

an international multilateral treaty which set the conditions of international transportation by air.

## ■ wash sale

is the sale of a security or instrument and the subsequent purchase with no economic interest. It can be motivated by tax or reporting purposes. It is generally deemed to be a sham transaction. It can also be construed as creating fictitious trading activity.

## ■ wastage

loss of goods due to handling, decay, leakage, shrinkage, etc.

## ■ wasting asset

is a derivative instrument that may expire worthless after a stated time or event. Options, Rights and Warrants are three wasting assets.

## ■ waybill

1. a document prepared by a transportation line at the point of shipment for use in the handling of the shipment showing the point of origin, destination, route, consignor, consignee, description of shipment and amount charged for the transportation service and other services connected with the transport It is similar in point of information to a bill of lading..
2. a document containing the description of goods which are part of a common carrier freight shipment. Shows origin, destination, consignee/consignor and amount charged. Copies of this document travel with goods and are retained by originating/delivering agents. Used by carriers for internal records and control, especially during transit. It is not a transportation contract.

## ■ weakening

is a hedging or risk management term used to describe the relative loss of value between the underlying market and the hedge vehicle. It suggests that the cash or spot commodity or market is becoming less valuable relative to the futures or forward as defined by the basis.

## ■ weigh station

permanent station equipped with scales at which motor vehicles transportation property on public highways are required to stop for checking of gross vehicle and/or axle weights. Many states also use portable scales to comply with their weight limits. Often combined with port of entry facilities.

## ■ weight

in shipping, weight is qualified further as gross (weight of goods and container), net (weight of goods themselves without any container) and legal (similar to net, determined in such manner as law of particular country/jurisdiction may direct).

## ■ weight break

the point at which the weight of a shipment is large enough to be assessed the lower freight rates which are applicable to larger shipments, as per the carrier's tariff.

## ■ weighted average coupon

is the measurement of the gross coupons underlying a Mortgage Backed Security and weighted by outstanding balance of each mortgage.

## ■ weighted average life

is the measurement of a Mortgage Backed Securities time horison other than maturity. It considers the impact of all principal payments both scheduled and prepaid.

**■ weighting**

is the amount of a securities value relative to a portfolio. The amount committed to a particular asset class, industry or sector.

**■ wharfage**

a charge assessed by a pier or dock owner for handling incoming or outgoing cargo.

**■ whole loan**

is a mortgage, either commercial or residential, that has not been securitised.

**■ widening**

is a term often used in hedging or risk management activities. It refers to an increased spread or price differential between the underlying cash market and the futures market. It can also refer to the differences between two futures contract delivery months or two forward delivery dates.

**■ Wiener process**

is a type of Markov Stochastic process. It refers to changes in value over small time periods. Sometimes, this process is also called Brownian motion.

**■ wildcard**

is the unilateral choice of one party to a transaction. For bond futures, the wildcard or seller's option refers to the selection of coupon and allowable maturity to be made against delivery.

**■ will**

a legally executed document that directs how and to whom a person's property is to be distributed after death.

**■ wireability**

refers to securities issued in book-entry form and paid for by wire transfer.

**■ without reserve**

a term applied to a sale by auction indicating that no price is reserved (there is no minimum price.)

**■ work out**

is the process to cover a short or liquidate a long position. This activity can be the result of an error transaction, unsold inventory, or closing out a large position.

**■ working capital**

the amount of funds in the business required to finance the day-to-day operations of the business.

**■ World Bank**

the International Bank for Reconstruction and Development (IBRD), commonly referred to as the World Bank, is an intergovernmental financial institution located in Washington, DC. Its objectives are to help raise productivity and incomes and reduce poverty in developing countries through the granting of loans.

**■ world bank group**

an integrated group of international institutions that provides financial and technical assistance to developing countries.

■ **world trade clubs**

local or regional based organisations in the United States and around the world of importers, exporters, customs brokers, freight forwarders, attorneys, bankers, manufacturers and shippers.

■ **world trade organisation**

the international organisation which resulted from the Uruguay Round of GATT negotiations. It is intended to promote world trade and to settle disputes among member nations.

■ **writes**

is the term which represents the granting or initial selling of an option whether it is a put or a call.

■ **X**

is the Commodity Futures Symbol which represents the November Delivery Month.

■ **X or cross trade**

is a transaction that is not exposed to the public by outcry or usual trading practices. This type of trade is permissible provided it is done in accordance with the rules and regulations of the particular exchange and other regulatory organisations. The letter X can indicate this type of transaction on a ticker tape. It may be also used on a ticket or blotter.

■ **Y2K**

refers to the Year 2000. It is often associated with a computer software problem frequently referred to as the Y2K bug. This is the inability of software to recognise dates greater than December 31, 1999.

■ **yard (freight)**

unit of track systems within certain area used for storing cars, loading/unloading freight and making up trains over which movements not authorised by timetable or train order may be made

■ **yellow sheets**

is the daily quotation reports which indicates interdealer quotes for corporate bonds. Most corporate bonds are traded in the Over-The-Counter (OTC) market.

■ **yield**

is the rate of return on an asset. It is frequently expressed as a percent of the current market price.

■ **yield curve**

refers to the graphical or tabular representation of interest rates across different maturities. The presentation often starts with the shortest term rates and extends towards longer maturities. It reflects the market's views about implied inflation/deflation, liquidity, economic and financial activity and other market forces.

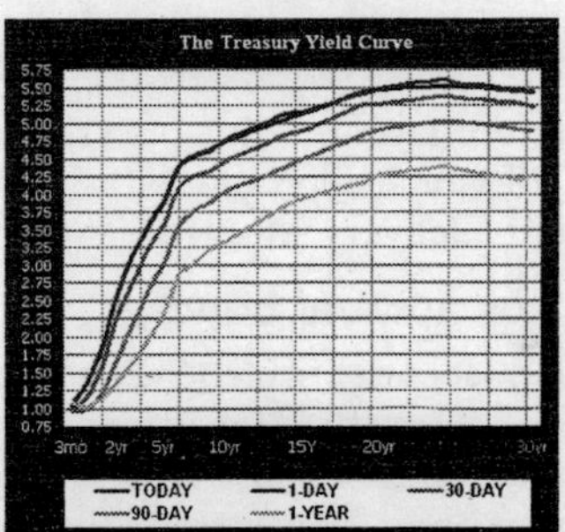

■ **yield to call, option or event date**

is akin to Yield to Maturity but adjusts for a short life expectancy. It is the rate of return which is measured by the current expected income stream relative to the prevailing market price assuming that the asset is held until the exercise of the first option or termination event. If the instrument is trading at a discount, then the yield to call, option or event date, will be greater than the coupon rate. If the instrument is trading at a premium, then the yield to call, option or event date, will be less than the coupon rate.

■ **yield to maturity**

is the rate of return which is measured by the current expected income stream relative to the prevailing market price assuming that the asset is held until maturity. If the instrument is trading at a discount, then the yield to maturity will be greater than the coupon rate. If the instrument is trading at a premium, then the yield to maturity will be less than the coupon rate.

■ **z**

is the Commodity Futures Symbol which represents the December Delivery Month.

■ **z or accrual bond**

is a security which has accretion characteristics. Its balance grows much in the sense of a zero coupon bond, however it is subject to prepayments or other events.

■ **zero coupon bond**

is a security which the interest and/or principal has been discounted to be offered at less than the stipulated principal or coupon amount due at maturity or early option payment. These securities effectively behave like treasury bills or other paper offered at an original discount. Zero coupon bonds can have conversion factors and other features implicitly embedded or explicitly stated.

■ **zero curve**

is a yield curve comprised of the yields of zero coupon bonds arranged over time. Frequently, this arrangement is graphically portrayed starting with the shortest maturities and progressing to the longest maturities. This curve would provide the basis for pricing other securities using iterative or interpolation techniques.

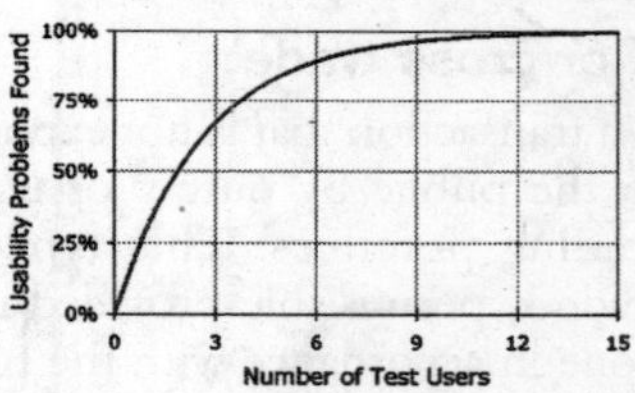


■ **zero-minus-tick**

refers to a trading transaction made at the same price as the preceding one but the preceding one was lower than its predecessor.

■ **zero-plus-tick**

refers to a trading transaction made at the same price as the preceding one but the preceding one was higher than its predecessor.